The Snow Storm by Lynn A. Co...
When Michael Farley goes out ...
he doesn't expect to find a woman half-buried in the snow. He
takes her home to thaw out, and Angela Harris immediately
becomes a help with the widower's two young sons. . .and a
source of his attraction. If he proposes marriage, will it be for
love of the woman or her cooking?

Image of Love by JoAnn A. Grote
Mantie Clark lives with her brother and his wife and is raising
her deceased brother's children. She doesn't mind adding Lane
Powell to the family's Christmas circle as another brother, but
after losing her first love to the War Between the States, she is
not interested in a suitor. A moonlight ride starts to soften her
resolve, but the risk of loving may be too great for her scarred
heart.

Dreams and Secrets by DiAnn Mills
Emma Leigh Carter works at the Jones Inn near Philadelphia
and enjoys her new task of arranging the Christmas gift exchange for the staff. Thad Benson is the shy stable manager
who goes quietly about his business. Will Emma guess that the
gentle man in the stables could be giving her such thoughtful,
romantic gifts during Christmas week?

Circle of Blessings by Deborah Raney
Stella Bradford has finally found the love of her life. It doesn't
matter to her that he is her English professor at the university
or that he seems to be hiding something from his past. But
convincing her father that James Collingwood is the man she
should marry is going to be a daunting task.

A CURRIER & IVES CHRISTMAS

Four Stories of Love Come to Life from the Canvas of Classic Christmas Art

Lynn A. Coleman
JoAnn A. Grote
DiAnn Mills
Deborah Raney

BARBOUR BOOKS

An Imprint of Barbour Publishing, Inc.

The Snow Storm ©2002 by Lynn A. Coleman
Image of Love ©2002 by JoAnn A. Grote
Dreams and Secrets ©2002 by DiAnn Mills
Circle of Blessings ©2002 by Deborah Raney

Cover art: Corbis, Inc.

Illustrations: Mari Goering

ISBN 1-58660-552-6

All Scripture quotations are taken from the King James Version of the Bible.

Published by Barbour Books, an imprint of Barbour Publishing, Inc., P.O. Box 719, Uhrichsville, Ohio 44683, www.barbourbooks.com

 Member of the
Evangelical Christian
Publishers Association

Printed in the United States of America.
5 4 3 2 1

A CURRIER & IVES CHRISTMAS

THE SNOW STORM

by Lynn A. Coleman

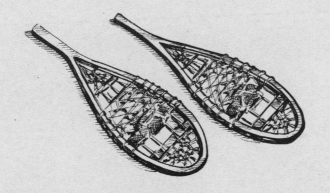

Chapter 1

1875

Michael pulled the lapels of his thick woolen coat across his chest. The wind whistled in his ears. Small ice particles bit his nose and upper cheeks. His beard, heavily laden with ice, felt like it could snap off. The squall hit with such force, it sent the animals into hiding. Not that he'd noticed until it was too late. Thankfully, Noah and Sam were safely tucked away at the house. For once he'd insisted they finish cleaning their rooms before hunting. It would not have pleased Julie to see the house in such disarray. He had tried to keep up the place, but with two boys and a heap of chores, there wasn't much a man alone could do.

Michael ducked a branch leaning low across his path. Numbness settled in his right hand. The rifle he carried got colder and heavier by the moment. "I shouldn't have come out today," he mumbled and shifted the rifle to his left hand.

Christmas was a mere six days off, and a Christmas goose had been the boys' desire. He should have waited. He pushed his legs forward. The snowdrifts came up to his knees. He couldn't blame the boys for wanting something different for Christmas dinner. The thought of ham and beans on Christmas didn't appeal much to Michael, either. How he missed Julie's fine cooking. "Lord, I miss her. Why'd You have to take her?" he groaned his familiar prayer. For the past year he'd been asking, and there appeared to be no answer. At least not one he could settle with. "It ain't natural for a man to raise young 'uns alone."

Noah had become quite the young man. His gentle spirit came from his mother. Sam was a bit too much like his father. The poor boy couldn't sit still long enough for a flea to catch him. Noah took to books and learning just like Julie. Sam fought it from day one. Michael snickered. Past memories surfaced, when the roles had been reversed and his parents had tried so hard to get him to concentrate.

Crack.

A tree limb snapped above him. Michael dove out of the way. A snow bluff cushioned his fall. He turned back and looked at the fallen branch. It probably wouldn't have killed him, but it could have knocked him out. And in this weather, blacking out inevitably led to death. He felt his body temperature dropping. Pushing himself up, he brushed off his cloak of snow.

"Keep a steady eye," he cautioned himself. Talking to himself seemed to get more natural with each passing day. Julie had been his confidante and friend. No one else lived near them. They were miles from town; folks weren't all that inclined to come for a visit. Michael wasn't too inclined to invite anyone, either. He had enjoyed the solitary life until he met Julie. Oh, how she'd changed his world. His heart tightened in his chest. "Stop thinking about her now and get a move on."

He rounded a corner of the path and stopped dead in his tracks. "What is that?"

He dropped his rifle and ran to the lump of woolen clothing. He brushed off the snow. "A woman," he gasped. "What's a woman doing out here?"

What did it matter? She was either dead or pretty nearly so. Michael pulled off his gloves with his teeth and felt her bluish skin. "Cold." As if it would have been anything else.

He placed his fingers under her nose. A feather of a breath passed over the top of his forefinger. "Lord, she's still alive. Help me."

Michael scooped up the woman. Blond hair spilled out around the edges of her hat and scarf. *What is she doing out here, Lord?* he wondered.

"I don't know if you can hear me, Miss. But I'll get you warm." Michael kicked his rifle up with his foot and wedged it between her back and his arms.

Michael pumped his legs harder, running toward his house. Energy coursed through his veins and pushed him forward. Moments before, it had taken all his strength to keep pushing his own body. "Lord, help me," he panted.

His house came into view. He could smell the wood fire burning in the stove.

A slight moan tickled his ears. "You're going to be all right, Miss. I'll have you in the house soon."

She didn't respond. "Father, be with her. Help her warm up," he prayed as he stepped up the front stairs. The front door resisted his attempts to open it.

"Noah! Samuel! Open up," he barked. Of all the times for

the boys to lock the front door. The howling winds screeched through the trees. *They must be scared,* he reasoned.

Noah opened the door. His eyes widened. "What's that?"

"A woman. I found her nearly frozen on the path. Help me." He placed his rifle by the door.

"What can I do?"

"Start heating some water. She'll need something warm to drink."

Sam bounced off the stairs. "Hi, Dad! Did you get us a— Who's that?"

"I don't know, Son. She was on the path. Go grab me your momma's quilt from my bed."

"Yes, Sir." Sam scurried down the hallway.

Michael laid the fragile woman in front of the woodstove. He pulled at the frozen buttons on her cloak and removed it. Next he worked on her boots. Her toes were pale and blue. Frostbite could be a real problem.

Sam ran in with his brown curls bouncing. The boy definitely needed a haircut. "Here, Dad."

"Can you get me a couple pairs of wool socks?"

"Yes, Sir." Samuel stared down at the frozen figure. "Is she. . . ?"

Dead. The poor boy had seen his mother after she'd passed on. Michael reached over and held his son's hand. "No, Son, she'll be all right. We just have to get her warmed up."

Samuel nodded and ran back to the master bedroom.

"Water's on, Dad. What do you need now?"

"Help me take her dress off."

"But she's a girl, Dad," Noah protested.

Michael took in a deep breath. He didn't have time for modesty. On the other hand, what would this woman say once she came to and discovered he had removed her clothes? *Lord, I wish Julie were still here.* He turned to answer Noah. "I know, Son. But she needs to be dry."

"Can't we just wake her up and tell her to take off her dress?"

"If she could wake up, we wouldn't need to tell her. I'll take her dress off. You just help me hold her."

"Can I keep my eyes closed?"

Michael held down a grin. "Yes, you can keep your eyes closed." Michael was beginning to wonder if he could keep his eyes closed, too. Taking a deep breath, he reached out to the top buttons. The fact that they were on the collar of her neck was a blessing. "Why does women's clothing have to have such tiny buttons?" he mumbled.

"Dad, she's waking up," Noah called.

Michael's hands were mere inches from the woman's buttons when he saw the look of confusion change to horror. He pulled his hands away quickly. "I found you half-buried in the snow. You need to take off your wet dress. You need to get warm—and quickly. Can you stand?"

"I–I don't know." Her brilliant blue eyes beckoned for answers.

"Then you'll have to remove your clothing here by the fire. The boys and I will turn our backs and close our eyes. Your honor is safe with us, Miss."

She tried to reach her buttons. Her fingers were still too numb. Michael groaned. "I'll unbutton. Can you slip the dress off?"

She nodded.

Michael refused to look at the poor child. She didn't need to be embarrassed. He was embarrassed enough for the both of them.

Noah and Sam obediently turned away from the woman,

and Michael didn't doubt that their eyes were closed as well.

"Who are you?" he asked, trying to ease the situation.

"Angela. Angela Harris."

Angela trembled and pulled the covers closer. *How could I have gotten so confused and twisted around in the storm? And who is Michael Farley?* His two sons stared at her as if she had two heads. Of course, given that she was huddled in front of their woodstove in a cocoon of quilts and woolen blankets probably had something to do with it. She had been shaking for hours. Her teeth had chattered long enough, she wondered if they would break.

Michael Farley had left to tend to the animals in the barn after setting a pot of beans and ham to warm on the stove. Somehow the smell of food helped ease her worries. Angela rubbed her arms vigorously, her eyes scanning her surroundings. The house suffered from the lack of a woman's touch; it was relatively clean but cluttered. The soot on the walls from the stove hadn't been cleaned off in a long time. *Why is it that men don't notice these things? Did God give them less than perfect eyesight?*

"Are you feeling better?" the older of the two boys asked.

"Some. Noah, right?"

"Yes." A smile erupted on his young face, a handsome boy with a thin frame, dark hair, and blue eyes like his father.

"Why were you in the snow?" the younger boy, Samuel, asked.

"It wasn't snowing when I left my house."

"This storm sure did move in fast." Samuel sat with his legs crossed beside her. "Why were you walking alone?"

"I had some thinking I needed to do."

"Grown-ups," Noah huffed, then settled down next to Samuel. "Dad's been doing lots of thinking since Ma died."

"I don't like to think. I like to play." Samuel smiled. His cheeks were lightly peppered with brown freckles, his head crowned with a massive amount of curls. Some of her girlfriends would die to have hair like that; and to think, it was on a boy. Sometimes she really wondered why God favored some men with items women would love, like curls and really long eyelashes.

"Playing is good, but thinking is important, too. I wager you do more thinking than you think."

"Huh?"

"Tell me, what's your favorite type of play?" Angela inquired. It helped get her mind off her frozen body.

"He's always building things," Noah answered.

"Yeah, I built a boat in August."

"A boat. That's quite a task. Tell me, how did you build it?"

"I took a hunk of wood and whittled it."

"So you looked over the piece of wood and decided which end would be the bow and which would be the stern?"

"Yeah." The boy beamed.

"Sorry to say, but you were thinking. You had to decide the best way to proceed with the task. Once you did, you set out to do it. All of that is thinking."

"Never thought of that." Samuel's grin slipped.

Angela chuckled, then coughed.

Noah jumped up and got the mug of tea. "Here, drink this."

"Thank you."

"Where do you live?" Samuel asked.

"In town."

"How come we've never seen you before?"

"I'm usually busy working inside my house. My father counts on me to take care of it."

"Dad does that for us," Noah offered.

"Wish I had a big sister like you who could take care of us. Dad doesn't know how to cook anything besides ham and beans."

"No sir," Noah defended. "He cooks bacon and eggs."

"That doesn't count, Noah. That's breakfast. I miss Mom's cooking."

"Whoa, boys, no need to fuss."

The front door slammed open. A cold blast of air ran across her warm nose. Angela shook at the sight of Michael Farley. Something was wrong. She reached for her dress and found it dry. "May I use a private room to change back into my own clothes?"

She had on a pair of men's thick undergarments, but they didn't seem quite big enough for Michael. She'd guessed they'd belonged to his wife. *What was her name? Ja, Jen, Ju. . .Julie. Yes, that was it, Julie.* Angela didn't want to return to the cold, but she couldn't see herself staying here. If he'd give her directions, she'd be on her way.

"You may use my room." Michael shook off his coat and hung it on the peg near the front door. "How's the beans, Noah?"

"Ready to eat."

"Good, I'm starved. We'll eat when you've changed, Miss Harris." Michael waved her off.

Immediately she jumped up, held her quilt wrap around herself, and scurried off to the back bedroom. She gasped seeing the unmade bed, clothes piled in the corner—or were they on a chair? Who could tell? At least the front room had some order to it. This room had none. Angela tossed the quilt on the bed. She slipped off the men's underwear and wished she had left them on. Dancing from foot to foot, she hurriedly clothed herself in her feminine garments. The dress needed a good pressing, but it was dry and it was decent. Something she could wear in public. Although that quilt felt mighty warm and comfy. She glanced back over to the crazy quilt. She'd seen a similar one before, but this one had been made with silk cigar wrappers. She wondered who had smoked all those cigars. Had Michael? There had to be a story behind that quilt. But why was she interested? It wasn't hers, and she was simply passing through. She reached the doorknob and placed her hand on the iron thumb rest, then looked back at the bed and the quilt. Angela released the door and marched back to the bed and made it.

Upon entering the kitchen a few minutes later, she grinned at the solemn faces of Noah and Samuel. Beans and ham every night would get old on her, too. She could relate. "Dinner smells wonderful." She grinned. "Thank you."

"Set yourself over there." Michael pointed to a chair beside Samuel.

The heavy cast-iron frying pan seemed to weigh but a feather in Michael's hands.

"I'll leave after dinner. Can you give me directions back to town?"

He plopped the pan down in the center of the table and narrowed his gaze. "You ain't leaving."

Chapter 2

"W hat?"

Michael didn't realize he had raised his voice. "Storm's still blowing; you can't leave."

"But. . ." Her hands trembled. Upon further examination, he noticed her entire body shook.

"You're still cold. Don't you know you can catch consumption? Get back in my room and put those undergarments back on and both pairs of woolen socks. You need to get warm." What was she thinking? *Why aren't women more practical about their clothing, Lord? It just doesn't make sense.*

Angela dropped her fork back to the table and timidly walked past him.

Alone in a strange house with strange men, she has reason to be nervous, he figured. *Especially with a man who has forgotten just how sensitive a woman can be,* Michael silently rebuked himself. Noah and Samuel scooped their beans and stared at their plates. He'd been too gruff. *Why'd she have to be a woman, Lord?* He could handle men. His knack for soft speech had died with Julie, and a beautiful blond with flawless skin wasn't going to get him to open up that area again. She'd just have to accept his ways. After all, it was his house, and he was in charge.

Angela reappeared with the woolen socks on her feet. Her dress seemed tighter around the waist. She'd put the long underwear on as well. *At least she listens.* He scooped up more of his beans and took his eyes off the alluring creature. Even dressed like that, she appealed to his senses.

"After dinner you can go through my wife's belongings. They're in a chest in my room. Take what you need." He didn't need to be sweet, but he could be polite.

"Thank you." She spread the linen napkin on her lap. "How long do you think this storm will last?"

"Hard to say." Michael forked his dinner. Beans just about every night was getting old, extremely old. Perhaps he should consider hiring a woman to come in and cook and clean a couple times a week. Noah and Sam would love it. So would his own gut.

Angela clasped her hands and bowed her head in prayer. Michael stopped chewing. Prayers before dinner were occasional at best, though he still did evening prayers with the boys before they went to bed.

"I apologize for being an imposition. I do thank you for rescuing me." She picked up her fork and scooped up some beans. Her mouth stopped chewing instantly. Then, as if checking her responses, she swallowed the tasteless beans. Angela dabbed her mouth with the napkin and replaced it on her lap. "May I cook for you while I'm here?"

Michael bit his inner cheek to keep from grinning. He'd be a fool to turn down a woman's cooking. Even the worst cook in the world would manage better than he. Hadn't the boys complained enough in the past few days about their constant meal of ham and beans? "I won't pass it up. As you can tell, I'm not much of a cook."

She nodded, but refused to speak her thoughts. *Angela Harris must have been raised by a refined woman,* he mused. The town was bringing in new folks every day, but Michael had kept to himself. *How long has she lived in the area?* he wondered.

An awkward silence filled the room.

Noah reached over and touched Angela. "I can't wait to eat your cooking." His grin was infectious.

"The boys and I have been hard-pressed for a good meal for a long time."

"I'd be happy to help. Do you have some molasses?" Angela put down her fork.

"Yeah, on that shelf over there."

She scooped up the frying pan and returned the contents of her plate to the pan. The boys did the same.

"Do you mind?" she asked.

"Of course not." What else could he say? Admittedly he wanted to return his plate to the frying pan as well. But he held back. He couldn't appear too eager, could he?

Michael watched as she worked her magic with the beans. The fresh aroma that filled the room had his stomach gurgling. Maybe, just maybe, Angela was an angel from heaven sent to help his household. He'd been thinking about hiring someone. Perhaps she was up to the task. She couldn't live too far away if she'd gotten twisted around in the woods.

"Where do you live?" Michael asked.

"In town. My dad owns the feed and grain store."

Harris. Of course. He should have put the names together. Frank Harris was a fine man, an honest man. He'd never had any problems doing business with him. Which meant she'd been living in the area for years. Why hadn't he seen her before? Where did she keep herself? Surely he would have noticed Angela before, wouldn't he?

"I know your father."

Angela turned and smiled. "He's a good man." She removed the hot pan from the woodstove and set it on the table. She served the boys, then herself. Her gaze caught his, silently asking if he would like some. He wanted to accept, no question, but there was more than enough on his plate to feed his belly. He blinked his negative response.

"Hmm, good." Noah smacked his lips. "You gotta have some, Dad."

"It's wonderful," Sam mumbled.

"Samuel, don't speak with your mouth full. And, Noah, I'm sure it's wonderful, but I have plenty on my plate."

"It's your stomach," Noah quipped as he dove his fork in for another hearty scoop. "Thank you, Miss Harris. This is great."

"Perhaps you can tell me what you added to the beans to make the change in them?" Michael asked.

"Just a little bit of molasses and a small spoonful of your brown sugar."

Michael nodded. He could do that. Maybe he didn't need to hire someone, just get someone to teach him how. No, he didn't have time to learn how to cook, plus care for the land and livestock. He scooped another forkful, dreading the next bite. His appetite gone, he pushed himself from the table and went outside to bring in some extra wood for the night and first thing in the morning. The wind howled, driving the snow in swirls around him. The trees bent before the onslaught, groaning in protest. The storm was a bad one.

⟋⟍

Angela didn't know what to make of Michael Farley. He obviously wasn't happy that she was there, but he was too decent a Christian to put her out into the storm. Her father must be worried sick with her being gone so long. *Father, God, give Papa peace. Let him know I'm all right.*

She made herself useful and started cleaning up the dishes. Unfortunately, as she began to clean, she couldn't keep herself from also washing down several shelves. Dust and grime were piled thick upon them. *How long ago did he lose his wife?* she wondered.

A blast of cold air filled the room. Michael Farley stood with his arms full of wood. "Boys, get the door," he hollered.

Angela resisted the urge to assist him. He seemed to be a gentle bear of a man who had a growl that could send folks running. Was it the anger over his loss? What did it matter? *This is temporary until the storm lets up enough for me to go back home. Home.* Her heart sank. She'd have to inform her father that she couldn't marry Kevin Mason. He was too old, anyway. Her twenty-one to his thirty years worked for some, but. . . She shook the thought away.

He was a kind enough man, she supposed. But shouldn't a woman have feelings for her husband? Some sort of attraction? She brought the images of Kevin back to her mind. Nothing. . . not one stir of emotion, good or bad, came from his image. And certainly not like the stir of her emotions over Michael Farley. She was drawn to him in an irrational manner. She should be frightened but instead felt secure in his home. She wanted to bury herself in his chest and feel the security of his embrace, as if she'd already experienced it. The image, sense, whatever, seemed so real, yet she'd never met the man before today. Angela worried her lower lip. This didn't make sense. She'd known Kevin for years. Never, not even once, had she wanted to be in his embrace.

Samuel broke into her thoughts. "Miss Harris, do you wanna play?"

"What would you like to do?"

"Parcheesi. It's a new game. Daddy bought it for us." Samuel held the boxed game in his hand.

"I'd love to. I don't know how to play it, so you'll have to teach me."

"It's easy. I'll teach you." Sam's chest swelled with pride. He was cute. He seemed to have his father's eyes, but it was hard to tell under all those brown curls.

"Can I play?" Noah asked.

"Everybody can play," Sam announced. "Dad, will you play, too? We can have four players."

Michael dusted off his shirt and woolen pants, cracking the first smile she'd seen on his lips since she'd met him. "It'll be a good way to spend the evening."

Accenting his point, the wind howled and whistled through the cracks in the door and window casings. Angela rubbed her arms at the mere thought of the cold blasts of Arctic air. She should have known by the absence of birds in the trees that a serious storm was coming. Thoughts of Kevin and a pending engagement had driven her deeper into the woods than she'd ever gone before. Getting turned around in an unfamiliar area wasn't good. She knew better.

Angela sat down at the table where Samuel had placed the interesting board game.

"Ya need a five to get out of your spot." Sam pointed to the area closest to Angela and handed her four red wooden pegs.

"You need to get all four pieces in here, but you have to go the long way around," Noah added.

It seemed relatively simple. Angela relaxed and tossed the dice that had been handed to her. She had to stay put, no fives. Perhaps this game would take longer than she expected.

The game progressed until Michael landed on the space where her piece was and sent her back to her base. "Hey."

He gave a disarming grin. "Sorry, those are the rules. If you land on a spot where someone else is, you send him back to the beginning. If he has two pieces on the same space, you're blocked and can't move forward."

"No one told me that." Angela looked over the board to see if she was in striking distance of anyone. This could be fun. Michael had a piece not too many spaces in front of hers. Angela blew on the dice and rolled again.

"Gotcha." The room erupted in laughter.

Angela's heart pounded seeing the love and compassion Michael had for his sons. The way he took time with them was a rare gift. She scanned his features. His coal black hair seemed such a rich crown, with his dark eyebrows accenting blue-gray eyes that crinkled slightly at the edges when he smiled. His full beard required a good trim.

His gaze caught hers. Angela shivered. A glimpse of his soul seemed to appear in his eyes. She broke the connection and looked back down at the board game. Noah was leading with three pieces in home.

"I got you, Noah." Sam smiled.

"I'll still beat you," Noah said proudly, but the disappointment of having to bring that one piece all the way around the board again showed in his face.

Angela peeked up at Michael again, his eyes hooded and guarded. Strangely, disappointment settled over her. What was compelling her to want to know this man? Why did she feel so close to him, even though they'd never met?

Sam passed her the dice. She shook and tossed them. A three and a four. She counted out the spaces forward and removed her hand.

"Why didn't you knock Sam back to his base?" Noah demanded.

Angela scanned the board. "Oh dear, I missed that."

"I don't mind." Sam gave her a big toothy grin.

"Now, Noah, it's just a game, Son," Michael admonished.

"I know."

"And this is Miss Harris's first time playing. She's bound to miss a few things."

Especially if my mind is on silly things. She'd never been one to swoon over a man. Even in school when the girls would giggle and wiggle because a boy walked by. It never bothered her. They were just boys, nothing special. Why was Michael Farley bringing up all these silly thoughts and feelings? He'd done nothing to show he was interested. *You'd best get a handle on these emotions, or you're in for a real heartache.* Angela caught a glimpse of Michael's wink. Heat rose in her cheeks.

~

Later that evening Michael found himself in his bedroom unable to rid his mind of Angela's tempting image. It didn't mean a thing. She was a stranger, a mere child. A grown child but way too young for him. Not that he was interested in pursuing a relationship. Julie, his true love, could never be replaced. But there was something about Angela's mannerisms that drew his attention. The house lacked the womanly touch. The boys were totally enamored with her. Perhaps it was time to give serious consideration to hiring someone to come and clean his house and cook the meals. Michael rubbed his beard. It was thick, just the way he liked it for winter—giving him good protection from the cold. He caught a glimpse of himself in the mirror. The ends of his beard were ragged. He needed a good trim to be more presentable.

Presentable—for whom? Angela's golden hair, rich and full, again flooded his mind. The strands seemed to be spun with golden rays from the sun. Pure sunshine, and oh, how this house had lacked sunshine for so long. Michael's heart ached. He turned toward his bed. Memories of Julie's emaciated body lying there flooded him. He dropped to his knees. "Oh, God, why? Why did you have to take her? I know death was better than the life she lived that last year, but why illness, Lord? Why Julie? Lord, I'm trying to do right by the boys, but I can't do it alone."

A gentle knock on his door caused him to jump from his penitent posture. He walked over.

"Mr. Farley," Angela whispered.

He cracked the door open a couple inches.

"What is the matter?" he asked.

"I hate to ask, but I'm having trouble falling asleep in these. . .these. . . Well, you know. And I was wondering if maybe your wife had some flannel nightgowns."

Julie's things? No. On the other hand, he had given her permission to wear Julie's dresses. Michael cleared his throat. "Yes, there are some in her trunk. Just a minute and I'll get one."

Why, oh why did he offer her Julie's clothing? Because he knew she wouldn't be comfortable in her own soiled dress. *You were being practical,* he reminded himself. Michael opened the chest and fought back the images of his wife wearing the various articles. Briskly, he ruffled through the clothing and pulled out two flannel nightgowns. With a couple quick steps, he stood by the door and thrust the gowns toward his unexpected houseguest.

"Thank you. I'm sorry to impose."

"No imposition; you're welcome." He couldn't close the door fast enough. Her soft blue eyes, the color of wild cornflowers, drew him. He wasn't looking to replace Julie. Attraction was for younger men. He had enough to think about without fighting an attraction to Miss Harris. Yes, he'd have to remind himself to call her Miss Harris, to think of her as Miss Harris. That would help.

He hoped.

He flopped on the bed. An image of Julie lying beside him warmed him. Yes, Julie, his beloved, his friend. Michael closed his eyes and savored the moment. "I don't want to be bitter, Lord. I do miss my wife." He shifted the covers and found himself hugging Julie's pillow. More evenings than not he found himself reaching out for it, for some form of comfort. When would he get over his loss?

He methodically counted down tomorrow's chores. This storm would change some of his daily routines. He'd make oatmeal for breakfast. The boys weren't all that partial to it, but it would warm their bellies and keep them full until lunch.

A flash of Angela working in the kitchen earlier that evening raked over his frayed nerves. The sweet aroma of the beans after she'd altered them. . .her angelic face. . . .

Michael jumped from the bed and paced. How would he survive having such a tempest in his midst for another day?

Chapter 3

A cool draft licked at Angela's nose. She scampered over to the woodstove. Wrapped in a woolen blanket, she tossed in some additional logs. Angela shivered and pulled the covers closer. Before the rest of the household woke, she dressed in her stiff, soiled clothes and the men's undergarments. She had to admit they were warm. Last night, asking Michael Farley for a nightgown had been embarrassing but necessary. He couldn't expect her to live and sleep in the same clothes for days.

She lit a lamp in the kitchen and gathered the necessary ingredients to make biscuits. Hopefully she'd have enough time in the kitchen before the others woke up. Angela eagerly went to work. Helping was the least she could do for saving her life and giving her warm shelter during the storm. She'd awakened a couple times during the night when she'd heard the shutters rattling against the house.

She checked the bread oven attached to the side of the woodstove; its temperature was perfect. In a large frying pan, she fixed generous slabs of bacon. She placed the tray of biscuits in the bread oven and set the table. A small bowl of honey, a small mound of butter, and the table was ready. Hearing footfalls upstairs, she scrambled eggs in the frying pan and put it on the stove. The coffee's rich aroma filled the room as the hot water seeped through the coffee grains.

"What smells so good?" Noah asked as he bounced down the stairs.

"Breakfast."

"Smells great." Samuel's smile reached to the corners of his eyes.

Michael's bedroom door creaked open. "You didn't have to cook for us."

"I wanted to. Come, sit down, and I'll serve." She knew she was being forward in the man's house, but all night she couldn't stop thinking about Michael.

The boys jumped into their seats. Michael stared over at them. "Boys, you're forgetting your manners. Wash up."

"Yes, Sir," they said in unison.

"Thank you." Michael's gaze softened. A flutter worked its way down Angela's spine, and she knew it had nothing to do with the cold. *Why'd I put on that long underwear? Step outside for a minute; that will cool you down,* she chastised herself.

Michael took two giant steps toward the door. "Feed the boys. I'll eat when I finish in the barn."

"But—" The door slammed shut. She wanted to protest his leaving without eating, but she also knew their exchange had been one of mutual attraction. He wasn't ready. After all, he loved his wife. The best she could figure from what the boys had said and didn't say, their mom had died a year ago and had been sick for a long time before she passed away.

"Homemade biscuits!" Samuel grinned.

"We haven't had homemade biscuits in a long time." Noah tucked his napkin under his chin.

"I hope you like them. They aren't as light and fluffy as I like to make them, but there wasn't a lot of time to sift the flour and allow them to rise."

Noah reached across the table and took two biscuits. *Good thing I made the whole batch,* she mused.

"Dad must be real worried about the animals. Ain't fit for someone to be out in that wind." Noah chomped down on his biscuit as bits of crumbs fell from his full mouth.

"Slow down, Noah, there's plenty for everyone."

He closed his lips. "Sorry, Miss Harris."

"You're forgiven. Did you say your prayers?"

Samuel bowed his head. "We forget sometimes. Momma wouldn't like us forgetting our prayers."

"Well, let's say them and then enjoy the wonderful breakfast the Lord is allowing us to have."

The boys nodded their heads and clasped their hands, waiting for her to lead them. *Lord, help me not to overstep my boundaries here.* "Dear Jesus. . ."

She led the morning prayer and the boys concluded with a hearty "Amen."

"How'd you learn to cook so well?" Samuel asked.

"My mother taught me. But she passed on a few years back, so I've been taking care of my father and brothers for several years. Thankfully, my brothers have married, so I only take care of Papa now." Angela began to wonder how long Michael would be in the barn.

"It ain't fun, losing your momma," Samuel sniffed.

A wave of compassion washed over Angela. She remembered

her own moments of anguish after her mother passed. "No, it isn't. But after awhile you get used to it, and you remember all the good times you had with her."

"I wish I'd spent more time with her, knowing she was dying." Noah held his fork in midair, staring off in no direction in particular.

"I remember those same feelings. You feel guilty that you should have done more. Fact is, we probably couldn't have. Takes awhile to get rid of those guilt feelings and replace them with anticipation of seeing her again in heaven."

Noah gazed into her eyes. Tears threatened to fall, but the brave young man held his own. Angela's own eyes filled partly for her own loss and partly for the pain she saw in the boy's eyes. "I miss my mother, too," she barely whispered.

The room fell silent as she and the boys took a moment to reflect on their losses. *Great, just great.* She was responsible for this downward turn of emotions. *Lord, help me say the right thing here.* "What are you boys doing for Christmas?"

Samuel grinned. "Dad said he'd try to get us a Christmas goose. That's when he found you."

"Oh dear, he brought home a lady instead of a goose. Just don't call me a goose lady."

The boys erupted in laughter.

"Seriously, how do you prepare the house for Christmas?"

"Mom would set the house up real fancy-like. But men don't need fancy things," Noah stated and went back to his eggs.

"Oh, I suppose ribbons and such are too feminine."

"I like the way Momma made the house pretty," Samuel mumbled with his mouth full.

"Yeah, it was special," Noah added softly.

Ah, so this is why she was here. Well, besides the fact that Michael had saved her life. But the Lord wanted her here to make their Christmas special. Angela scanned the room. How could she dress up the place?

"If this storm keeps up, I'm going to lose some livestock," Michael muttered as he fussed with the bales of hay. He'd lined every wall with hay to keep more heat in the building. His stomach ached for the tasty food that waited for him in the house. But he couldn't stay in there. Not now. Not until he got control of his emotions. Why he'd ever agreed to letting that woman help with the cooking was beyond him. Wasn't the old saying lesson enough—a way to a man's stomach, and all that? Michael groaned. He wasn't going to allow his stomach to dictate his emotions. He'd starve for the next couple days if he had to.

Finished in the barn and with the wind howling, he had little choice but to make his way back to the house and face this new temptation in his life. After all, he wasn't really attracted to her, he reasoned. Loneliness and not having Julie around simply had gotten the better of him.

"The biscuits are great, Dad." Samuel smiled and sat up. He was working on something, and Michael sneaked a glance to find out what. Looking for a clue, he surveyed the room and stopped at Angela.

"I've put your breakfast in a pie tin and set it on the stove. Hopefully it's still warm."

"Thank you." Michael hung up his winter coat and hat and headed for the stove. He found a pie tin wrapped in a towel with a mound of food under it. Temporarily putting his plan of starving out the window, he sat down at the table. The first mouthful—pure nectar. His stomach rumbled in agreement.

The kitchen appeared brighter. Michael scanned the cupboards and shelves. They sparkled. Angela stood at the sink with her hands buried in sudsy water. Michael cleared his throat. "I appreciate the warm breakfast, but you really don't have to clean."

She turned to him and slowly raised her gaze to meet his. Azure eyes warmed his heart. *God, help me. I'm. . .*

"No trouble at all. I'm glad to help."

Michael looked down at his plate. *Much safer.*

"Dad?"

"Yes, Noah." The biscuit melted in his mouth. How long had it been since he'd had a decent meal?

"Sam and I are working on something for Christmas and—well, we were wondering if you wouldn't mind staying in your room."

A grin slid up his cheek. "Not a problem, Son. I have a thing or two I need to work on myself."

Noah's grin widened.

"Whatcha making, Dad?" Samuel dropped his charcoal stick and came over toward the table.

"Now, Son, it wouldn't be a surprise iffin I told you."

"I suppose, but did you build me a sled?"

Deepening his voice, Michael said, "Samuel."

"Sorry, Sir." Samuel's shoulders slumped.

Michael reached out and brought his youngest son to his lap. "You wouldn't want the joy of the surprise ruined by me telling you, would you?"

"No, but if it was a sled, I could use it now."

Michael laughed. "If, and I do mean if, it is a sled, you couldn't use it until this storm passes."

Michael's heart drummed as Samuel leaned against him. "Daddy, Angela says that after some time you feel better about losing Mommy. Is that true?"

What on earth was the woman telling his sons? "Yes, I believe it is." *But how long would it take?* Michael couldn't conceive an end to this misery.

"Angela said it was hard at first when her mom died."

Michael pushed down the knot in his stomach. Angela knew what she was talking about after all.

Angela came up beside them. "Sam, why don't you let your papa finish his breakfast?"

Samuel pulled away, and Michael looked toward the half-full plate. Eating was the last thing on his mind at the moment. "You can sit beside me while I finish, Son."

Samuel wiggled down and sat on a chair. "What are you making, Son?" Michael plunged his fork deeply into the hashed brown potatoes.

"Dad!" Samuel groaned. "You just said I couldn't know."

"Oh, well, I'm a grown-up. You can tell me."

"Nah uh! Angela, do I have to tell Dad what I'm making him for Christmas?"

"Nope. Your papa will just have to wait, same as you."

"Aw, shucks. Hey, Noah, what are you working on?"

Noah laughed. "Not gonna get it from me, Dad. Good try, though. Come on, Sam, let's take this upstairs so Dad can't see."

Michael laughed and noticed Angela smiling. "What did you put my sons up to?"

"Pardon, Monsieur. You must have me confused with

another," she feigned, placing a hand to her chest.

"And the woman speaks French as well."

"Not really. You don't mind that I helped the boys, do you?" She sat down beside him.

Lord, why am I so attracted to her? "No, not at all. It will help them with this long day."

"What are you working on for the boys?"

He leaned closer and whispered. "I'm just about through whittling some toys for them." He glanced at the stairway. "And I did make that sled for Samuel."

"I love Christmas. It's such a rich opportunity to share God's grace with others."

"It reminds me of when I was a child. I was a lot like Samuel." Michael eased back from her and returned to his breakfast. She smelled heavenly, cooked wonderfully, and she was way too appealing on the eyes. *Lord, help me.*

"That doesn't surprise me." Angela smiled.

"Oh?"

"You've barely sat still since I entered your home."

Am I that obvious, Lord? "Sorry."

"No apology necessary. The boys and I have talked." She placed her silky smooth hand upon his. "I understand their loss, and I'm sorry for yours. I can't imagine how hard it must be to raise a family on your own. At least my father had me to help. And all four of us were older."

He lifted his thumb to caress her hand, then stopped. What was he doing? He pulled his hand back. "I'd best get to work before the boys come down. Make yourself at home."

The chair scraped the floor. He put his dirty plate beside the sink. "I'll be in my room if you need anything."

Angela blinked. *What were you thinking?* she asked herself. She went to the sink and cleaned Michael's plate. How dared she reach out and touch the man? Where was her common sense? Her mother had raised her well. She knew better. Or at least she thought she knew better. She'd never reached out and touched a man like that before. Well, no one but her father. But fathers didn't count. They weren't men, just fathers. *Oh, that sounds highly intelligent.*

One thing was certain, she couldn't marry Kevin, not if she could be so attracted to another man. The fact that Rosemary Cloutier had been visiting her father more often hadn't escaped her notice, either. Had her father found another woman but refused to marry her as long as Angela was in the house? Was that the sudden rush to get her married to Kevin?

Angela tore into the mounds of debris in the family area. Piles of old clothing, shoes. . .her hands stopped at a picture. *Julie,* she thought. *So that's where Sam gets his curls.*

"Let me have that." Michael's harsh tone startled her.

"She's very pretty."

"Yes, she was." Michael collapsed in a chair. "You don't need to be cleaning my house."

"Sorry. You said to make myself at home and, well, since my mother died, that's what I do. I clean, I cook, I sew. . .whatever is needed."

Michael nodded.

Angela sat down on the bench opposite him.

"I'm sorry," he said. "I guess I've let the place get. . ." He turned the picture face down on his right thigh.

"How can you possibly keep up with running the farm, the

boys, and the house?"

"I've been thinking about hiring someone to come in a couple times a week to cook and clean. Would you be interested?"

"I don't know; I'd have to pray on it and. . ." She paused. Should she tell him about Kevin and her father's attempts to marry her off? "I'm not sure what my future holds at the moment."

Michael's eyes stayed fixed on his wife's upside-down picture. "One should pray," he mumbled.

What was he thinking? Had he slipped into a world of old memories with his wife? And why does it bother me if he has? Am I. . .no, I can't be, there's nothing there to suggest such a foolish thing. Other than the hammering of her own heart when Michael came close. *This is too strange, Lord. How can a reasonably intelligent woman fall in—* No, she wasn't in love, she was in lust. No, it wasn't lust, it was attraction. *How can I be so attracted to this man, drawn to him? Want to help him. Want to help his sons. It seriously doesn't make sense, at least not logical sense.*

She'd heard about love at first sight but had never experienced such a thing and thought it rather foolish. A woman took time to develop an acquaintance with a man before she opened her heart to him. That was the proper order of things. Not the misguided emotions she felt at the moment.

"What's going on in your pretty little head?" Michael asked. Her cheeks flamed.

"Dad," Noah called out.

Chapter 4

I t didn't hurt nearly as bad when he looked at Julie's radiant image. Michael set the picture on the small table by the divan. "Excuse me," he said, getting up to answer his son's call.

He caught a glimpse of Angela hiding her embarrassment. She was a beautiful woman. Could he keep his attraction to her from growing if she were to accept his offer to clean and cook for them?

He hiked up the stairs two at a time.

Why'd you have to offer her the job? he wondered. *Because you know she's not afraid of hard work. Just look at the way she tackled this place.*

Noah stood behind his partially opened door. "Dad," he whispered.

Michael leaned closer.

"Sam and I want to make something for Miss Harris for Christmas."

"That's a fine idea, Son." He prayed the boys weren't getting too close to the angel downstairs. "What do you have in mind?"

Samuel came up behind him. "Well, she's a girl, and we aren't sure what girls like. We thought we'd better ask you since you were married to a girl."

Michael held down his grin and scratched his beard. "Seems to me girls like fancy things. Like hat boxes and jewelry and stuff."

"We ain't got none of that stuff." Sam sighed.

"Ah, but in your momma's trunk there is some lace and fancy woman's fabric she'd bought before she got sick."

"Do you think Mom would mind us using it?" Noah released his grip on the door.

"I think your momma would be pleased that you used it as a gift." He prayed Julie would understand. Pleasing Angela was no longer something the boys alone wanted to do, but a desire stirred deep within him to do something special for her.

"Give me a minute and you can come join me in my room. We can go through your momma's things."

His sons' eyes twinkled with excitement, and it didn't surprise him to find a grin spreading across his own face.

A heavenly scent caused his nostrils to flare.

"What's Miss Harris making now?" Noah asked, rubbing his stomach.

"I don't know, boys, but I think we're in for a real treat."

"She's a good cook," Samuel declared.

"Yes, she is. Too good," he muttered, turning his back on the boys. Bit by bit, every tasty morsel that passed his lips fueled his desire to get to know her.

Downstairs, he found Angela in the kitchen. The table was littered with flour, bowls, and a variety of other things, her movements quick and fluid between the stove and the table. "What are you doing?"

"Baking. Sorry about the mess, but I'll clean it up."

"I mean, what are you baking?"

"Oh, just a few things I thought the boys might enjoy."

Michael's shoulders slumped. *She's cooking for the boys. Of course she is. She isn't...* No, he wouldn't finish that thought. He didn't want to be reminded about the angelic temptation taking over his kitchen and his heart. It was better this way. More pure, more right. God had sent her, their own Christmas angel, to furnish them with a wonderful holiday.

"Michael," she whispered.

"Yes?" His pulse quickened.

"If it's all right, I'd like to make up some special things for your Christmas dinner. The boys said you were hunting for a Christmas goose, and there are some things I can bake to make the meal special for all of you."

At least he was included in her "all of you."

"I won't stop you if it's what you'd like to do. The good Lord knows our stomachs could use some tasty meals."

"Thank you. And, Michael?"

He stepped closer. She smelled of cinnamon. Who'd have thought the smell would be so appealing? Her gaze met his — the warmth of her blue eyes, the widening of her pupils. Desire lurked beneath the surface. He saw it. She couldn't deny it. He couldn't deny it.

He reached for her hand. "Angela." Her name struggled to the surface and tumbled over his lips.

Noah and Sam's footfalls assaulted his ears. He released her hand and quickly stepped back. What had come over him?

"Dad, can we go in your room now?"

He cleared his throat and tore his gaze from Angela's. "Give me a minute, boys."

41

Angela swallowed hard when Michael left her side. What had come over her? Over him? *Lord, stop the storm outside before this one inside of me brews into a tempest,* she prayed.

"What ya making?" Samuel asked, scurrying up on to the bench next to the table.

"I thought I'd make you a surprise."

"For me?" Samuel beamed.

"Yes, for you." She tapped his nose with her floured finger.

Noah laughed. "Your nose is covered with flour."

Samuel brushed off the white covering.

She might have desires for the boys' father, Angela admitted ruefully, but she definitely had fallen in love with the boys.

Michael called them from his room.

Samuel dipped his finger in the cookie batter. "Hmm, good. I like cookies."

She gave him a playful swat on his backside as he scurried off to join his father. She heard some whispering and turned just in time to find Noah getting a finger full of the cookie batter. "If you keep that up, there'll be none left to cook."

Noah smiled and ran off to his father's room.

What she didn't expect was to find Michael's finger in the bowl a few minutes later.

"Stop that." She swatted her dishtowel at him.

"But the boys bragged about it so much I just had to taste it for myself." Michael winked.

"You're the parent. You should show by example," she chastened.

"Do you mean to tell me your father never dipped his finger in your mother's cookie dough?"

Angela grinned. Her father had been caught on more than one occasion stealing a taste. "I didn't say that."

"I rest my case."

"Oh, you, go do something." She shooed him off.

"In a minute." Michael reached in and took another scoop.

"You're worse than the boys."

Michael grinned and scurried back toward his room.

"Men." She smiled. "They're just little boys in a larger frame, Lord."

"I heard that," Michael called back to her.

Joy washed over her, hearing the laughter in his voice. God might be using her to help bring healing into this house, but she'd have to watch the ever-growing attraction between them. If she didn't know better, she'd think they'd nearly kissed.

Impossible.

Was it? Angela flopped down on a chair. How was she going to tell her father she couldn't marry Kevin without telling him how attracted she'd become to a stranger? But was Michael Farley still a stranger? Angela nibbled her lower lip.

The wind howled. "And when is that storm going to end?" she muttered. *I need to get home. I need to get some sanity back into my life.* She turned and faced Michael's closed bedroom door. Did she really want to leave this haven? Here people weren't telling her what to do. She wasn't their slave. She did the chores because she wanted to. She was appreciated. She'd gotten more thank-yous and praises for her cooking from these three than she had in the past year with her father.

Kevin didn't mind her cooking, but he didn't compliment it, either. In reality, Kevin wanted a house servant more than he wanted a wife. Oh, she supposed he loved her on some level.

Why, she couldn't imagine. Apart from his obvious appreciation of her looks, they had nothing in common. He liked the things she didn't, and she liked the things he had no interest in. No, she couldn't marry Kevin.

Michael's huge frame, dark hair, and wild blue-gray eyes came back into focus in her mind's eye. "Oh my." She fanned herself. "Work, I need to work."

Angela went back to making the cookies, stew, various breads, and some sweet jam to put on the Christmas goose. Yes, they would have a Christmas feast fit for a king. They deserved it. Desire meshed with reality. She wanted to participate in the meal with them. Perhaps the storm would continue for five more days. Reality weighed heavily on her shoulders. She should be home with her father, in her own home, in her rightful place, not enjoying some winter fantasy her mind had concocted.

Five more days.

She'd never survive it. After all, hadn't it been only twenty-four hours since she woke up in front of the Farleys' woodstove?

"Stop the storm, Lord. I need to go home."

Michael worked with the boys. He prayed Angela would accept the boys' hard work as precious gifts, even though they weren't something a refined woman like herself would purchase in a store. They had taken an old hat box of Julie's and covered it with new fabric. Gluing and pinning the lace around the border had given him fits. His fingers were more punctured than after several days of working with wire fencing. *How do women sew with these things?*

"Do you think she'll like it?" Noah asked.

"I'm sure she will."

"What is she going to do with it?" Samuel scrunched up his nose.

"I imagine she'll put precious things in there or perhaps a hat."

"But our hats hang on a peg by the door." Noah wrinkled his forehead.

"True, but ladies' hats are more delicate."

"Why?" Samuel's innocent question made Michael more aware of how isolated he'd kept the boys since Julie's death. He needed to change that. He needed to take a trip and visit her parents and perhaps his own.

"God made women more delicate, like a lady's hat."

"But why?" Noah leaned back on his elbows. "Female barn animals do as much as the male animals, sometimes more."

"True, but even there, look at the size of a cow compared to the bull."

Noah's eyebrows rose.

Michael continued. "With people, God made it that man would work and provide for his family, but that the woman would help take care of the house, raise the kids, feed us delicious meals, and stuff like that. They are still just as busy, but it's different work."

"Can Miss Harris be the woman for our house?"

Michael's gut twisted. "It doesn't quite work that way, Son. A man and a woman have to fall in love and know that God has a plan for them to marry. Like your mother and me."

"But. . ."

Noah interrupted. "Dad would have to kiss her."

"Oh." Samuel pulled his knees up to his chin. "Like Billy kisses the girls at school?"

"Sort of."

Michael wondered just what Billy was doing in school and why the teacher wasn't aware of it.

"Dad, I don't think you ought to chase Miss Harris like Billy does. The girls scream and run away from him."

Michael chuckled. "Trust me, Son, I'm not going to be chasing Miss Harris for a kiss. And before you get any more foolish ideas in your head, a man can hire someone to come into his home to do the cooking and cleaning. And I'm in a mind to do just that."

"Can you hire Miss Harris?" Noah beamed. "She cooks real well."

"I'll mention it to her, but she has other responsibilities at her home."

"I like Miss Harris, Dad. I hope she can work for you, too."

The question was, Did Michael want to hire Miss Harris, given the obvious physical attraction between them? She was too young to be an old maid, so trying to hook her claws into him didn't figure. But he couldn't for the life of him think of one good reason why she'd be attracted to him. His beard and his hair were wild and woolly. His house was unkempt. *Must be a reaction to me saving her life.*

He rubbed his beard. *Why am I attracted to her?* No, he couldn't allow that attraction to grow.

"Julie," he sighed, putting her things back in the trunk.

He came across her sewing kit and some warm, plaid, flannel fabric. He clutched the material to his chest. She'd purchased this shortly before she became ill. She'd planned on making new shirts for him and the boys.

No, he couldn't let his attraction to Angela grow. Too much would be lost.

Chapter 5

Angela fought her thoughts all afternoon and into the evening. The boys had loved their supper, and so had Michael, although he failed to give her more than a simple thank-you. Having him work in his room was a welcomed relief from the tension building between them all day.

The evening wasn't a total loss. Reading to the boys before they went to bed had been a blessing. Hearing Michael read the Christmas account from the Gospel of Luke blessed her as well. He had a deep, rich voice, and hearing him read the Word of God drew her closer to the Lord—almost as if He were right there in the room telling the story Himself.

The front room, dining area, and kitchen were finally clean. She hadn't worked this hard in a long time. Angela leaned back and stretched her spine. Even fall cleaning hadn't been this difficult. Fresh laundry hung in the living area. They wouldn't smell as fresh and clean as if they were hung outside, but the constant howl of the wind reminded her there was little chance of laundry doing anything but freezing outside.

"Miss Harris," Michael called out to her. At some point during the day, he'd regressed to using her formal name. "What are you doing now? Can't you sit still for a moment?" Michael huffed as he made his way through the hanging clothes.

Angela looked down at her toes. "I'm sorry. I didn't mean to upset you."

"Look, you're not here to be my slave. You may have to work day and night for your father, but in my house—"

"I'm not my father's slave."

"You could have fooled me. You can't rest, can you?"

"I can. I just feel I'm more useful helping you out." Her eyes began to water. Try as she might to stop them from overflowing, she couldn't. *He is trying to be nice,* she reasoned, but his words stung.

"Miss Harris." Michael lowered his voice. "Angela, you don't have to do all this."

"I want to. I feel useful."

"I appreciate your help, truly I do, but you must stop and rest. You're pale and weak. Don't forget you almost died out there." He raised his hand to her forehead. "You've got a fever. Please sit down and relax."

Angela sat down on the divan. Exhaustion swept over her.

"Now, it's my turn to serve you."

Angela sat up.

Michael gently pushed her back down. "Hush now. I'm going to make us some tea. I'm quite capable of that."

Angela leaned against the small feather pillow on the divan. She shouldn't have pushed herself so hard. With the inside of her wrist, she felt her forehead. Her temperature was elevated. A draft hissed through the window. A shiver swept over her. She grabbed the quilt she'd draped over the divan earlier and covered herself.

"Glad to see you're being reasonable. I don't need you falling ill. It's bad enough your father's going to be worried sick over you. He won't be pleased if I don't take the best care of his daughter." Michael handed her a piping hot mug of tea.

Angela wrapped her hands around the mug and let the heat warm her. "I wish there was some way to contact him."

"The wind appears to be settling down some. Hopefully the storm will end during the night."

Angela glanced at Julie's picture. "How did she die? If you don't mind me asking."

"Lung sickness or consumption. The doctor wasn't certain which. She withered away before my eyes. It's a horrible way to go."

"I'm sorry. My mother got some infection, and it just poisoned her entire body. Perhaps that is why I feel the need to keep everything so clean."

"Perhaps."

Angela sipped her tea. Michael gently rocked back and forth in the chair. What could she say? They were both lost in the memories of death and dying. Heaven was looking better every day.

For the first time in over a year, Michael allowed himself to think about others in this world who suffered. He and his sons were not alone.

He combed his beard with his hand and cleared his throat. "Angela, thank you for helping. I know I've let the house go. Have you thought about coming to work for me?"

"Do you think it wise?"

"I don't understand. Because I'm a widower and you're single?"

"No, but that is a point to consider." She pulled the quilt higher up to her chin. "I'm thinking more in terms. . . " She paused and looked away. "In terms of what happened earlier."

"Nothing happened." Only because sanity had entered his clouded brain just in the nick of time.

"Fine, believe what you will. But you and I both know what we saw in each other's eyes."

Heat filled his cheeks. The temperature on his neck rose a notch or two. "Nothing happened and nothing will. I love my wife."

"I see." She closed her eyes and bowed her head.

Was she praying? He could control his emotions. Foolish thoughts would not, could not, rule his actions. "I'm—"

"Please don't say it. You'll only make things worse. I don't understand what happened earlier any more than you do. But whatever this is, it is more real than the past two years with Kevin."

"Who's Kevin?" The words slipped from his lips.

"Kevin Mason has been attempting to court me for two years. He and Father have decided we should get married. I can't marry him. I won't marry him. A woman has to feel something for her husband. Something akin to what I felt earlier, I daresay. I won't marry a man I don't love."

"No one should marry someone without love." Michael clasped his hands together, fighting the desire to reach out and hold her hand. Marriage was hard work. He'd been stretched in more ways than a team pulling a plow during his marriage to Julie. He couldn't imagine tackling a life with someone he didn't care for.

"Thank you. Father will just have to understand."

"Would you like me to talk with him?"

"Would you like him to force you to marry me?"

"What?"

"Face it, we've been alone together for two days. How do you think he'll be feeling about my honor?"

"For pity's sake, Woman, was he raised in the Dark Ages? I merely rescued you from death. Am I supposed to marry you because of that?"

Angela giggled. "No. I'm just saying that if you speak of private matters with my father, he will be concerned about my honor."

"Oh. I get your point." He leaned forward, placing his elbows on his knees.

"Papa will be fine with your rescuing me."

"Let's not get your papa riled then. I don't need any more trouble."

Angela chuckled.

"I still could use a housekeeper."

"I'll pray about it, Michael."

"That's all I ask." Michael stood up. "Do you need anything?"

"No, I'm fine, thank you."

"Then I'll say good night. I'm certain I have a lot of work cut out for me in the morning."

"Good night."

He placed his hand upon her shoulder and gave it a gentle squeeze. "Rest, Angela; you've worked too hard."

"I will. I promise."

"Good night." Before another wave of emotion took over, he thrust his feet forward and worked his way through the maze of clean laundry. *Were there really that many clothes I had piled around the house?* he wondered.

Opening his bedroom door, he glanced at the piles of clean and unfolded clothing—the piles of only-worn-once-and-could-be-worn-again clothes and the mound of filthy clothing that needed immediate attention. He closed the door. Angela didn't need to see this mess.

Michael groaned. She'd been in his room the day before. She had seen it. Buying a new pair of pants instead of washing the old was ridiculous. But he'd found himself doing that on more than one occasion when he was in town. "Lord, I need a maid. I wouldn't mind Angela, but she is temptation like I've not experienced in a very long time. Heal her, Lord. Keep her from getting sick. In Jesus' name, amen."

Michael found himself snuggled in bed and for the first time since Julie's death not reaching for her pillow. His eyelids closed. His nightly prayer changed. He hadn't asked the Lord to give Julie a message from him. Instead, the image dancing through his mind was of Angela.

He punched his pillow and buried his face deep within it, stifling a scream. "God, help me. I can't give in to this. It's too soon. Forget too soon, it's impossible. I can't open my heart to lose it again. Please end this storm before I do something foolish."

Angela's chest felt heavy, tight, making it hard to breathe. "No, God, please help me." She jumped up and felt dizzy.

"Are you all right?" Michael called from her left.

"I–I need some tea."

"Sit, I'll fix some up for you. How's that fever?"

She felt her forehead. "I think it's gone." If that was the case, then she wasn't as sick as she thought. Her back ached. Her legs ached. It hurt to even lift her arms. *What's wrong with me?*

He came up beside her and gently felt her forehead. "You're going back to bed." He lifted her and carried her to the divan. "I'll remake my bed with fresh sheets. You're spending the rest of the day in bed."

"No, I—" Angela cleared her throat, abating the threat of a cough.

"This is not up for debate, Angela. You're going to do exactly as I say, understand?"

Angela couldn't argue; she had no strength. She'd overdone it yesterday. She knew it, he knew it, and now her body was fighting it.

"Give me a couple minutes. Drink your tea."

She reached out and clasped his hand. "Thank you."

"Just get better," he said through clenched teeth.

She leaned her head back down on the pillow and closed her eyes. She took in a deep breath. *Praise You, Lord, I didn't cough,* she prayed, then allowed sleep to take over. She was tired; she just needed to rest. She'd be all right. If only she could convince Michael of that.

Pleasant dreams cascaded over her. She drifted off. Her spirit soared, it was spring, flowers bloomed, birds sang in the trees. "Oh, Michael." She found herself embraced in his arms. "How can I love you so?"

"Women," Michael mumbled as he fought to keep his temper. "What was she thinking?"

He pulled the sheets off his bed. The open windows would cleanse the air while he kicked up the dust and cleaned his room. "If she sees this dirty laundry, she'll force herself out of bed and work again. She's got a death wish, God. What is she trying to prove, anyway? That I'm a lousy housekeeper? I know that. Noah and Sam know it."

Michael shoved the dirty linen in a sack, then stuffed his filthy clothes in the armoire. While she rested, he would finish the laundry and do his clothes and any of the boys' that needed doing. He opened the cherry armoire he'd made for Julie when they were first married and piled the not-so-dirty clothes inside.

He spun around in a circle. "Not too bad." He put on fresh sheets, lit the small stove, and closed the window. "God, heal her. I don't need her father coming after me."

"Who did laundry?" Sam asked, following his brother down the stairs.

"Miss Harris. Noah, please get a kettle full of water and put it on the woodstove in my room."

"Sure." Noah headed into the kitchen.

Sam pushed himself up on his toes to try to look over the laundry. When that didn't work, he bent down and looked under them. "Where's Miss Harris?"

"On the divan, but I'm putting her in my room. She needs more rest."

Sam stood ramrod straight. Michael knew the child was thinking of his mother. The slight twitch of his right eye was a sure sign. A tick caused, the doctor said, by strong emotions. Michael hadn't seen it for months. *God, please don't let her get seriously ill.* "She's going to be fine, Son. She just worked too hard and needs more sleep."

Sam bent his head down. "Oh. Guess we'll have ham and beans tonight, huh?"

"Maybe. I think she made some beef stew yesterday."

"Really?" The boy beamed.

"Yes. Now, I must get her to my room. Excuse me."

Sam pulled back a plaid flannel shirt and followed his progress through the laundry jungle. *Lord, don't let these boys suffer another loss. It's too soon.*

The golden mane of hair cascaded over her pillow. Her skin seemed pale, but a slight blush of color painted her cheeks. Rather than disturb her, he lifted her and carried her to his room. Gently he placed her on his bed and covered her in a cocoon of quilts and pillows.

In her sleep she pulled the covers up over her shoulder and rolled to her side.

Michael left her, and Noah placed the kettle on the woodstove. "She going to be all right, Dad?"

"I believe so, Son." Michael placed his hand on his son's shoulder. "Are you hungry?"

"Starving. She made biscuits and sweet rolls, I think."

"Sounds wonderful. Come and help me by taking down the dry laundry while I fix up some flapjacks and bacon."

Noah patted his stomach. "Storms can be a blessing."

Michael gave a light chuckle as he closed his bedroom door.

"Who cleaned your room, Dad?" Noah asked.

"I did."

"You cleaned, Dad?" Sam asked, tugging on two shirts hanging on the line.

"I can clean; I just don't have much time for it."

"Mom used ta say you didn't clean, you just stuffed the furniture full of the dirty laundry."

Michael cleared his throat and looked at his feet. "Well, don't you go telling Miss Harris that. She's done too much.

She was weakened from that storm."

Noah smiled. "Your secret is safe with us, Dad."

Michael managed to get six good flapjacks for the boys. The other half dozen were slightly charred. "Grows hair on a man's chest," his father used to say. Personally, he'd rather have a hairless chest and a belly full of good food.

The wind seemed to have calmed down. "Boys, I'm going to head out to the barn and check on the animals. Don't go waking up Miss Harris, now."

"No, Sir." He watched the boys climb the stairs. Perhaps they were still working on their Christmas gifts.

Christmas! The goose he'd promised for the boys. Michael bundled into his wool coat and headed out the front door. The blast of cold air caused him to pause. He pulled up his collar and tried to work his way through the deep piles of snow. *Noah and Sam will love playing in this.*

He retreated to his porch and took his shovel. The only way he'd get to that barn today would be to make a path.

Michael had no idea how long he'd been out in the cold, but his hands were numb and his back stiff. He'd fed the livestock and walked easily back to the house along the path he'd carved out. He'd need to reweave his snowshoes if he hoped to hunt with this much snow.

Stepping inside the house, he found the heat stung his body. He'd been out too long. Snow was still falling, but the flakes were larger. Soon the storm would end, and he could bring Miss Harris back to her home.

The door to his room stood wide open.

He stepped closer.

Sam stood beside his bed. "Are you still sleepy?"

Angela rolled over and held Sam's hand. "I'm feeling pretty rested. You up for another game of Parcheesi?"

"No, I need help making Daddy his present."

Michael stepped back.

"How can I help you?"

Sam leaned over and cupped his hand to Angela's ear.

"I think that's a splendid idea." Angela smiled.

Samuel stood up straighter and puffed out his chest. "He'll be so surprised."

"Yes, he will."

Michael stepped back farther, deeper into the family room. He hurried back to the front door and opened and closed it loudly. "Hey, everyone, I'm back."

"Daddy." Sam came running from the bedroom.

Michael saw Noah in the kitchen wagging his head. Michael winked at him. Noah held back his grin. The joy of being a family was warming this house again, and all because of a golden-haired Christmas angel. *Thank You, Lord.*

Chapter 6

By evening the storm had cleared, and the sky turned a brilliant blue before the sun set. "I need to get home." Angela sat down beside Michael at the kitchen table and held a hot mug of tea between her hands. "My family must be worried sick."

"I'd take you home, but are you strong enough to be out in that cold?"

"If I bundle up enough, I'm sure I'll be fine."

"Noah, Sam, I'm going to take Miss Harris home. I'll be gone for awhile. You boys promise me you'll stay inside while I'm gone." Michael turned to her. "Have you ever worn snowshoes?"

"Afraid not."

"I'd take you with the wagon, but the snow's too deep for my oxen. We need to leave right away if I'm to get back before dark."

"I'll be ready in two minutes." She rushed into Michael's room, put on her own clothing, keeping the long undergarments on. Lacing up her boots seemed futile. They were delicate in-town boots designed for style, not for tramping around in the woods. What had she been thinking when she left home? Finished, she jumped to her feet and greeted the family.

Samuel hugged her first. "You'll come and visit sometime, won't you?"

"I'll try, but I'm certain it will be after Christmas."

He nodded his head of curls and stepped back, swiping his eyes with the back of his hand. Angela took in a deep breath. She loved the child and would miss him, too.

Noah extended his hand. "Thank you, Miss Harris."

Such a little man, she thought. Angela pulled him into her embrace and kissed the top of his head. "You're welcome, Noah."

Michael grabbed the woolen lap blanket from the back of the stuffed chair and draped it over his shoulder.

"Time's a-wasting, Miss Harris." He opened the door and a blast of cold air instantly flooded the house.

"Bye, boys, I'll miss you." Angela waved.

"Bye." Noah looked down at his feet.

"Bye." Samuel sniffled. Noah put a protective arm around his brother's shoulders.

Tears threatened Angela's eyes. She turned and left the two precious boys she'd grown so attached to. How was it possible in only forty-eight hours?

"Here, put this around your shoulders. I'll hook the snowshoes up for you." Michael bent down and grasped her right foot. She eased it up slightly for him to attach the large, funnylooking contraption. She knew they worked. She'd just never needed to wear them. Her father's work always kept them in town. If she wasn't inside, she walked the streets after they were cleared.

"You ought to purchase a pair of real boots. These things aren't good for anything except to look at."

"Yes, I should. I don't do much walking around in the woods."

He fastened the other snowshoe to her left foot.

"Now when you walk with these, the trick is to lift your foot straight up and then set it straight down. We tend to drag our toes when we walk. With snowshoes, it's more like walking like a soldier on a march."

"Okay."

"Go ahead. Try them out." Michael sat down on a barrel and put his on.

Angela worked the awkward contraptions, lifting her legs straight up then down, just as he'd instructed. She turned back to see the boys looking out the window and grinning at her. *If nothing else, I've provided some entertainment for the family,* she snickered to herself.

Michael reached out his hand and helped her work her way down the path to the front gate of his property. It seemed to take forever to get that far. Walking in snowshoes would take practice.

"Angela, I know this will sound forward, but I need to carry you, at least until we get close to town. I'll never make it back to the boys before sunrise, let alone sunset."

Should she let him? He'd carried her once before, but that was different. She'd been numb from the cold. Now she would have to give her consent. She thought back on Noah and Samuel alone in the house. They'd been alone before, but she didn't like it. "All right, Michael. I'm sorry I don't know how to walk in these things."

"Takes some practice. Unfortunately, we don't have time."

He hoisted her up into his arms, and she wrapped hers around his neck. "You'll stay warmer this way," he mumbled.

Warmer was one thing. Holding him, or rather being held by him, sent waves of desire as well as comfort over her. How could that be? Why would she feel desire one moment and security and comfort as if she belonged in his arms the next? She focused on his blue-gray eyes. "Michael?"

He caught a glimpse of desire in her cornflower blue eyes. He held her tighter, then released her slowly. "No, Angela. I can't."

"I'm sorry," she mumbled.

Why'd the woman have to be so desirable? Not to mention her cooking abilities. It wasn't fair. Life wasn't fair. Hadn't he learned that last year when Julie died?

She turned her head and watched the path before them. He'd taken a shortcut through the woods rather than following the road to town. They traveled in silence.

Dogs barked in the distance. "Who's out there hunting, now?" Michael asked.

"Possibly someone looking for that Christmas goose," she quipped.

"Don't remind me."

"Oh, Michael, I'm sorry I've caused you so much trouble."

"You haven't." He shifted her in his arms. She tightened her grasp around his neck. "Sorry, I'll warn you next time."

"Thank you. Do you think you'll be able to get a goose for the boys in time for Christmas?"

"I'm going to try." *Good, talking about the boys and Christmas is a safe subject*, he reasoned.

"They're really excited about the things they've made for you."

Michael smiled. "I'm excited, too. They need joy in their lives."

"Yes, they do."

"It hasn't been easy since Julie died. At first her family came and helped for awhile, but once they saw I was determined to stay in the area and build the farm, they moved back home. I think they thought I'd have to send the boys to them. Truthfully, there were days I thought about it. I'm not sure having them live with me is best."

"Oh, don't even think that way. Of course it's best. You just need some extra help."

"Which brings us back to the question I asked you the other night. Will you come work for me, Angela?"

He could see the edge of town in the distance. The barking of the dogs was getting closer. Odd that someone should hunt so close to town.

"No, Michael, I can't."

"Why not?"

"You know as well as I." Their gazes locked. Who would break away first? Her hands fumbled behind his neck.

"Michael," she whispered. Her warm, delicate hand stroked his cheek and beard.

He dropped her. "I'm sorry," he said, feeling his face warm.

"Well, I've heard of cooling a person off, but. . ."

"Sorry, Angela, I didn't mean to drop you. I just didn't. . ." How could he explain it? That her hand touching his face so startled him he lost his composure?

"Help me up," she ordered and stretched out her hand.

"Sorry." He helped her to her feet and started to brush the fresh snow off her. But when he came close to her hands, he pulled back. He felt like he was eight years old again and having his first serious crush. Of course that girl, Vivian, had never known anything about it. She'd sit down beside him, and he'd be unable to move, unable to breathe.

"Michael Farley, you are the most ridiculous man I've ever met!" Angela's voice interrupted his thoughts. "If I'd given Kevin a quarter of the interest I've shown in you, he'd have persuaded my father to have us married years ago."

His face flamed. "I can't."

"Hmph. You can; you just don't want to. There is a difference."

"But—"

"Look, I know you loved your wife, and I know it still hurts to not have her a part of your life. But the way we feel for each other is real. That's why I can't work for you, Michael. It would never work."

The howling of the hounds closed in upon them.

"Angela!" she heard someone calling.

"Angela!" someone called again.

"Over here," she screamed. The dogs stopped barking.

"They're looking for you," Michael offered.

And apparently you aren't, she silently observed. She turned to Michael. "Before they come, I have one more thing to say. God brought us together for a reason, Michael. I know it; and if you search your heart, you know it, too. You know where I live. If you ever decide to. . ."

"Angela!" her father's voice choked out her name. He came running toward her.

"Papa, I'm okay. Michael Farley found me in the woods and brought me home before the storm hit."

Her father extended his hand. "Thank you, Mr. Farley."

"Not a problem, Mr. Harris," Michael said as he shook

the man's offered hand.

"Want to come to our house for some hot coffee before you head back home?" her father offered, holding Angela tightly.

"No, Sir, thank you anyway. The sun's getting ready to set, and Noah and Sam are waiting on me."

"Thanks again. I'll get all the details from Angela."

"Thank you, Mr. Farley," Angela said formally. "I appreciate everything you've done for me." She fought the desire to wink at him. Her father would surely catch that maneuver.

"You're welcome, Miss Harris."

He understood the subtle shift to the formal greeting. For a thickheaded man, he did have some sense every now and again.

"I love you, Papa. I'm so sorry. There was no way to connect with you sooner."

"Now, now, Dear. You're safe; that's all that matters. No one could go out in that storm. We just started searching for you about an hour ago."

Folks started gathering around, and Angela gave an abridged version of getting twisted around in the woods when the storm hit and getting so cold that sleep overtook her. Soon the crowd worked their way to town and dispersed to their homes, while she and her father made their way to the feed and grain store.

Being in her father's arms sent a wave of security over her. Angela waited until they were in the house and alone before she spoke.

The teakettle whistled. Her father removed it and poured the hot liquid into the teapot. "Why'd you go into the woods?" he asked, sitting down opposite her.

"Papa, I had to think about Kevin. I can't marry him, Papa, I just can't."

"Why, Dear?"

"I don't love him. He's nice and all, but there are no sparks, no desire. Shouldn't a woman have desires for the man she's going to marry?"

Her father looked down at the table.

"I know we don't talk about these matters," she persisted. "But Momma isn't around, and you have to know."

He coughed. "I understand. But what am I going to tell Kevin?"

"Tell him no. I'm sorry that sounds harsh but. . ." She poured the tea into the cups. "Papa, I'll tell him if I must, but he spoke to you."

"No, I'll speak to him. He's a good man; he'll understand. Besides, if he learns that your anguish over the decision to marry him sent you out into the woods, he'll never forgive himself."

"Please, don't tell him. I don't want to hurt him. He's not a bad man. He's just not my man." She sipped her tea to avoid telling her father who she felt her man was. She couldn't shake the certainty that she and Michael should be together. Perhaps it would just take more time. *Perhaps when he's over the death of Julie, he'll be able to see for himself.* But how long would that take? *Oh, Lord, don't let it take years.*

Chapter 7

Michael returned home before the sun fully set over the horizon. Its fiery display in the sky was no equal to Angela's lecture. The woman had passion and a boldness he'd not seen before in anyone of the opposite sex. Even if he could get past Julie, was he willing to explore living with a woman so bold? Nope, the tempest was gone. He was safe now.

"Hey, boys, I'm home."

"Hi, Dad, we're upstairs working. You can't come up," Noah called down.

"I'll be down here. When you're ready for bed, come on down." Michael moved into the kitchen. On the table sat a fine loaf of apple and raisin bread. He hacked off a large slab and topped it off with the whipped butter Angela had left in a small bowl on the table. His stomach grumbled with appreciation.

He went to the stove and heated up his pot of coffee. Everywhere he looked he saw traces of Angela. The decorative way she'd set up the house for Christmas. The breads, rolls, pies—the woman was a cooking machine. Of course, he and the boys were eating machines. If he could only convince her to come work for him.

Memories of her touch sent a shiver down his spine. No one had affected him like that, not since Julie. Perhaps she was right; the temptation would be too great. Besides, he wasn't ready for another relationship.

He poured himself a large mug of coffee and went into his room. The first thing he needed to do was unload his armoire of his dirty clothing. Inside the tall chest he found a packet wrapped in some of Julie's material with a note attached.

"Michael, please put these out Christmas Eve after the boys go to bed. Consider them a gift from Julie and myself."

He opened the packet and discovered the flannel shirts Julie had started to make for the boys with the material she'd purchased just before she'd taken ill.

His heart thumped. "Angela, Julie. . ." He held the shirts to his chest. "Lord, Angela is an angel sent from You."

In his mind he heard a whisper of a voice reply, "Not really."

The heavenly image of Angela's golden hair and cornflower blue eyes flooded his mind.

"Dad!" Samuel yelled.

"Saved by reality." Michael refolded the shirts and put them in the bundle. "In my room, Son. Give me a minute."

He placed the package in the armoire and closed the doors. "Come in, Sam."

"Dad, I was thinking."

When Sam started thinking, it was time for Michael to put up his guard. "What about, Son?" Michael sat down on his bed, which he noticed was made with fresh linens. *That woman.* He wagged his head from side to side.

Samuel crawled up on the bed and sat beside him. "Well, Miss Harris, she helped us with your presents."

Michael nodded his head. He would wait to see where this was going.

"And well, you see, I was thinking. I was thinking that maybe we all ought to make something for her."

"Son, we already did that. We don't have much time for another gift."

"I know."

Noah entered the room. "But if we all worked together, Dad, don't you think we could do something more?"

"Possibly. What did you boys have in mind?" Michael tapped his knee for Noah to join them.

"She likes to cook, but we can't make pans, can we?" Noah asked.

"No, Son, I'm not a blacksmith. I'm afraid that's something we couldn't do."

Samuel scanned the room. Michael followed suit. "What about a sewing box like ya made Momma."

"Yeah, but bigger. Momma's sewing stuff was always all over the place."

"Hmm." Michael scratched his beard. "I have some cherry in the barn."

"Cherry?" Sam scrunched up his nose.

"It's a type of wood, a hardwood with a nice design in the grain. We'd have to work real hard to have it ready by Christmas. Of course, we wouldn't have it oiled by then."

"We need to give her a finished present, Dad." Samuel stood up on the bed and placed his hands on his hips.

"I suppose you're right."

Noah went over to his mother's sewing box. "Why don't we just fix up Mom's and give it to Miss Harris? I ain't gonna learn to sew, are you, Dad?"

"No, but—"

"Mom wouldn't mind, Dad. She doesn't need a sewing box in heaven 'cause she didn't take it with her," Sam surmised.

The boy was dangerously close to being too intelligent for his own good. "No, I suspect you're right."

"What do you have in mind, Noah?"

The three of them huddled over Julie's sewing box and planned.

On Christmas Eve, Angela realized she hadn't stopped baking and knitting for days. She had to make something more for the boys. The shirts were really from their mother. The question was how she would get the items to Michael's house without him noticing it until it was too late.

Kevin Mason took the news that they wouldn't be getting married rather nonchalantly. In some way she felt he seemed relieved. Like he'd asked for her hand out of duty or maybe just out of guilt for eating all those free meals. Whatever the case, he was now out of her life. He'd come over only once during the day and then simply visited her father in the store.

Dreams of Michael grew stronger each night. She prayed for him. She prayed for herself. She prayed for them. She prayed to get the images out of her mind. It was utter foolishness to fall so deeply for a man she barely knew. But having spent two full days with him and the boys, she felt she knew him better than she knew her own father, if that were possible. She groaned and went to the oven to check on her pumpkin pies.

"When are you going to stop baking, Angela?" her father asked as he entered their private living quarters.

"This is the last until tomorrow."

"Is there anything left to cook? There's just the two of us."

"I know, but. . ."

"All right, I can't take it another moment. What happened at the Farleys?"

"What?"

"Don't go giving me those innocent eyes. Tell me straight, Daughter. Did you fall in love with Mr. Farley?"

"Oh, Papa, I think so. I can't stop thinking about him. Day and night. Night and day. It's impossible." She sat down at the table.

Her father pulled out a chair for himself. "I see, and does he feel the same way about you?"

"No, he wants to hire me to clean his house and cook his meals."

His bushy eyebrows rose. "Why didn't you take him up on the offer?"

"Papa, I couldn't. What if. . ." She felt the heat of embarrassment rise on her cheeks.

"That bad, huh?"

She nodded. What could she say? And how was it her father understood such feelings? A fleeting thought that he was once a young man in love slipped through her mind.

"Look, I can't say that you should or shouldn't take the job. But Farley, he don't get out much. When do you think you'll see him again?"

"I don't know, Papa. I was kind of bold."

"What are you saying, Daughter? Please tell me you did nothing we should be ashamed of."

"No, Papa, nothing like that. I merely told him once he

was over his wife, he should come see me."

"I see. You know it takes a man awhile."

"I know, but—"

Her father raised his hand. "Hush, Child, I have something to say. I suppose you've probably figured out I've been seeing Rosemary Cloutier."

"Yes. Are you going to marry her?"

"Nothing like getting to the point of things, huh?" He grinned. "Well, she's told me to get serious or move on."

Angela laughed out loud. "Men, what is it about you? Papa, I know Mrs. Cloutier will never replace Momma, but if you love her. . ."

"That's just it, Child. It takes a man awhile to realize he can love another woman and not disrespect his first wife. You see, I love your mother very much, and the mere thought of thinking of another woman as my wife. . .let's just say it was none too comfortable."

"You're saying I should be patient?"

"Yes." He pushed his chair back and got up from the table. "It's only been, what, four days since you met him?"

"Five," she corrected.

"Five whole days, an eternity," he mocked and went to his room.

He did have a point, and patience didn't suit her well. "God, give me strength. I don't think I can wait two years like Mrs. Cloutier."

⌒

Michael kissed Noah and Sam after finishing their prayers together. They'd had a delightful couple of days preparing for Christmas, everyone huddling in their own corners of the house, busily making gifts in secret and working together on Angela's gift. "Good night, boys. I'll see you in the morning."

"Night, Dad." Noah snuggled under the blanket up to his chin.

Michael pulled the covers up over Sam's chest and tucked the boy in.

"Daddy, is it really Jesus' birthday?"

"No one knows for sure, Son, but it seems as good a day as any, don't you think?"

"Yeah, but how come we don't know what His real birthday is?"

"Because they didn't write it down back then."

Samuel raised himself up on his elbows, undoing the tucked-in blankets. "Why didn't they write it in the family Bible, like we do now?"

Michael chuckled.

"Because Jesus was part of the Bible, Silly," Noah added with a hint of disgust in his voice.

"Noah."

"Sorry, Dad. Sorry, Sam." Noah rolled to his side.

Samuel wiped his nose with the cuff of his shirt. Michael thought of correcting him but couldn't afford the time. "Good night, boys," he said again, getting up from beside their bed.

"Dad," Samuel called out in his singsong voice.

"Do you want coal in your stocking, Son?"

"No, Sir."

"Then I suggest you get some sleep."

"Yes, Sir." Samuel scurried under the covers and squeezed his eyelids shut.

Michael thought he heard Noah say something about babies

under his breath. Another thing he'd have to let pass if he was going to finish his gift for Angela.

He'd worked hard each night after the boys had gone to bed. At first it was difficult thinking about giving Julie's sewing box to Angela, but soon it seemed like a very practical thing to do. However, he didn't want Angela feeling like she was getting Julie's leftovers. Together with the boys, they had worked to refinish and also add a little bit to the box.

What he was working on would be an addition to the box or could be used as something entirely different. Carving the angel in the top of the small box he'd designed for pins and needles, or perhaps small pieces of jewelry, had been the hardest part. Putting the box together, while difficult because of the small size, wasn't anything compared to the intricate work on the angel.

Michael prayed as he worked the small chisel to carve the fine lines of the feathers within the wings. "Father, she definitely brought a change in this household, but I don't know if there should be anything more between us. I'm grateful, but I'm not sure if I'm ready for a wife. Angels are messengers, Lord, and I got the message."

A small voice rumbled around in his head. *"Did you?"*

Chapter 8

"Merry Christmas, Father." Angela hugged her father and gave him a gentle kiss on the cheek.

"Merry Christmas, Child. Did you sleep well?"

"Yes, Papa."

"What is our agenda today? I know you did not cook all this food for us. Where are we going?"

"I thought we could invite Mrs. Cloutier over for Christmas dinner."

"Did you think to extend an invitation at church last evening?"

"Yes." She winked.

"We are to have guests, then? Good, good, a house is merrier with more people. Are your brother and his wife invited to this special event?"

"Of course. Father, why do you think I wouldn't invite the entire family?"

"No reason, Child. I seem to be the last to know of your plans."

"I wanted to surprise you."

"And who else did you invite?"

"No one. Just the family and Mrs. Cloutier, of course. You will be making her part of the family shortly, won't you, Father?"

A deep rumble of a laugh filled the room. "In my own good time, Child. And I'll not fancy you pushing me one way or the other."

"Never, Papa."

He wagged his head and went back to his room, no doubt to dress for the guest. The one family she wanted to invite had been the Farleys, but Michael hadn't been in church last evening. She'd so hoped to see him and the boys. He should have been able to get his oxen and sled out by now. At least she had hoped he would have. It mattered little. She could not be forward and approach him. She'd already been far too forward than was proper for a woman of good breeding. Of course, she never did complete her studies at finishing school, not after her mother died.

Who was she kidding? She had reached out and touched Michael in a very forward manner. She knew it. He knew it. And he'd run from her faster than a fox with his tail on fire.

Well, if God has it in mind for the two of us to get together, it will take a major miracle. Something equivalent to getting a mule out of a pool of molasses, I daresay. She would pray and she would try to be patient, or she would be single the rest of her life. No man could have her heart, not after Michael Farley had put his brand on it, however unknowingly.

She placed a large pot on the coal stove and poured in a couple gallons of fresh apple cider with several large cinnamon sticks and a few cloves, then let it simmer. She put the pork rib roast she'd prepared the night before in the oven, stuffing the meat with slices of apples and raisins.

Angela sat by the tree and waited for her father.

"Smells heavenly, Angela."

She inhaled deeply. The aroma of cider mixed with the scent of spices from the pork roast filled her nostrils, and her heart warmed with joy. It was a holiday of rejoicing. Today marked the day when God started the process to bring man back to Himself. It wouldn't be complete until Easter and the resurrection, but each year it was a good reminder of just how miraculous it had been to bring a Babe into the world to bridge the storm of sin.

"Thank you, Father. Come, I have something for you."

"Don't you want to wait for the rest of the family?" Her father smiled, his bushy eyebrows rising up his forehead.

"No, Papa, I want to give this to you now. You'll understand once you've opened it."

"All right, Daughter. If you insist." She could tell by the gleam in his eyes that he, too, still had the heart of a child when opening gifts. "But first, we must pray and thank the Lord for this glorious day."

"Yes, Papa." She held out her hand, and his thick, rough hand grasped hers.

"Father," he began.

Her mind drifted to Michael, to Noah and Samuel. Did they appreciate the gifts she'd made for them? She prayed she hadn't overstepped her bounds by finishing those shirts. Admittedly, she had had to redo Noah's because he'd grown so much. Samuel would fit the one Julie had intended for Noah.

"And, Lord, we come before You on behalf of Mr. Farley and his family."

Angela's head shot up, then relaxed.

"He's a kind man," her father continued, "but he's had a

mess of trouble with his wife takin' ill like that. It's hard on a man raising young ones on his own. We ask You to go before him in all he says and does."

Angela bit her inner cheek. Father did understand what it was to have children without a wife. But Michael had it worse. He didn't have a daughter, and both boys were still young, though Noah couldn't be told that.

"We praise You for all that You've done for us this past year. And we ask only that You give us a wonderful day with our family today. In Jesus' name, amen."

"Amen." Angela choked down her emotions. God had blessed them this year. Everyone was healthy. She wasn't engaged to Kevin—was she ever thankful for that. And Papa was getting ready to find himself a wife in Rosemary Cloutier. Yes, life was good. So why did she ache inside for Michael? For Noah? For Sam? And most of all for what could have been with Michael and herself? *Oh, God, You know my heart. I give it to You. Tread lightly, Lord,* she prayed.

"Daddy, Daddy, wake up!" Samuel shook him until he opened his eyes.

"What, Son?"

"You've got to see, Daddy. The house, it's beautiful. Where'd all the presents come from?"

"I don't know; we'll have to check." Michael slung his feet over the side of the bed. If he figured right, he'd gotten about two hours' sleep. He'd spent the night cleaning and putting up the remaining Christmas bows and decorations that he and Julie had collected over the years. He'd even chopped some sprigs of pine to put the bows on. If he did say so himself, he'd done a pretty fine job of it. Of course, he'd be dragging the rest of the day.

"Come on, Dad." Samuel tugged on his pajama sleeve.

The rest of the morning was a blur. The boys were so excited, and Michael fought an exhaustion headache—or was it the constant reminder of his Christmas angel and her present sitting under the tree?

"Dad, can we take Miss Harris her present?" Noah asked.

"What about Christmas dinner?"

"I ain't hungry."

"Me, neither," Samuel added, jumping up and down. "Can we please take her her present? Please, Dad. Please."

"All right. But first I need a nap." Not to mention it wasn't even eight o'clock in the morning yet.

"All right, Dad." Noah slumped his shoulders.

"Just an hour, boys. Then we'll leave. I promise. You can wake me up. Will that be all right?"

Sam nodded his head. Michael retreated to his room. He needed just a tad bit more sleep if he was going to address Angela. The woman demanded all of a man's keen senses.

Michael collapsed on his bed. Visions of Angela's golden hair calmed yet revived him all at the same time.

A short while later, Michael jumped out of bed, put on his Sunday best, and found the boys playing with the toys he'd carved. "You boys, get dressed in your church clothes. I'll hook up the sleigh."

"Really?" Sam jumped up.

He grinned. "Really. Come on, get a move on."

The boys ran up the stairs faster than he'd seen them go in a long time. Michael carried the new and improved sewing kit for Angela. He'd decided that gift would come directly from the boys. His more personal gift would come from him, when the boys weren't looking, he hoped.

If anything was decided last night, he definitely didn't want Angela removed from his life. What that meant in terms of them and a future relationship, he didn't know. At least he'd consider the possibility.

He hitched up the sleigh with the oxen, and the boys came running out of the house. No boots, but they did have their winter coats semi-fastened. Michael chuckled. *If Angela were here. . .* Nope, he wouldn't think that far.

"Where are your boots, boys?"

"In the house," Samuel said innocently.

"Noah, go grab boots for you and your brother. Samuel, bring the woolen lap blanket from the back of the sofa. You never can tell if another storm will blow in."

"Yes, Sir." The boys spun around and reentered the house. Michael climbed up and waited for his sons. "Thank You, Lord. They're good boys. You've blessed us."

The sleigh ride made the trip into town much faster than the day when he'd walked Angela home. Still, it took a lot more time than he thought it would. "She's going to be surprised, huh, Daddy?" Samuel said for the umpteenth time.

"Yes, she'll be surprised."

"I can't wait," Noah exclaimed. "We worked so hard. She's going to like it, isn't she, Dad?"

"I'm certain of it. You boys did an excellent job."

"Can she be our new momma, Dad?" Samuel asked.

Michael swallowed the ice ball in his throat, nearly dropping the reins. "That's in God's hands, Son."

Noah smiled and winked at Samuel. What did he say wrong there? The boys were up to something. What, he wasn't certain of, but he'd need to watch them like a hawk. No sense leading Angela on when he wasn't sure himself. Or was he?

Angela stirred the hot cider and inhaled deeply the warm, homey scent. Memories of Christmases past, her mother at the stove preparing the cider, filled her. No longer did she feel the heartache of the loss. Instead she experienced profound gratitude that her mother had been such a great example of a godly woman.

Angela ladled a mug full of the warm cider. The pork roast sizzled to the point of near perfection. All the guests had arrived and were sitting in the front parlor around the Christmas tree. For the first time in her life, she felt—

What do I feel? Strange, alone, as if I'm not really a part of the family. But that's not really it. I am a part, but just not fully connected. "Face it, Angela," she mumbled to herself. "Your mind is on another family."

She fussed with the decorative settings on the table. Part of her gift was the meal she'd prepared. Father sat beside Rosemary on the sofa, his arm resting across her shoulders. *Perhaps a spring wedding,* Angela mused.

Just then, she heard someone coming up the back stairs to the apartment. She listened intently. More than one person was coming. She walked to the back door.

A small knock was followed by some muffled voices. *Who can it be?* She opened the door. "Noah, Samuel."

"Merry Christmas, Miss Harris," the boys chimed in, their cherub faces grinning from ear to ear.

"We brought you a Christmas present." Sam puffed up his little chest.

"We made it," Noah offered.

"Oh, my. Come in, boys, come in." She glanced at Michael standing behind his sons. Had he intentionally held the piece of furniture in front of his eyes, or was he lifting it over the boys' heads so they all fit on the landing?

"Who's here?" her father called from the front room.

"The Farleys."

Michael lowered the piece and smiled. Angela thought her heart would burst. Had he had a change of heart, or was he doing this for the boys? He was a good father, and no matter how hard it might be for him to see her, he'd still do what was best for his sons.

"Come, join the family in the front parlor. Have you eaten?"

"No, but it sure smells good in here." Samuel leaned toward the stove.

"We have plenty. Would you like to join us?" She glanced up to Michael.

"Can we, Dad?" Noah cried.

"We didn't mean to—"

She placed her hand on his arm. "Of course you didn't. You're welcome to join us, Michael."

"If you don't think we'll impose, we'd be honored." He winked.

He winked, Lord. Oh my. Does he—

Stop it, Angela, stop making things out to be more than they are.

After brief introductions, the boys presented their gift to her. She recognized the piece, but they'd added legs and another drawer. "See." Sam opened up a door on the side of the piece. "Momma always said she needed more space."

Noah interrupted. "We added this area for your spools of thread."

"Boys, this is wonderful, and to think you've made it. It's so special." She reached out and kissed them both. "Thank you, thank you very much."

A special gift and a sacrifice for Michael. Her heart was full.

Rosemary and Angela's sister-in-law, Cynthia, went to the kitchen to finish preparing the meal.

Papa made light conversation with Michael about next spring's planting. She looked at Michael while the boys played quietly on the floor with some toys her brother had brought out from his old room. Now she felt content, as if her world were falling into place. Michael had to know they were meant to be together. He had to feel it, too. Didn't he?

They shared the meal, and everyone complimented her cooking. Cynthia and Brad went home shortly afterward. Papa escorted Rosemary home. The boys played outside in the snow.

Finally she and Michael were alone.

"Angela." Michael's voice was barely above a whisper.

"Michael, thank you for the sewing box."

"That's from the boys. They wanted to give it to you."

"But—"

"Shh." He touched his finger to her lips. Her legs wobbled. "I have a gift for you, but I wanted it to be a surprise, and I guess I'm selfish. I wanted to share it with you privately."

"Oh?"

He reached into his pocket and pulled out a bundle wrapped in pink silk. He tenderly placed it in her open hand. "Open it, please."

"Michael, I–I. . ."

He gave a light chuckle. "Just open it."

She obeyed and pulled the scarlet ribbon tying the silk cloth together. Her hands trembled. "Michael, it's beautiful." She traced the delicate angel on top of the box. "You carved this?"

"Yes, it's a box for needles, pins, anything small."

She opened the lid.

"You do wonderful work, Michael."

"I had great inspiration." She caught his gaze. "Angela, I don't know how to say this so that it sounds right. I'm not a man given to great words, and on more than one occasion I sent my wife crying because of what I said."

She nodded for him to continue.

"I can't get you out of my mind. I'm not sure if I'm ready to open my heart, but I want to. I'm afraid, Angela. I don't know if I could go through the heartache of losing someone I love again. Does that make sense?"

"Yes. Father shared with me about his own struggle of not feeling he was dishonoring my mother by allowing himself to have feelings for another woman."

Michael's posture relaxed.

"I know the Lord sent you to us. You've turned my world upside down and helped me get my focus back. I want you in my life, Angela. I just don't know if that means I'm ready to ask you to be my wife."

Angela let out a nervous giggle. "Oh, Michael, why don't we just take it one day at a time? I believe we should court before we start talking marriage."

Michael laughed. "You may be right there." He wrapped her within his arms, pulling her closer. "I think I've fallen in love with an angel, a golden-haired angel."

Angela placed her hand upon his chest. "I know I've fallen in love with a grizzly bear."

Michael roared with laughter. "I can roar."

"Oh yes."

"Be patient with me, Angela. I don't want to hurt you, but. . ."

"You loved your wife, and you didn't think it was possible to fall in love again."

"Yes. How'd you know?"

"Like I said, I had a talk with my father."

"Oh, right. Why does a man feel like he's the only one who's ever had these feelings? I know others have lost beloved wives, but. . .I just don't get it."

"Michael, the storms of life affect us all. Yet we also experience the joys of life, and God gave us a unique gift in love. It's so personal we can't imagine how anyone else feels these things as we do. But we know in our own minds that others do. I think it's just one of those great mysteries of God."

He leaned back on the sofa and thought for a moment. "You're a wise woman, Angela. I think you might be right there." He pushed a wayward strand of her hair behind her ear. "May I kiss you?"

Please! she wanted to scream. Instead, she nodded slightly. *What would it be like to. . .*

Oh, Michael. She wrapped her arms around him. The tender kiss deepened.

"Daddy's kissing Miss Harris!" Samuel screamed.

Instantly she and Michael pulled apart from each other. Heat rushed to her cheeks.

Noah came running to the doorway. "Did you kiss a girl, Dad?"

"Yup, and I think I'm going to be doing more of it." Michael took Angela's hand tenderly in his own.

"Eww, Dad, you don't kiss girls." Sam's nose scrunched up.

"You do when you're older, Son. And if you love them." Michael winked.

Epilogue

Two years later

I'll be back as soon as I can." Michael grabbed Angela from behind, wrapping her in his arms.

Angela turned around within his embrace. She combed down his winter beard with her fingers. "I wish you didn't have to go."

"I know, but if we're going to have a little one, I need to have this wood milled."

Angela smiled. They'd been married for six months, and the Lord had granted them the blessing of a child due in another six months.

"Promise me you'll call on the boys if you need something lifted."

"I promise." Life couldn't get any better than this. The year and a half of waiting for Michael to know beyond the shadow of a doubt that she and he were meant to be together had been hard some days. But most of that time they had spent wisely, slowly developing their friendship. And she'd accepted his offer of a job. It had given her more time to be with him, time they desperately needed.

"Don't forget Father and Rosemary will be coming for Christmas dinner."

"I'm honored to have them in our home any time, you know that."

"Oh, and I have a surprise for you."

Michael held her tighter. "What else could you possibly surprise me with? I'm so excited about the baby, Honey."

Angela giggled. "I can tell. I told you last night about the baby coming, and here you are off to get the wood milled for the baby's crib. You do realize it will be a few months before the baby is born, don't you?" she teased.

He nibbled the nape of her neck. She squirmed to get away. He tightened his hold.

"I know how long it takes, Angela."

"You could have fooled me," she said with a wink.

"Keep it up," he threatened playfully.

"Mom, Dad, we're going outside," Noah called out from the living room.

Angela broke free from Michael's hold.

"Bundle up, boys," Michael called back, not breaking his gaze from Angela's.

"Daddy, can I go to the mill with you?" Sam asked.

"No, Son. I need you to help your mom while I'm gone. Besides, you get to stay and play in the snow."

"Oh yeah." Samuel ran to the front door.

"Button up, Sam."

"Yes, Ma'am."

The door flew open and the boys tumbled out with boots flopping and jackets half-buttoned.

"I'll get them to finish dressing before I leave." Michael chuckled.

"Thanks."

"Now, where were we? You said you had a surprise for me?"

Angela wiggled her eyebrows. "I believe I do, but if I tell you, it won't be a surprise, will it?"

"Now that's not fair. I told you I was painting the windows and doors of the house the color of your eyes."

"True, but you can't keep a surprise."

"When do I get to see this?" Michael demanded, hands on his hips.

"Soon, real soon."

"You keep this up and I'll have to take you over my knee."

"You and what army?" she teased, knowing those to be fighting words.

He lunged forward. Swiftly she avoided his capture.

"Angela. . ."

"Later, Dear. The boys are watching."

He turned and saw their mittened hands cupped on the windows, their faces glued to the action. He turned back to her. "You don't fight fair."

She pulled the dishcloth off the hook and swung it over her shoulder. "Life's not fair, Darling. It's what we make of the storms and whether we allow God's joy to come in after them."

"You're right. And before another one brews, I'm taking the logs to the mill. I'll be home as soon as possible."

"I'll keep your dinner warm."

"Thanks. By the way, if I haven't told you I loved you this morning, consider yourself told." He winked.

"Boys watching or not, you better tell me better than that," she challenged.

Michael groaned but embraced her just the same. "I love you, Angela."

"I love you, too, Michael. Come home quickly. I'll be missing you."

"And I you." He kissed her gently on the lips. "Thank you for being patient with me."

"Thank you for loving me. I don't know when I've been happier. Go now, and hurry home."

She waved at Michael as he left, leading the team of oxen that were pulling the sled loaded with logs. As Samuel waved to his father, Noah bent down and made a snowball. Angela chuckled. She knew Samuel would soon be attacked.

LYNN A. COLEMAN

Lynn makes her home in Miami, Florida, with her husband of twenty-eight years, serving the Lord as pastors of Christ Community Church. Together they are blessed with three married children and seven grandchildren. Lynn writes for the Lord's glory. She also hosts an inspirational romance writing workshop on the Internet, manages an inspirational romance Web site, and serves as advisor of the American Christian Romance Writers, an organization she cofounded. She loves hearing from her readers. Visit her Web page at www.lynncoleman.com

IMAGE OF LOVE

by JoAnn A. Grote

This is my commandment,
That ye love one another, as I have loved you.
JOHN 15:12

Chapter 1

Minnesota, 1869

Mantie Clark stood at the schoolhouse door, smiling as she watched the children don their winter coats. She shivered and drew her green shawl more closely about her shoulders. Winter had arrived early this year, even by Minnesota standards. The wool coats and colorful mufflers and mittens were welcome against the bite in the air.

The children's chatter and laughter filled the cloakroom. Their energy contrasted sharply with the quiet discipline they portrayed in the schoolroom.

She wished each child good-bye as they hurried through the doorway and into the chill outdoors. Each returned the farewell, most with a mittened wave, though their attention was on the freedom beyond the door.

"See you at home, Jesse and Jenny." Mantie patted her nine-year-old nephew and ten-year-old niece on their shoulders as they passed.

A six-year-old girl with blond braids tugged at Mantie's skirt and held up hands encased in black mittens. "My fingers don't work. Will you tie my hat?"

"Of course, Susannah." Mantie smiled and knelt beside the banker's daughter. Swiftly she secured the black knit hat. "There you go."

"Thanks, Teacher."

Five minutes after she dismissed school, only one child remained. Eight-year-old Nathan Powell stood silently beside her in the doorway, watching the street. He held his floppy brown felt hat in mittened hands, respectful of the rule not to wear hats inside.

"Do you remember how to find your home?" Mantie broached the question gently. Nathan was the only child in town she didn't know. Today was his first time at school.

"My brother said to wait. He said he'd come get me when school was over."

"Then I'm sure he'll be here soon. Doesn't your brother go to school?"

The look he gave her indicated he thought her comment stupid, but his voice remained properly respectful. "He doesn't have to go to school. He's a man."

"I see." She wondered how old the brother was. Any male over twelve seemed a man to an eight year old.

Nathan continued to watch the village lane, which led past a scattering of log and clapboard homes to the short, straggling business street. The only movement on the street was the children laughing and teasing each other on their way to their homes, their winter clothing splashes of moving color against the snow-covered ground. Books swung from leather straps at the children's sides. Snowballs arched through the air.

Jesse scooped up a handful of snow, hurried up behind his

sister, Jenny, and stuck snow down the back of her coat. An indignant yell resulted. Jesse ran off laughing amid loud but meaningless threats from Jenny.

Mantie shook her head, still smiling. *Things haven't changed much from when I was their age,* she mused. A bittersweet memory of Colin Ward bombarding her with snowballs at the ripe old age of ten whisked her into the past. Colin had been the new boy in town. She'd been too young to know the attack and the gleam in his brown eyes meant he found her attractive.

She touched the cameo locket at her throat, sighed, then closed the door on both the winter scene and the past. "Why don't we wait inside where it's warm, Nathan?"

He walked with her into the schoolroom, rather reluctantly, she thought. He kept his brown wool jacket buttoned up and his darker brown mittens on. Instead of standing beside the stove at the front of the room, he moved to a window and stared out.

"How many people are in your family besides you and your brother?" Mantie sat down on a desk near him and tried to draw him out.

"None."

Her heart twisted. His parents must be dead, like Jesse and Jenny's parents. She hated that any child needed to live through that.

Her gaze slid over his clothes. The jacket, corduroy pants, and high-buttoned black boots looked new. They weren't fancier than the other children's clothes but were in better shape than most. His brother must make enough money to provide well for Nathan. She searched her mind for the newcomers to town. "Is your brother the new blacksmith? Everyone is excited to finally have a blacksmith in town."

He shook his head. "No."

"What does your brother do? Is he a farmer?" New farmers still flooded the area, enticed by the rich soil that until seven years ago had belonged to the Sioux. Former soldiers, tired of the war between the North and South, embraced the land that the Homestead Act offered them for nothing but the sweat of their brow.

"He bought the livery stable."

She hadn't realized the stable had a new owner. The boy didn't seem eager to discuss his family. Perhaps he'd open up on another topic. "What do you think of our schoolhouse? It's only three months old." To Mantie, it still smelled of newly planed wood and fresh paint.

The boy shrugged.

Mantie smiled. "I suppose boys don't get excited over new school buildings like adults do. Until now, the children in town went to school in a room over the general store, so you see why I think this building is special."

He continued to stare out the window.

Was he reticent because he was terribly wounded over his parents' deaths? *Please find a way to heal him, Lord.* She wondered how long ago he'd lost his parents—and how. Apparently there wasn't a sister-in-law to help raise the boy, since the family was made up of only Nathan and his brother. Or perhaps Nathan didn't consider a sister-in-law family.

"Did the other students tell you that I'm not the teacher? I'm helping out today because the teacher is down with the croup."

"They said the teacher is a man." His voice announced he didn't particularly care.

"Yes, Mr. Wren. I think you'll like him. He loves children and loves to teach."

Silence.

The door opened. Nathan turned, hope written large on his wide face.

Mantie stood and turned around to greet the newcomer. A tall young man entered the room, his gate quick without a sense of rush. Like Nathan, the man held his beige hat in his hands. The friendly gaze from blue eyes beneath pale brown hair swept over her to the boy. "I'm sorry I'm late, Nate. I was helping a customer." The gaze moved back to Mantie. He nodded, smiling. "I'm Lane Powell, Nathan's brother."

"Mantie Clark."

Nathan moved quickly to stand beside his brother. Mantie noted with approval that Mr. Powell rested a hand on his younger brother's shoulder.

The man's clothes were shades of brown and tan, like Nathan's. Unlike Nathan's, the older brother's clothes showed signs of wear. A patch covered one corduroy knee. Sweat stained the broad-brimmed hat. He brought a scent of horses and hay and leather, but it was mild next to the animal smells on some of the farmers she knew.

Nathan looked up at his brother. "She's not the teacher. The teacher's sick."

Mantie bit back a laugh. "That's right. I hope Mr. Wren will be back Monday. The croup caught him."

"He's not alone in that, I hear."

"No. A number of students stayed home today. Nathan tells me you bought the livery stable."

"Yes. The new blacksmith, Abe Newsome, is my good

friend. When he decided to move here, Nate and I decided to join him."

He isn't as secretive as Nathan, she thought. "I hope you'll like it here."

"I'm sure we will. Town's new, but not so new as the towns to the west. That's where Mr. Frank, the former livery stable owner, headed. You probably knew that."

"No. I'm surprised to hear he left. Usually news in this small town is common knowledge before the weekly newspaper comes out on Fridays."

"Mr. Frank said he's itching to try business in one of the towns on the prairie. This is far enough west for me. Peace is older than those prairie towns, but it shows lots of promise. It's nice to see people so excited about building it together."

"Yes, I think so, too." People were eager to leave behind the miseries of the war that had ended four years earlier and look ahead to a more promising future. She didn't correct him by saying people thought of the rolling lands around Peace as prairie. Descriptions of prairie to the west told of flatter lands with trees only along rivers. Here much of the land was treeless, but the hills north of the river, where she lived, reminded her of the Big Woods to the east. "The town still needs an assortment of skilled tradesmen. We've not a cabinetmaker or shoemaker or milliner, for instance."

"Is the town offering free lots to people with those skills? Have to say, that's what convinced my friend Abe to move here."

"The town fathers consider a blacksmith more important than most trades, evidently. I know of no other trades for which free land is offered."

"Certainly not for the livery. What does your husband do?"

Mr. Powell's inflection hinted at the simple curiosity of a newcomer rather than interest in her as a woman.

She lifted her chin slightly. "I'm not married. I live with my brother, Walter Clark, and his wife, Alice. He has a position with the railroad here."

His eyes lit with recognition. "Oh, yes, I met him briefly."

Silence fell between them. Nathan shifted impatiently, his boots scuffing against the wooden floor.

Mantie returned to the business required of her as schoolmistress. "I noticed Nathan brought his slate today." She smiled down at him and looked back at Lane. "He'll need to purchase a reader and an arithmetic book. You can find them at the general store. The proprietor will know what Nathan needs."

"Thank you kindly, but Nate brought a reader and an arithmetic book along from Wisconsin. That's where we moved from. Guess Nate forgot to bring the books with him this morning."

She smiled at Nate once more. "It's easy to forget things in the excitement of starting at a new school."

Nate flushed and looked at the floor, but Mr. Powell beamed at her. Appreciation for her understanding of his brother shone from his smiling eyes.

"There's no school tomorrow, Nathan," she reminded him, "so don't forget to bring your books on Monday."

He looked up at his brother. "Tomorrow's Thanksgiving. We had a play today about the first Thanksgiving and the Pilgrims and the Indians who helped them. I didn't have a part since I'm new."

"Next year you'll have a part," Mantie assured him. "The women will make Thanksgiving dinner for the town tomorrow. Everyone is invited. It's a tradition." She didn't reveal the reason for the dinner. Bachelors outnumbered married men two to one. The married women felt it their obligation to ensure the bachelors ate at least one good home-cooked meal each year. "The children will give the play for the town tomorrow." An idea struck her. "Nathan, would you like to help by introducing the play? It's an important job. You'd only need to learn a few lines."

Nathan didn't look eager. "In front of the whole town?"

"You won't be alone. I'll be there and so will all the other children. You can wear the black paper hat and collar Jesse wears in the play. When you're done with your speech, you can return them to him."

"What do you say, Nate? I'll help you with your lines," Mr. Powell encouraged.

"All right, I guess."

Mantie clasped her hands lightly in front of her. "Thank you. You'll be a big help to me."

In small letters she wrote a few sentences, which took up both sides of his slate. He read the words aloud, slowly.

"Perfect." She beamed at him. "Be careful carrying the slate home so you don't brush the chalk off."

Mr. Powell frowned slightly. "Miss Clark, where is this play going to be given?"

"Here, at the schoolhouse."

"Here?" He looked around.

Her gaze followed his. No wonder he looked doubtful. The room held no tables—only desks and a few benches along the walls. "I assure you, tomorrow there will be tables. We'll set boards across the desks and use the benches. People may need to eat in shifts, but that only adds to the fun. It gives people more time to visit." She laughed. "It may seem unusual, but it's better than meeting at the saloon, which is where public meetings were held before the school was built. Church meetings are held here, too."

Mr. Powell grinned. "Sounds like the school needs a carpenter more than a livery stable."

She laughed with him. "I hope you and Nathan will join us for both the play and dinner."

Immediately she regretted her words. Would he think them a personal invitation? Her intention had been simply to extend welcome to a new member of their small community. "We're all like family here." Would that sound to Mr. Powell like the lame afterthought it was?

If so, he didn't show it. Instead he looked pleasantly surprised. "Thank you. We'll be there with bells on. My cooking is good enough for everyday, but a holiday demands something better, don't you think, Nate?"

Nathan shrugged but grinned.

"Good. We'll see you tomorrow then." Mantie began briskly picking up papers from the simple, handmade teacher's desk.

Mr. Powell seemed to hesitate, but she kept her attention on her work.

"Come on, Nate. We're keeping Miss Clark from her duties. Likely she's eager to get home after a day herding you youngsters. Good-bye, Miss Clark."

"Good-bye." She didn't look up until she heard the door close behind them. Lane Powell seemed a nice enough man, but she didn't want to give a hint that she might like him to show her anything but friendly interest. Romance wasn't in her future.

Chapter 2

Lane shut the schoolhouse door and followed Nate down the steps. It was a beautiful day, but his mind remained inside the school. There was something about that schoolmarm-for-a-day that appealed to him. He liked that she found a way to make Nate feel a part of the school by including him in the play at the last minute. He liked her intelligence, liked that she smiled easily, and liked her pretty green eyes. He especially liked that she was friendly without being flirtatious or shy. *Is she the one, Lord?*

Lane cleared his throat. "Miss Clark seems like a nice lady to start your school days with here."

Nate shrugged. "I guess."

"Meet any boys your age?"

"No."

Lane swallowed a sigh of exasperation. He'd hoped the move to Peace would be good for Nate. Instead, Nate grew quieter every day. "Thought I saw a couple kids pass by the livery stable after school who looked about your age."

"No one is eight like me."

"Close?"

"One boy is nine."

"What's his name?"

"Jesse."

At this rate, it was going to take the entire walk back to the livery to get two full sentences out of the boy. "Does this Jesse seem friendly?"

Another shrug. "I guess so. He didn't tell me he's going to beat me up."

Lane chuckled. "That's a good sign."

"Two older boys said they're going to beat me up."

"Why?"

A shrug. "Jesse said they want to prove they're tougher than me." A look of disgust crossed Nate's face. "Isn't that stupid? They're ten. Of course they're stronger than me."

"Sounds like you're smarter than they are."

Nate looked pleased at that.

Lane was tempted to ask what Nate planned to do if the boys bullied him to a fight. He decided against it. Boys hadn't changed much since he was young. Sometimes a fight was hard to avoid. Some kids seemed born bullies.

"Jesse says the boys who want to fight me think they're tougher than everybody else and are always trying to prove it. Nobody else likes them much."

"What else does Jesse say?"

Shrug. "He lives on the other side of the river."

"Does he have brothers and sisters?"

"Only a sister. She's ten. Her name is Jenny. Miss Clark lives with them. She's their aunt."

Now there's some worthwhile news, Lane thought. "What about their parents?"

"They're dead. Their dad died in the war. So did Miss

Clark's beau. He and Jesse's dad died in the same battle, fighting side by side."

"I see."

Was that why she was still Miss Clark instead of Mrs.? A lot of women lost brothers and beaus in the war, but it would be especially difficult to lose both in one day. Sounded like she might be helping raise her brother's children, too. Maybe that's why she wasn't married. Many men didn't like taking on a ready-made family along with a wife. He'd never thought much about the issue one way or another.

Strange that he hadn't. Any woman who married him would have to not only accept but also love Nate. Lane couldn't imagine refusing to do the same for any children dear to the heart of a woman he loved.

He'd been barely more than a boy when he'd entered the war. When the war was over, his first responsibility had been to find a way to support himself. He knew he couldn't support a wife right away.

Besides, he hadn't met anyone he wanted to marry. For the last two years, he'd been asking the Lord to bring into his life the woman God meant for him. He wanted more than someone to help him with the everyday chores and to bear his children. He wanted a woman for whom he would be a special blessing and who would be a special blessing to him.

Miss Mantie Clark's green eyes smiled in his memory.

Is she the one, Lord?

The small white clapboard house smelled of baking pies and wood smoke when Mantie entered. The warmth in the house felt good to her chilled cheeks. She hung her fox-trimmed, hooded, gray wool cloak on the pegs on the entry wall, set her books and gloves on the trunk beneath the pegs, and hurried into the kitchen.

"I'm sorry I left you alone with all the Thanksgiving baking, Alice." Mantie reached for an apron while apologizing to her sister-in-law.

"I don't mind as long as you're up early tomorrow to help me with the turkey." Alice grinned and brushed a dark brown lock of hair behind her ear. "Or perhaps the most diligent work will be keeping the family away from the baking tonight. We'd hate to go to the dinner tomorrow without dessert."

Mantie slipped the gray-and-blue-plaid apron over her head and tied it behind her back. The colors clashed with the navy-and-green plaid of her dress, but as long as the material was protected, it didn't matter. She picked up the quilted potholders, scorched from use, and lifted the cover from the deep pot on top of the cast-iron stove. Simmering vegetable soup, thick with barley, set her stomach protesting in hunger. "I didn't even smell the soup for the pies when I entered. Soup always tastes especially good on a cold evening like this."

"I'm sure Walter will complain we aren't having meat and potatoes, but I didn't think it necessary with the large meal tomorrow."

"You always feed him well. He's put on a few pounds since you married last summer. It must be your good cooking. Or perhaps it is that he is so content with you."

Alice stopped beside the oven, about to open the door with the hot pad Mantie had set down. Pleased surprise filled her deep blue eyes. "Do you truly think he is content?"

"Absolutely. There's a restfulness about him when he's with you that wasn't there before."

A smile played on Alice's lips as she removed two maple

syrup pies from the oven and set them on wooden slats to cool.

Twenty-year-old Alice sometimes acted the mother to twenty-five-year-old Mantie. Normally, Mantie didn't mind. She'd been the homemaker for her brother Walter and their late brother Howard's children, Jesse and Jenny, for more than five years. It was sometimes difficult handing control of the household over to Alice, but Mantie knew it was only right for Alice to be allowed that place in her husband's home.

Mantie's thoughts turned from her brother's marriage to Lane Powell's news. "Did you know Mr. Frank sold the livery stable?"

"Yes. He's moving farther west. Walter told us at dinner last night. Don't you remember?"

"I must have been wool gathering." She frowned. Likely Colin had filled her thoughts. In the five years since he'd passed, she'd thought of him almost every waking hour. She forced her attention back to the present. "I met the new owner today."

"Of the livery stable? Where?"

"He came by the school to walk his brother home."

Alice dipped a long-handled wooden spoon into the soup pot. "His brother? Don't you mean his son?"

"No. Evidently it's only the two of them. The rest of their family is dead. His name is Lane Powell. His younger brother is Nathan."

Alice grinned. "Another bachelor. Maybe this one will catch your heart. You've turned down all the others in town."

"You're exaggerating."

"Mm." Alice blew on a spoon filled with soup. "Those who haven't asked to court you are afraid to. You're chillier than a Minnesota blizzard toward the poor bachelors."

"I'm not breaking any hearts. The men aren't interested in

me because I'm me. They are only interested because so few single women live in the area."

"A fact for which most of the single ladies are thankful. But not you."

Mantie touched the cameo locket pinned at her throat. "Those women are welcome to the men in this town. There isn't one man here who lives up to Colin."

Alice stared at her a moment, then put the lid back on the soup kettle and laid down the spoon. She walked slowly to Mantie's side and rested her hand on Mantie's arm. "Sometimes," she said gently, "I wonder if you're building your memories of him into something no man can live up to, memories even Colin could never have matched."

Pain jabbed at Mantie's chest. Though gentle, the words were still a reproach. Mantie seldom allowed herself the luxury of speaking of her continued love for Colin. She well knew that her family believed the five years since Colin's death had provided ample time for her to put her love for him behind and start a life and family with another. Alice's comment, however, was the closest anyone had come to putting that sentiment into words.

"Colin isn't replaceable like a china plate that's been broken."

"I'm sorry. I didn't mean—"

"I know you didn't." Mantie walked to the open shelves built into the kitchen wall to retrieve bowls for the evening meal, glad for a reason to walk away from Alice's touch. She tried to calm the anger that roiled in her chest. *Alice doesn't know anything about losing the man she loves,* Mantie reminded herself. *She doesn't know what it's like falling asleep every night remembering his kiss and waking every morning remembering you won't see him that day. How can I expect her to understand?*

Mantie and Alice arose Thanksgiving morning before day-break. It was pleasant working near the stove. The winter night had chilled the house as usual. They prepared stuffing while the oven heated. By the time Walter, Jesse, and Jenny awoke, the aroma of roasting turkey filled the house.

When the dinner preparations were almost done—long after the breakfast of eggs, bacon, and oatmeal sweetened with maple syrup—Alice and Mantie left the kitchen to change from their working dresses.

"Wear that beautiful emerald-green swirled silk you made last month," Alice urged. "It brings out the green of your eyes."

"I planned to save it for Christmas."

"Why? There's no one who will see it at Christmas who won't see it now."

"But it's always nice to have something new to wear for Christmas, and this is the only fancy dress I made. The other two are practical wools."

"All the more reason to wear it now. There aren't many special days to wear it."

"I guess you're right."

The prospect of wearing the emerald green cheered Mantie considerably. She poured cold water from the pitcher on her washstand into the matching porcelain bowl. The water refreshed her after the hours spent around the hot kitchen stove.

To keep her hair out of the way when she worked in the kitchen, she'd left it in the braid in which she'd bound it before going to bed the night before. Now she released her hair with quick fingers, brushed it out, and swept it up into a figure eight at the back of her head. She anchored the hair with tortoiseshell pins.

Slipping into her silk dress, Mantie checked her reflection in the walnut-framed mirror above the washstand. Alice was right. The color of the dress did make her eyes look greener. It was the prettiest dress she'd made since Colin died. Clothes hadn't seemed important after losing Colin and her brother Howard in the war. But when she saw the emerald-green swirled silk at the general store, a desire to wear the beautiful material leaped within her.

Mantie wrapped a narrow black velvet ribbon around the dress's lace neck and tied it in back. Turning, she looked over her shoulder at the mirror and smiled at the long ribbons hanging down her back, ending below the level of the mirror.

Finally she picked up the locket lying on the stand. The locket had belonged to her mother. Inside Mantie had placed a picture of Colin. Wearing the locket made her feel closer to them both. She touched the hidden button, and the locket sprang open. Colin's broad face stared back at her.

Would she ever stop missing him? Had God placed her in this town with so many single men because He wanted her to marry, to help someone build a family? She pushed away the thought and the guilt that accompanied it. She was so horribly lonely, but she couldn't imagine loving anyone but Colin.

With a sigh, she closed the cameo locket and pinned it at the neck of her dress. Some might think the pale blue background against which the cameo was set clashed with the green dress, but she didn't care. She wore it always. The townspeople were accustomed to seeing it. If anyone other than family knew it carried Colin's image, they didn't say so.

Her fingertips rested against the cool ivory of the cameo. "I love you, Colin," she whispered.

Chapter 3

L ane Powell's gaze swept the crowded schoolroom. He grinned at Nate and Abe. "Seems Miss Clark's prediction that the entire town would be at the Thanksgiving dinner was accurate." So many people filled the room that the warmth was stifling.

"Sure smells good. My stomach's growling," Nate complained.

"Mine, too. Smells like turkey and ham." The aromas were strong, in spite of the fact the meals had been cooked elsewhere. Lane spotted a makeshift table where there might be room for three more if the men didn't mind squeezing together a bit. He made his way through the crowd, nodding at the few faces he recognized. Nate kept close on his heels, and Abe followed.

Lane tapped the shoulder of a man whose brown hair was graying at the temples. "Excuse me. Room for a few more here?"

"Sure thing. More the merrier." The man dug an elbow into his neighbor's side. "Scoot over."

Lane and Nate sat down beside the man. Abe made his way to the other side of the table. The men looked askance at Abe's wide chest and huge arms but made room for him, to their own crowded discomfort.

A high whistle screeched through the room. It brought everyone's attention to a tall, skinny man in a black suit who stood on a chair at the front of the room. A grin split his long, narrow black beard. "Greetings, everyone."

"Greetings to you, Pastor."

"Howdy, Reverend."

The pastor rubbed his hands together briskly. "Let's thank the Lord for His bounty."

All heads bowed. At the end of the pastor's prayer, "amens" rumbled through the room.

"Remember, men," the pastor warned, "no snoose and no cigars. This is a schoolhouse. There'll be a church service here tonight, and I expect to see all of you. Let's show the Lord you meant it when you thanked Him for the food these women have prepared."

A burst of energy followed as women bustled about the room with plates and bowls heavy with food. Silver clanked against china. Men's voices rose in conversation and easy joking with the women.

Lane caught sight of Mantic moving between the closely spaced benches, a bowl of mashed potatoes carried high above the heads on either side of her. In her dress of shimmering green, she looked more beautiful than he remembered.

She set the bowl down on the table in front of him, reaching between Abe and his neighbor to do so. Straightening up, her gaze met his. Her smile blazed, setting his heart aglow.

"You made it." Her smile shifted to welcome Nate. "Hello. Are you ready to introduce the play after dinner?"

Nate nodded and returned her smile with a shy one of his own.

Lane indicated Abe with a wave of his hand. "This is the friend I told you about, the new blacksmith." He introduced them.

Abe nodded at her greeting, his gaze not quite meeting hers. Lane was accustomed to his friend's bashful nature around women. Abe only spoke to members of the fairer sex when he couldn't find a way around it. The man whose strength and size intimidated other men was as timid as a hare when it came to women.

"Hey, Miss Clark." The man beside Lane vied for Mantie's attention. "You decide to marry me yet?"

Lane's breath caught at the man's bold comment. Mantie Clark was a lady, not the kind of woman one spoke to in such an uncomely manner.

A blush covered Mantie's cheeks, but she smiled gamely. "Tom Morrison, if I said yes, it would frighten you so, you'd skedaddle out of town before sundown."

Tom joined the other men in laughter. He waved his fork back and forth and lifted his eyebrows in a teasing manner. "One of these days, Mantie Clark, I'm goin' to quit askin', and then you'll be sorry."

She didn't reply but kept her smile as she turned away.

A man with curly red hair who looked to be in his mid-twenties stopped her after two steps. "How about marrying me? I could sure use some good home cooking like this every day."

A chorus of "Me, too" went up from the table.

Mantie shook her head. "And what's the benefit in that to me? I'd be better off opening an eating establishment and feeding the lot of you for money."

Chuckles mixed with groans.

Lane watched Mantie with admiration. She threw back the

men's teasing comments with charm, though their comments obviously embarrassed her.

"Hush up, you men." A young woman with black hair grinned from behind Mantie. "The women in town have decided there'll be no more marriages in this town until there's a proper church building to perform the ceremonies in."

A roar of protests greeted her announcement.

"Alice Clark, you take that back." A girl with red hair that waved in glorious color down her back stood with hands perched on narrow hips. "I'm to be married next week, and I'm not waiting for any church building."

Lane grinned as the bachelors visibly and audibly relaxed.

Alice handed a gravy bowl to a man seated near her. "That'll be the last marriage until you men pitch in enough money and labor for the church."

"No need for us to worry, Mrs. Clark," Tom Morrison spoke up. "You up and married Walt on us last summer. Torey here," he indicated the red-haired girl, "has agreed to wed young Spangler. Mantie won't court any of us. Hardly any women left for us poor old bachelors and widowers to marry."

"Notice you didn't come up with this church-first weddings-later idea until you married Walt," the man beside Abe challenged.

Alice laughed with him. "I wasn't about to give the best-looking man in town a chance to back out of marrying me."

The women headed back to the front of the room, where platters and bowls covered the teacher's desk.

"Lack of women in this town's not such a joke," Tom Morrison informed Lane between forkfuls of turkey. "Single women are snatched up almost soon's they hit the county."

"That's right." The young man with red hair agreed. "Torey

there, she's barely turned seventeen. Moved here with her ma and pa two months ago."

"Now, Mantie Clark, she's different from the rest." Tom emphasized his point with a shake of his empty fork. "She and her brother have lived here for three years. She's turned down every man in town who's had the courage to ask to court her."

"Good woman, too," the redheaded man assured. "A man'd be lucky to have her for a wife."

Lane tried to avoid being obvious about his interest in Mantie, but he watched her throughout the meal. Most women he knew eagerly anticipated marriage. Many snatched up the first man who asked, especially after the war killed off so many young men. Why wasn't Mantie Clark interested in marriage? Was she still holding on to the pain of losing her beau?

Or had the Lord been keeping her for him? He was probably being fanciful, but he was attracted to her more than any woman he'd ever met. Had to admit, though, it didn't look likely she'd return his interest; and if what these men said was true, moving to Peace might not have been wise for a man looking for a wife.

Lane discovered he liked the easy bantering among the townspeople. Mantie's description had been correct: The people here were like one big family. Warmth filled his chest. Maybe he'd made the right decision following Abe to this young town.

As Mantie had warned, men continued to crowd into the church. Those fortunate enough to find seats at the first serving gave up their places to others as soon as they completed the main course. Pie was eaten standing up along the walls or in the cloakroom.

After the meal was over, dirty dishes were piled into baskets to be taken home and washed, and the few leftovers were stored temporarily. While the baskets were carried out to wagons and buggies, the men removed the planks that had made up the tables.

The children, their eyes shining, assembled in the cloakroom with Mantie. The adults took their places on the backless wooden benches and waited, sitting shoulder against shoulder to make room for as many as possible. Some men cheerfully offered to stand against the walls or sit on the floor.

Lane was pleased when Mantie's brother, Walter, sat down beside him. Walter introduced the black-haired Alice as his wife. Her pretty young face lit up when Lane was introduced as the new stable owner. "Walter told us about you. Welcome to our little town. You and your brother must come to dinner with us some night soon. I simply won't hear otherwise."

"Thank you, Ma'am. We'd be honored." The prospect of dinner at the home of the elusive Mantie pleased him. He wanted to know the woman who turned away most of the single men in town.

"Perhaps this Sunday?" Alice inquired. "You do close the livery on Sunday, don't you?"

"I only accept business on Sundays when it can't be helped," he replied cautiously. It often couldn't be avoided. People needed stables and transportation when they needed them. However, he didn't go out of his way to work on the Lord's Day.

The audience quieted as Nate made his way to the front of the room through the men seated on the floor. A tall black paper hat rested on his ears and hid his brown hair. A round black-and-white collar embraced his neck and stuck out over his shoulders. When he reached the front of the room, the audience broke into applause.

Lane shifted in his seat as he watched Nate's face grow red. Would the boy have the courage to say his few lines?

"Ladies and gentlemen, we, the students of Peace school, invite you to join us in reliving the first Thanksgiving in this bount. . .bounti. . .bountiful land."

Lane held his breath. *Keep going, Nate. You can do it,* he urged silently. Nate's panicked gaze met his. Lane smiled and nodded.

Nate pressed his lips together before starting again. "The Lord. . .the Lord led the Pilgrims to the shores of this great land. The natives welcomed them with kind and generous hearts." His voice grew stronger and the words came quicker. "Together they shared the bounty of the fer. . .fertile land. Celebrate that day again with us now."

He kept his gaze on the floor as he made his way back to the cloakroom amid a spattering of applause.

Lane knew the rest of the play was as important for the parents of the other children as Nate's presentation had been to him, but he could barely wait for it to be over. He wanted to tell Nate how proud he was of him.

When the play ended, Lane made his way to the cloakroom. It was filled with parents and children finding each other. The children still carried or wore their simple aprons and paper and feather hats that made up most of the costumes.

Lane rested his hand on Nate's shoulder. "You did a fine job. I'm proud of you."

Nate stuffed his hands into the pockets of his corduroys and kicked at an unseen pebble. "I stammered, and I almost forgot part of it."

Suddenly Mantie stood beside him. "Anyone could stammer over some of those big words. And you didn't forget anything. You were wonderful."

Lane could have hugged her for her kind words. "See there? If the teacher says so, it must be true."

"She isn't the real teacher," Nate grumbled. But Lane noted the twitch of Nate's lips and knew the boy was struggling not to smile.

He winked at Mantie. "Nope, but she does pretty well in a pinch, don't you think?"

Nate shrugged.

A girl and boy stopped by. Mantie introduced them as her niece and nephew, Jenny and Jesse. Lane remembered Mantie had said that the hat Nate wore for the play was Jesse's. The boy wore it now and carried the paper collar. Nate's gaze lingered hungrily on the hat. Lane glanced about. All the other children appeared to be taking their simple costumes home with them. Nate hadn't a costume of his own, of course. Lane's heart sank. He should have anticipated that.

"You did good, Nate," Jenny said.

"Thanks."

Jesse grinned. "My hat was almost too big for you. Good thing Mantie stuffed that handkerchief inside it to make it fit better."

Nate colored.

"Here." Jesse held out the collar. "You should have part of this costume since we shared it."

Pleasure followed surprise on Nate's wide face. "You mean it?" He took the collar before Jesse could reply.

"Don't think that collar will fit beneath your jacket," Lane said. "Why don't you let me hold it while you get ready to go?"

Nate handed it over with obvious reluctance.

"Say," Jesse started, "a bunch of us boys are going skating down by the mill. Do you want to come, Nate?"

"I don't have any skate blades."

"That's all right. Come anyway. Lots of the kids don't have skates. It's just as much fun to slide around in your boots and pretend you're skating."

"It's too early for the ice to be hard enough to skate on the river yet." The very thought of the children out on the ice tightened the muscles in Lane's stomach.

"But winter's been here forever," Jesse protested.

Lane grinned. "It just seems like forever. I don't think it's been cold enough for the ice to be safe."

"Mr. Powell is right," Mantie agreed.

Jesse screwed his face into a scowl. "Aw, Mantie."

She shook her head. "You must stay off the river."

"Why don't you go sledding instead? If you do that, I promise to check the ice every day and let you know when it's safe for skating," Lane promised.

Jesse's scowl deepened. "I don't have a sled."

"I do," Nate piped up.

Jesse looked at Nate. "That all right with you?"

"Sure. I have a toboggan."

"Oh, will you let me ride on it?" Jenny's eyes were wide with eagerness.

Nate glanced from her to Jesse. "I thought only boys were going."

Jenny groaned. "Mantie, make them let me play."

"Why don't you see if you can talk some of the other girls into going with you?" Mantie suggested.

The corners of Jenny's lips drooped, but she didn't protest.

The children moved away, Jenny to look for a playmate, the boys to retrieve Nate's jacket from the other end of the cloakroom.

Lane smiled at Mantie. "Thank you."

"For what?"

"For making Nate feel welcome here."

"I think Jesse is the one making him feel welcome."

"It isn't only Jesse." As he spoke the words, Lane ruefully thought, *I wouldn't mind if Miss Mantie Clark went out of her way to make me feel more welcome here, too.*

Chapter 4

M antie bowed her head slightly to the slender man with the long, narrow black beard. "Good Sunday to you, Reverend."

"And to you, Miss Clark."

She slid her gloved hands into her fur muff and followed Alice through the schoolhouse door and down the wooden steps, moving cautiously. The steps were swept free of snow, but they were still slippery. Safe after the last step, she allowed herself to look up and drink in the beauty around her.

When they'd arrived for the church service, fog had covered the ground like a shade drawn tight down against the night. Now it was lifting, leaving behind bare tree limbs and pine trees encased in ice. Horses, blanketed against the cold, their white breath blending into the white landscape, waited at white wooden hitching posts.

"Morning, Mrs. Clark, Miss Clark." Lane Powell's greeting pulled Mantie from her reverie. A gentle smile reflected from the gray eyes that met her gaze.

Beside him stood Abe, whom Mantie remembered from the Thanksgiving dinner. Lane quickly introduced his friend to Alice.

To Mantic's surprise, Alice responded with bright enthusiasm. "Mr. Newsome, I'm pleasured to meet you. My husband told me he'd met you. Won't you join us for dinner today along with Lane?"

Abe shifted, looking uncomfortable. "Thank you for the invitation, Ma'am, but I won't be able to make it. One of the farmers who came to church this morning needs new shoes for his horses." His voice wasn't loud and booming as Mantie had expected. There was a rumble to it, to be sure, but the voice was quiet and unassuming.

"Surely he doesn't expect you to work on the Lord's Day." Alice sounded shocked.

"I hate to ask him to make an extra trip into town, Ma'am. Hate more to let a horse go longer than necessary without proper shoeing. Don't expect the Lord minds much when our work relieves a bit of pain for another, even if the other is an animal."

Mantie wasn't sure whether the reverend would agree, but she liked Abe Newsome's consideration for a creature's pain.

"You'll be wanting to put the horses in the livery stable, I expect," Lane said. "Feel free to do so."

Abe nodded. "Hooves need to warm up before shoeing after being out in weather like this. Always hate to shoe horses in winter."

Mantie suspected from Abe's demeanor that he was glad for an excuse to avoid the dinner. But why? Most bachelors jumped at the chance for a meal cooked by a woman and leaped faster when it meant spending time in the presence of an unmarried woman such as herself. Curious, she watched Abe as he lumbered across the snow toward a farmer who stood beside a wagon set on runners.

Walter stopped beside them, only to lead Lane away to introduce him to the local banker.

As soon as the men were out of earshot, Mantie turned to Alice. "So that's why you swept pine needles over the parlor carpet this morning. You invited the town's newest bachelors to dinner without telling me. How could you?"

"Walter and I want to make them feel welcome here." The twinkle in Alice's eyes confessed the incompleteness of her answer.

The Clarks hadn't ridden to church. As the little group started home, Jenny, Jesse, and Nate ran ahead. Walter and Alice walked together, so Mantie hadn't a polite reason to refuse when Lane Powell fell into step beside her. To her relief, he kept their conversation friendly but impersonal, asking many questions about the young town.

The stone bridge near the mill was slippery. His gloved fingers touched her elbow as they crossed, ready to support her if needed, but he removed them when the river was behind them. Mantie knew from experience that a number of the bachelors in town would not have acted in such a gentlemanly manner. She appreciated both his concern for her and his restraint.

"Walter, do go build a fire in the parlor stove," Alice insisted as soon as they entered the house. "We'll want it warm and cozy for visiting after dinner."

Alice had prepared a pot roast early that morning before church. Though she'd made sure the fire was no longer burning when the family left for the service, she'd left the roast and vegetables warming in the oven while the family was gone.

As Mantie and Alice completed the meal preparations, the men visited in the kitchen because the parlor wasn't yet warm. Mantie made sure Jesse sat between her and Lane during the meal, frustrating Alice's plans. Alice wrinkled her nose at Mantie as their gazes met across the table.

Everyone welcomed the raisin pie Mantie had made the night before. The children gobbled up their portions, in spite of Alice's gentle reprimands to eat slowly, and were done before the more manner-conscious adults.

"Can we go outside and play?" Jesse asked eagerly as soon as he swallowed the last bite of piecrust.

Mantie touched the tip of her napkin to her lips before replying. "We have company, Jesse."

Jesse clasped his hands in his lap and pressed his lips together. Mantie could barely keep a smile from forming. *The energy of youth is so difficult to contain,* she thought.

Jenny sought Lane's expertise. "Do you think the ice is ready for skating?"

"It looks pretty thick to me." Jesse's voice held only a small waver of doubt as he looked at Lane for confirmation.

"Well, I don't know." Lane methodically folded his napkin and laid it beside his plate, the children squirming all the while. He rubbed his chin with his index finger. "Rivers don't usually freeze hard enough for skating before Christmas. Might be you'll need to wait until then."

A groan rose from the three children.

A grin burst across Lane's face. "I spoke with the local ice cutter yesterday. He says the ice is plenty thick for skating as long as you stay a safe distance from the dam."

"Yeah!" Jesse's chair scraped across the wooden floor as he pushed back from the table. Jenny and Nathan followed suit.

"Did anyone say you could leave the table?" Alice asked.

Jesse's excitement dropped from his face, replaced by disbelief. "But. . ."

Walter rested his hand on Alice's. "Won't harm any great world plan to let them leave the table early this once, will it?"

Mantie's stomach turned over at the sweet smile he gave his wife and the way Alice easily capitulated to him. Mantie touched the locket at the neck of her gray wool gown. She and Colin would never again share tender glances.

The children noisily donned their coats. Jenny and Jesse hurried to their rooms to retrieve their skate blades.

Alice smiled at Walter. "Why don't you and Lane visit in the parlor while Mantie and I clean up the kitchen?"

Lane looked a little uncomfortable. "I hate to appear unappreciative, but I'd like to head to the river with the children. It being Nate's first time there, I'd like to check it out."

"But I thought the ice cutter said the ice is fine," Alice protested.

Mantie allowed herself a small smile. It appeared Alice's attempt to bring Lane and Mantie together for the afternoon was crumbling, and this time Mantie wasn't the one avoiding the situation.

"I trust the ice cutter's knowledge," Lane said. "After all, he knows how thick the ice is. Still, I'd feel safer if I were there this first time. I can check out some of the areas where the current might make the ice thinner and warn Nate and the others to stay away from unsafe spots."

"Why don't we all go?" Walter looked from Alice to Mantie.

"We don't have skates," Alice protested.

Mantie suspected her sister-in-law was thinking more of the defeat of her matchmaking plans than of her lack of skates. Outside in the snow and cold, with Lane's attention on the children, the atmosphere would not be as conducive to budding romance as it would be in the parlor.

"It might be fun to watch the children," Mantie said. "And now that the fog's lifted, it's beautiful out."

Alice conceded with an exaggerated sigh. "All right."

Mantie smiled. She truly liked her sister-in-law. Alice was beautiful, animated, and very good for Walter. In the past she'd honored Mantie's desire to avoid encouraging the town's single men. She hoped Alice's broken plans would discourage her from trying again.

By the time the adults left the house, the children were out of sight. Their laughter drifted back along the road to the river.

Tall jack pines covered the hills. Their greenery was still encased in shimmering ice, as were the winter-barren limbs of deciduous trees. With the brilliant blue sky for a background, the ice-encrusted trees reminded Mantie of the ivory cameo set against blue.

When the group rounded a bend in the tree-lined road, Mantie could see the stone bridge spanning the river at the bottom of the hill. On one side of the bridge stood the mill, its wheel frozen into the millpond ice. Bright scarves and mittens highlighted the more muted colors of jackets as boys moved about on the ice, shovels and brooms pushing back the snow. The sound of metal scraping ice drifted up the hillside alongside children's calling voices.

When they reached the riverbank, Lane scanned the area. "It seems they've selected a good spot." He and Walter went out on the ice, stopping every few yards to sweep away snow and check the ice for cracks and depth.

When the men returned, Lane said, "The ice looks good here."

Walter agreed. "Think I'll gather some wood and start a small fire up on the bank. The kids will want to warm up after a bit."

Already the children were setting aside their shovels and brooms and fastening the leather straps of their skate blades over their boots.

Lane reached his hand out toward Mantie. "Would you like to check out the ice along the river's edge with me, Miss Clark? Just for a short ways. We can count on some of the kids wandering. Too tempting to check out what's around the bend."

Mantie hesitated, then removed one of her gloved hands from her muff and allowed him to clasp it. Footing could be tricky on the uneven ground along the riverbank.

As she and Lane started down the bank, she caught Alice's triumphant look. Frustration squiggled through Mantie. Alice obviously thought her attempt to push Lane into Mantie's life was progressing in spite of the change in plans.

Around the bend the noise of children's laughter and skates against ice diminished. Soon the quiet of the woods surrounded Mantie and Lane. He stopped and looked up at the jack pines towering above them, closed his eyes, and took a deep breath. "I love the silence of snow-covered woods in winter."

"I do, too." She spoke softly, as he had, not wanting to disturb the peace that filled the forest.

He squeezed her hand and smiled. "Hard to believe Peace is such a short distance away." He pointed at a snow-shrouded bush beside the river. "Look."

A rabbit quivered beneath the branches, its nose twitching.

Together, they watched it for a few minutes. Finally they proceeded with their duty, and the hare raced across the ice and into the woods above the opposite shore.

Lane pointed out tracks of deer, raccoons, squirrels, foxes, and wolves. "The deer are the road builders in winter."

"What do you mean?"

"They make paths in the snow that shorter-legged creatures follow."

Mantie's gaze slid along one of the snow paths from the river's edge until she lost sight of it up the hill. "God must provide path makers for us when we need them, too."

"I expect He does." The smile in his eyes told her he liked her thought.

"I think we don't always recognize our path makers or the paths."

For a few moments he studied the path he'd shown her. "Maybe we don't recognize them because they don't look the way we expect."

When they'd checked the ice along the bank far enough to satisfy Lane, he tested the ice farther out himself before allowing Mantie to cross with him to the opposite side. They followed the bank back in the direction of the skaters.

She wondered what Alice was thinking. A quizzing regarding the time spent out of sight of the others likely lay ahead this evening. What would Alice think when she discovered Lane had spent the time pointing out animal life and their habits instead of romancing her? The thought brought a smile.

Alice's plan to treat the blacksmith to dinner had failed, too. "I'm sorry your friend wasn't able to join us today."

"Abe?"

"Yes. It was kind of him to help out the farmer on a Sunday." She smiled. "Most of the single men in town beg and cajole for an invitation to a dinner made by a woman."

He laughed, shaking his head. "Not Abe. He avoids women like they carried the plague."

"Why?" She snatched back her curiosity. "I'm sorry. It's not my affair."

They walked on for a few more steps. She was surprised when Lane spoke, answering her question.

"Women never seem to care for Abe. Maybe his size intimidates them. Or they don't like the smell of the forge that hangs about him or the soot beneath his nails. Maybe they don't think a blacksmith is gentlemanly enough for them. Or maybe it's that he's a bit shy around them. Whatever the reason, they don't like him. Rather, they don't give themselves a chance to find out if they might like him."

"I suppose some women might be put off by the appearance of a man like Mr. Newsome."

Lane grunted.

"I'd like to think," she continued, "that most women would get to know him before deciding he is undesirable. He's obviously a hardworking, responsible man. Since he's your friend, you must recognize other good attributes in him. In the end, it's a man's heart that's important."

Lane stopped and turned to face her. His gaze searched her eyes.

She gave a nervous laugh. "What?"

"I've been warned that you don't allow any man to court you."

Embarrassment surged over her. Did that mean he'd asked about her? Did he want to court her? She pulled her gaze away and began walking. "I can't see what that has to do with Mr. Newsome."

He fell into step beside her. "I thought since you have the same aversion to romance, you might understand Abe better than most."

"Are you trying to play matchmaker, Mr. Powell?" First Alice and now this man who'd been a stranger only a few days ago. Really, it was more than a woman should need to bear.

"Not for Abe, Miss Clark. Not for Abe."

The laughter in his voice spurred her to increase her pace. She focused her attention on the bend just ahead. Her foot struck something and she stumbled. "Oh!"

Lane grabbed her arm with one hand and grasped her about the waist with his other. "Steady there."

"I'm quite all right." She pulled away from him.

He kicked at the snow where she'd stumbled. "Here's your culprit. A twig caught in the ice."

She started again toward the bend.

"Miss Clark, I apologize." His hand at her elbow urged her to stop. "It wasn't my intention to insult you."

She lifted her chin and looked him directly in the eye. "If I don't want to court and marry, it's no one's business but my own."

"You're right."

His quick agreement only incited her anger. "If you must know, I loved someone once. He died."

"I know." His voice, like the look in his eyes, softened. "I'm sorry."

She stared at him, stunned. Where had he heard about Colin?

He squeezed her arm gently. "I spoke out of turn. I was wrong to compare your situation to Abe's. Please forgive me."

Her anger receded in the face of his sincerity, but at a loss for words, she simply nodded and turned away.

Her thoughts were in turmoil as she and Lane walked back to join the others. Realizing he knew of Colin made her feel exposed and vulnerable. She'd told no one in Peace but Alice about the love she'd lost. Certainly Alice wouldn't breach good manners so far as to reveal her loss to a comparative stranger. Walter must have told Lane of Colin; and if Walter had told of Colin's death, what else had he revealed?

Chapter 5

"Looks like the whole town's out to skate," Lane observed when they arrived back at the millpond.

He exaggerated, but not by much. The area of shoveled ice had been enlarged during their absence. At the far end, Jesse and Nate played with boys who were hitting a large flat rock along the ice with sticks and brooms. Parents and older children held the hands of little ones who were learning to maneuver on the ice. Jenny skated close to the river's edge with a girl about her own age. Mufflers and skirts floated on the breeze their owners created by skimming over the ice. Husbands and wives skated arm in arm. As always, seeing happy couples caught at Mantie's heart with memories of Colin and the knowledge they'd never again be together.

Lane touched Mantie's elbow and nodded toward a little girl who wobbled on shiny skate blades a few feet from them. Mantie recognized the banker's six-year-old daughter, Susannah. Golden braids hung below her black knit hat, framing a round, rosy-cheeked face. As they watched, Susannah's skates skidded out from under her. Undeterred, she pushed herself up and tried again.

Whomp! Her bottom hit the ice. Pressing her lips firmly together, she struggled once again to her feet.

Plunk! Back down. The front of her blades curved in front of her boot toes like smile lines. Susannah's mittened hands formed into fists. "Oh, my!"

Mantie and Lane shared a laughing glance.

"Shall we help?" Lane took Mantie's answer for granted and started toward Susannah.

Mantie followed, walking carefully on the ice. "Hi, Susannah."

Lane smiled at Susannah and held out his hands. "Need a hand up?"

Susannah let him take her hands. He lifted her in one swift movement to her feet.

"How about if Miss Clark and I each hang onto one of your hands while you skate between us?"

"Only for a little bit." Susannah lifted one of her hands toward Mantie. "I'm trying to learn to skate by myself."

Lane nodded solemnly. "Of course."

Susannah's skates thunked rather than rang against the ice. Mantie realized the girl was walking on her blades. "Try pushing your blade across the ice instead of stepping on it, Susannah."

Susannah tried. One foot moved out in front. Farther. Farther. "Help."

Lane and Mantie lifted the girl's arms until both feet were underneath her again.

Mantie tried once more. "Push your foot like this, Susannah. Just a little way at a time." She shoved the toe of her right boot forward. "See?"

Susannah nodded.

Mantie pushed the toe of her left boot forward. "O–oh!"

She thrashed about with her free arm. It was no use. She fell to the ice, pulling Susannah and Lane with her.

"Oh, my!" Susannah pushed herself off Mantie. "I think I'll

skate by myself, thank you very kindly."

Mantie's gaze met Lane's over Susannah's head. They burst into laughter.

Susannah levered herself with her hands against Lane's legs and stood up. A second later she sat between them again.

Laughter shook Mantie's voice as she inquired whether Susannah was hurt. Before Susannah replied, a man asked whether Mantie was all right.

She looked up to see Susannah's father. "Quite fine," she managed before breaking into another peal of laughter. She pulled her disarrayed skirt over her boots.

Susannah's father lifted the little girl into his arms. "I think we've had enough skating for one day, Susannah. Thank you for trying to help her, Miss Clark, but she's determined to do it herself, as you can see."

Susannah's protests drifted back to Mantie and Lane as the girl's father carried her toward the shore.

"The girl is pioneer stock for sure: stubborn and tough." Lane stood and with a grin helped Mantie to her feet. "You never learned to skate?"

"Whatever gave you that impression?" Mantie attempted a haughty expression but couldn't keep it up. She grinned back at him. "I haven't skated since I was a girl back in New York. My old skate blades now belong to Jenny."

He steadied her with a hand under her elbow. "Doesn't the general store sell skate blades? Or perhaps you didn't care for skating."

"I'm not sure whether the general store sells blades. I liked skating when I was young. I guess I haven't thought about it for quite awhile." Life's everyday duties had filled her days for so long. Spending time at things such as skating seemed frivolous.

Caring for the children and Walter, moving across the country after the war, and existing each day with the pain of losing Colin and her brother had taken all her strength.

Lane pointed to the riverbank. "Looks like Walt got the fire going."

The pleasant scent of wood smoke drifted on the air. A small group gathered about the flames with Walter and Alice. Nearby, boys lying belly down on wooden sleds sailed down the smooth riverbank and out onto the ice.

Mantie became aware of skaters watching her and Lane. She didn't mind people laughing at her fall on the ice, but she didn't want them thinking she and Lane were courting. With a sinking feeling, she realized it was already too late to stop such speculation.

When they arrived at the fire's welcoming warmth, Mantie immediately moved away from Lane to stand beside Alice. While Lane answered Walter's questions about the ice down-river, Alice nudged Mantie. Black brows lifted above eyes dancing with excitement and curiosity.

Mantie frowned at her and shook her head slightly, then pointedly looked away.

Jesse and Nate came up the slope from the river, red-cheeked and panting. Jesse's progress to the fire, made on his skate blades, was slower than Nate's.

"They must be exhausted," Mantie said to Alice. "They'll sleep well tonight."

Nate stopped beside Lane, waiting with obvious impatience for his brother to stop speaking to the adults. He broke in as soon as he politely could. "Can I go get the sled, Lane?"

Lane laughed. "Sure, if you think you have enough energy to use it."

"We're not tired, are we, Jesse?"

"Not a bit of it." Jesse dropped to the ground. "Wait for me to take off my skate blades, Nate."

"Looks like you were wrong," Alice said as they watched the boys race toward town.

"Yes," Mantie agreed. "I'm glad to see Jesse and Nate get along so well. I wasn't sure Nate wanted to make new friends at first."

She felt someone's gaze on her and glanced about. Lane was watching her with a smile. She realized he'd heard her comment and sensed his thankfulness for her concern for his little brother. His gratitude filled a place inside her with warmth, a place untouched by the fire before them.

Nate and Jesse's shouts announced their arrival with the sled.

"I've never seen such a fine sled," Mantie marveled to Alice.

It didn't look like the sleds with which Mantie was familiar. Instead of the usual lengths of wood that completely filled in the space between the sled's bed and the snow, these runners were made from metal and gave the sled the more delicate, graceful image of a sleigh.

Townspeople surrounded the sled. Men wanted to see how it was made. The boys merely wanted to ride it.

Nate took it for the first run. It whizzed past the crowd, down the bank, and onto the ice. Instantly the other children crowded around Nate, begging for a chance to ride.

"Nate looks like he's grown three feet, he's so proud," Lane confided to Mantie. "Just hope he realizes that this doesn't mean those kids want him for a friend."

"I think it's nice he's sharing it with them. It seems to ride more smoothly than the shovels and sleds with wooden runners."

"Have you ever ridden a sled?"

"No."

He reached out his hand. "We can remedy that."

She stepped back. "Oh, no." The town already thought they were courting. She wasn't going to cement the idea, tempted though she was to sail down the hill. Besides, she couldn't imagine a less elegant position for a woman than lying on her stomach racing head first down a snowy riverbank.

Lane gave in without a fight.

She wished he hadn't and was immediately disgusted with her contrary attitude.

She turned her back on the sled and shovels and walked down by the ice. Colin wouldn't have given in as easily as Lane. He would have badgered and teased and insisted until she rode down the hill whether she wanted to or not. In the end, she'd have loved it. She always loved everything they did together. He'd been so full of energy and fun and laughter. Her stomach tightened at the memory. He'd brought so much joy into her otherwise quiet days.

The longer Mantie watched the sledders, the more she wished she'd accepted Lane's challenge. The children's laughter, giggles, and shining eyes told of their fun. The way they ran up the slope, their sleds bouncing behind them, spoke of their eagerness to experience the exhilarating run again. Soon snow encrusted the clothing of all the children, but they didn't seem to notice.

With a bit of a swagger, Nate agreed to give little Susannah a ride. She sat in front, her eyes wide with excitement. "Hold onto the sides," Nate commanded. He sat behind her, reaching in front of her to grasp the sled's rope in both hands. She let out a squeal of delight as the sled gained speed, closing her eyes hard against the flying snow, bringing laughter from the crowd.

Jesse condescended to give Jenny a ride next. The other girls weren't as fortunate. "Sledding is for boys," Nate announced solemnly. Jesse nodded in agreement. Disappointed, the girls went back to the river to entertain themselves.

The brightness of the winter afternoon dimmed as the sun neared the horizon. The number of skaters and sledders dwindled as they headed toward home and warmth and dry clothes and supper before the evening church service. Alice left to begin preparing the family's meal. "Stay for awhile if you want," she urged Mantie.

Walter made sure the fire was out, spreading the embers and covering them with snow.

"Do we have to go? Can't I have just one more ride?" Nate begged.

"I think Miss Clark should have the honor of the last ride." Lane smiled at Mantie. "What do you say? Changed your mind yet?"

The temptation was too great. Most of the townspeople were gone. She grinned. "All right."

Nate sat down on the front of the sled. "You can get on behind me, Miss Clark."

Mantie shook her head. "I don't think there's room for both of us."

Nate relinquished his sled with obvious reluctance.

Rejecting the idea of lying on her stomach, Mantie knelt on the sled and grasped the sides.

"That might not be the best position," Lane warned. He explained how lying down kept the weight more evenly distributed over the length of the sled and showed her how it was easier to grasp the sides while lying down. "And of course, if you need to avoid a rock or tree, it's not as frightening to roll off if you're already lying down."

"Cheerful thought." She darted him a look of disgust and didn't change her position.

He chuckled.

"Will you give me a push, Jesse?"

Jesse obliged.

She barreled down the slope at a speed that felt considerably faster than when she'd watched others. The sled seemed to leap when it went over a slight bump in the path. Mantie's heart dropped from her chest to her stomach. Her weight pitched to one side. The next moment she lay in the snow, the sled on its side next to her.

She sat up and reached to brush snow from her eyes. Instead, she made it worse. Blinking, she looked down at her gloves. They were covered with snow. Her wrists stung from the cold of snow jammed into the top of the gloves.

Jesse, Jenny, and Nate raced up to her. "Are you all right?" Jenny asked, panting slightly.

"Did you like it?" Jesse asked. "Isn't it grand?"

"Yes, to everything." Mantie struggled unsuccessfully to find a way to get up with a modicum of grace. Jesse and Jenny each grasped one of her arms and tugged.

By the time she was standing, Lane had reached them. "You're going to try again, aren't you?"

She had the juvenile desire to stick out her tongue at his teasing tone and laughing eyes. Instead she righted the sled and pulled it back up the hill. He fell into step beside her. "How do you steer this thing?" she asked when they arrived at the top.

"You lean. It doesn't make sharp turns, of course, just kind of veers to the side you lean toward. Of course, it's better sometimes to try to find a straight course and keep the sled on it."

"Do tell. And where on a hillside does one find such a perfect course?"

He had the grace to smile sheepishly. "Why don't you let me go down with you once and show you how it's done?"

She wasn't sure whether that was a good idea, but she obligingly made room for him at the back of the sled. "Pull the rope tight and hold it with both hands," he instructed. When she'd done so, he reached his arms forward and grasped the rope, too. His breath was warm against her cheek, and she caught her breath at his closeness.

The intimacy was forgotten a moment later in the exhilaration of racing down the hill, flying past trees and shrubs. The bump that had thrown her earlier threatened to toss the two of them. She felt the sled start to lean to one side. "Lean!" Lane's yell sounded in her ear at the same time his arms pressed against hers. Together they shifted their weight. The sled shifted, too, and they hit the ground and continued their descent. Then they slid across the ice. Lane stuck out his feet and dug in his heels until they slowed to a stop.

It happened in a flash, but Mantie was aware of it all and exuberant at having mastered that silly lump of land, even though it took Lane's help to do it.

They stood up and she turned to him, smiling. "Thank you. It was wonderful." She felt as carefree as a child.

"Maybe next time you'll want to try it alone again. I think it's getting too dark to sled now."

She hadn't noticed how deep the shadows had grown. He was right, of course.

As she walked home with Jenny, Jesse, and Walter, Mantie relived the afternoon in wonder. She couldn't remember when she'd last had so much fun that she'd lost track of time.

Chapter 6

M antie, it's time to get up."
Jenny's voice broke through Mantie's sleep. "I'm awake," she mumbled.

Light, Alice and Walter's voices, the smells of oatmeal and bacon, and too little heat rose through the grated opening in the floor near the bed. The room was still gray in the early morning. Through half-opened eyelids, Mantie watched Jenny, with whom she shared the room, grab her dress and high-buttoned shoes.

Jenny opened the door and stopped. "Don't go back to sleep," she warned before hurrying downstairs to dress beside the kitchen stove.

I can't believe I slept this late, Mantie thought. Usually she was up early, helping Alice prepare breakfast for the family while Walter milked the cow and broke the ice in the water for the farm animals. At least she didn't need to be at school this morning. Mr. Wren had attended church services yesterday, hale and healthy.

She stretched, then drew the quilt back up beneath her chin. Its heaviness and warmth were so enticing. Just a minute or two longer couldn't hurt.

Images from yesterday afternoon at the river filled her mind: Lane pointing out animals and tracks in the quiet forest around the bend; Susannah's determined chin as she tried out her new skate blades; the color and sense of life the skaters brought to the river and millpond; the children's laughter; the excitement of skimming over the snow with Lane on Nate's sled.

Lane. She liked the way he played and laughed with the children. She'd enjoyed his friendly, but not too friendly, company. If only men could remain friends and not always try to court a woman.

She pushed the quilt back, sat up, and swung her feet over the side of the bed. Even through her stockings, the floor chilled her feet. She dressed quickly, pulling the warm but itchy wool stockings over her knees, donning her brown wool housedress and high-buttoned shoes. She left her braid. She'd brush her hair out downstairs. Looking in the mirror, she pinned the locket above her heart.

Shocked, she stared at the locket's reflection in the mirror. This was the first morning in years that she hadn't awakened with her first thought being of Colin. Troubled, she walked downstairs, yesterday's joy-filled memories smirched.

Clothes still draped over the rope Walter had strung across the kitchen the night before. Everyone but Alice had returned from the river wet to the skin and had needed a complete change of clothes for the evening service. Alice had scolded good-naturedly, warned they would all come down with croup, and heated apple cider to warm them.

Jesse and Jenny were ready to leave for school by the time Mantie entered the kitchen. The children's coats and accessories were still damp from the previous day. Mantie lent Jenny a dry pair of gloves, and Jesse wore the stained pair he used for chores.

Walter left with the children, he for work and they for school. Mantie couldn't avoid seeing the affectionate look and squeeze of the shoulders Walter gave Alice at the door before leaving. Although she was glad for her brother's happiness, the signs of their affection were a painful reminder of the life she would never share with Colin.

Mantie filled a bowl with oatmeal from the pot on the back of the stove and sat down at the table. As the children often did on cold winter mornings, they'd pulled the table closer to the stove. Mantie was glad they had. The extra warmth was especially welcome after the cold blast of air let into the kitchen with their leave-taking.

She checked the white porcelain pitchers on the table. The children and Walter hadn't emptied them. She poured warm maple syrup on the oatmeal to sweeten it and covered it with cream.

"Are you going to join me, Alice, or have you already eaten?"

"Mm." Alice set a cup of coffee beside Mantie's plate and seated herself across the table.

Mantie tilted her head and studied her sister-in-law's face. "Are you all right?"

Alice rested her elbows on the table and waved one hand in dismissal. "I'm not hungry, thank you."

Mantie shook her head. If Alice were a student, the teacher would accuse her of daydreaming. "I'm sorry I overslept this morning and left you to feed everyone and get them off to school and work."

"I didn't mind. Did you have a good time with Mr. Powell

yesterday? You do like him, don't you?"

So that was it. Alice's mind wasn't on breakfast and Monday morning chores. She wanted to know whether her matchmaking attempt had succeeded.

"He seems to be nice," Mantie conceded.

"Did he ask to see you again?"

"No."

"Oh. That's too bad. Of course, he still might ask you. Maybe he's scared off by your reputation."

"I hardly think—"

"Didn't he hint at liking you, even when you were alone together down the river?"

"No. I mean. . ." The memory of his laughing response when she'd asked whether he was trying to make a match between her and Abe flashed through her mind: *Not for Abe.*

Alice didn't seem to notice her hesitation. "I have something to tell you."

"Yes?"

"That is, Walter and I have something to tell you, but Walter thought I should tell you." Alice looked uncharacteristically embarrassed.

"Alice, you are not making any sense this morning."

Alice rested her hands in her lap, took a deep breath, and met Mantie's curious gaze. "We're going to have a baby."

Mantie blinked. "A baby? I mean, that's wonderful."

Alice smiled. Her shoulders lifted in a nervous shrug. "We think so. Walter is very excited about it."

"Of course he is. Are you feeling all right?"

"Oh, yes. I was sick when I got up this morning, but I'm fine now."

"Don't worry about getting up to take care of anyone for awhile. I can see to getting breakfast and all. When is the baby due?"

"The end of June." Alice rested her hand on her stomach. "My dresses are beginning to feel tight already."

"We'll need to make you some new clothes."

Alice reached across the table and clasped one of Mantie's hands. "I'm so glad you're here. I'm excited about the baby, but I feel safer knowing I have you to depend on."

Mantie smiled and squeezed Alice's fingers. "I'm glad I'm here, too. It will be fun to have a baby in the house, won't it?"

But later, cleaning soot from the kerosene lamp chimneys while Alice heated water for the weekly laundry, Mantie wondered how long Alice would welcome a sister-in-law in her home. At the moment, Walter's home was large enough to easily house his sister, nephew, and niece. He and Alice were only starting their family. Would Alice soon feel Walter's extended family was crowding her and Walter's family?

What else can I do but live here, Lord? I can't support myself, let alone Jesse and Jenny.

The young town desperately needed skilled people, but it didn't need any of her skills. She could teach, but neither the town nor the surrounding townships needed teachers. Men filled the available positions. The salaries the male teachers demanded cost the townships more than female teachers, but everyone agreed men needed the jobs more than women, especially women like herself who had relatives to support them.

She could sew, but the town already had a tailor, and a number of women took in sewing. She doubted she could make enough money to pay for room and board from sewing, even if she added laundry and ironing. Those needs were also already met by others.

She was a good cook, but she hadn't the funds to open an eating establishment.

Men served as clerks at the few businesses in town.

I'm letting my fears run away with my senses. Walter and Alice aren't kicking me and the children out of their home.

But the niggling fear remained, and her thoughts struggled with it while she and Alice performed the hot, heavy work of washing linens and clothing. Mantie couldn't imagine Walter and Alice actually asking her to leave. Still, things might grow uncomfortable between them. She wouldn't want to stay if she weren't genuinely welcome.

But where could I go, Lord? The question returned.

A number of unmarried men in town would gladly offer a solution. Her heart cringed from the thought. It was unbearable to consider spending her life as the wife of any man other than Colin.

Besides, she'd need to find a man who wanted not only her and her skills as a housekeeper, but Jesse and Jenny. Many men didn't care to take on the responsibility of children other than their own.

For that matter, she hadn't raised Jesse and Jenny by herself. She and Walter had raised them together. If she left Walter's home, would he want Jesse and Jenny to stay? Would Alice?

The thought chilled her heart. Jesse and Jenny had been the center of her life since their father and Colin had died. The prospect of life without them at its core was as bleak as a windswept prairie on a winter day.

Of course, she couldn't expect the children to spend the rest of their lives with her. One day they would leave to establish homes of their own. That was how it should be. One way or another, the day would arrive when she must live without them. She'd never allowed herself to face that fact before.

What am I going to do, Lord? I need to start building my own life. I can't expect Walter or the children to take care of me for the rest of my years. I know You must have a path for me. Please, make it clear.

The image of the animal paths in the forest flashed across her mind. She'd told Lane that we didn't always recognize God's paths and path makers. What had been his reply? She furrowed her brow, searching her memory. Oh, yes. He'd said, *Maybe we don't recognize them because they don't look the way we expect.*

Leaving Walter's home certainly didn't look like a path she expected, but she must be prepared for the possibility.

The morning had started with such joy-filled thoughts, and Walter and Alice's baby was marvelous news. But her own fears brought clouds that were missing from the bright winter sky.

Walter and Lane recognized a friend in each other. Often during the next weeks, Lane and Nate joined the family for supper and Sunday meals. Once, Abe came along, though Lane confessed that it took a bit of arm twisting.

Mantie heard Abe talking and laughing when he visited with Lane and Walter in the front room while she and Alice cleaned up the kitchen after dinner. But if she and Alice were near, Abe was quieter than the proverbial church mouse, and she could see the guarded look in his eyes.

"Is that the way I am around men?" she asked Alice. "Like I've built a fence around myself that says 'no trespassing'?"

Alice nodded. "Yes, I'm afraid so."

"That's why you said I'm colder than a Minnesota blizzard around them. I didn't realize how off-putting my manner is. I don't mean to be unfriendly with the men. I just don't want to encourage their romantic attentions."

"Lately, I thought I'd sensed a thawing. Is Lane Powell beginning to interest you?"

"Absolutely not."

Alice gave an exaggerated sigh. "Well, I can hope, anyway."

Mantie's fears of one day being unwelcome resurfaced. "Are you hoping to marry me off to get me out from underfoot?" She kept her tone light, hoping Alice wouldn't know how important the answer was to her.

"I'm hoping you find someone to fill your life with love and joy the way your brother does mine. I only want you to be happy."

Mantie slid her arm about Alice's shoulders and gave her a quick hug. "There's lots of love in my life."

"Not the kind I mean."

No, Mantie thought, *not that kind of love. There'll never be room for that kind of love in my life again.*

Chapter 7

One night when Abe had refused another invitation to join them for supper, Alice asked Lane about him.

"I feel guilty coming over here without him so often," Lane confided. "He lives with Nate and me. This part of the country's been without a blacksmith for so long that Abe can't keep up with the work. Works into the night, most every night."

Nate had told Mantie he preferred time at their house to hours spent in the two rooms he and Lane and Abe shared at the back of the livery stable. "Lane says we'll have a house of our own one day."

The first couple evenings Lane spent at their home, Mantie was wary. Would he press to court her? She treated him politely but made certain Alice didn't succeed in placing her beside him at meals or leaving them alone where an opportunity might arise for him to speak as a possible suitor.

Soon Mantie admonished herself that her fears were unfounded. Lane was friendly but appeared uninterested in pursuing a romantic involvement. Before long, Lane's and Nate's presences in the house felt as natural as her brother's and Jesse's.

She began to miss Lane on the evenings he didn't come.

Walter and Lane established a pattern of challenging each other to checkers after dinner while the children studied under Alice and Mantie's watchful eyes at the kitchen table. But if Nate or Jesse or Jenny needed help with their sums, Lane always gave it without complaint.

Whichever boy finished his lessons first received the reward of a game of checkers with whichever man won the first game. Mantie couldn't remember when Jesse had completed his lessons so quickly and with so little complaint.

"We're learning a new poem at school," Jenny announced one evening. "Abe would like it. It's called 'The Village Blacksmith.' "

"Longfellow's poem. A good one," Lane commented.

Mantie glanced at him in surprise. She hadn't thought of him as a man who read poetry.

Jenny nodded. "I like it, too. Mr. Wren says we need to memorize the whole thing, and it's very long."

Lane grinned at her. "You can do it. You're smart."

Her face brightened, and she stood a little taller. "Do you really think so?"

"I know so."

Alice leaned close to whisper in Mantie's ear, "That man would make a good husband and father."

Mantie smiled blandly back at her. "Yes. Won't some woman be glad?" She didn't admit she admired his way with the children. So many men preferred children be seen and not heard.

Nor did she admit that the thought of Lane married, his life centered around a family of his own, struck a chord of anticipated pain. *He is only a friend,* she hastened to reassure herself, but she suspected she'd miss him when he married.

As Christmas grew closer, days and evenings were filled with pleasant tasks and whispered, shining-eyed secrets. "Don't come in until I say so," became a common command from the children as they worked on Christmas gifts. Mantie and Alice worked on their gifts during moments stolen from other duties while the children were in school or after the children were in bed at night. Tempting odors elicited pleas for tastes as Alice and Mantie built up an assortment of cookies, pies, and sweetbreads.

When weather permitted, the family spent part of Sunday afternoons at the millpond and river. The Sunday before Christmas was no exception. Shadows grew long in the late afternoon as Mantie stood beside Alice, laughing at Lane and Walter playing crack the whip with Jesse and some other boys. Nate, having no skate blades, was sledding.

"I'm glad Walter has found such a good friend in Lane," Alice commented.

"He's been good for Walter," Mantie agreed. "Walter's always been a wonderful uncle to Jesse and Jenny, but Lane seems to have brought out Walter's lighthearted side. He's been so immersed in the responsibility of providing for the children all these years that he forgot how to play with them."

Alice grinned and patted her stomach discreetly. "He'll be well prepared to play with this little one."

Mantie smiled at Alice's anticipation.

Fun-filled shouts came from the ice as the human whip cracked and three boys tumbled. One of them landed beside a wooden sign Mantie hadn't noticed before. "Who put up that thin ice sign?"

"Lane. Walter told me Lane takes time away from the livery

stable every day to check the ice. Lane says he doesn't want any of the village's children losing their lives to the river."

The men and boys ended their game. Mantie studied Lane's face as he and Walter headed toward the bank. *He is a fine man,* she thought.

Alice smiled up at Walter. "Look at your red cheeks. I suppose it's time I head home to prepare something warm for our skaters."

"I'll go," Mantie offered.

Lane smiled at her. "Mind if I join you? I'm ready to get in out of the wind and cold, but Nate wants to sled awhile longer."

As they crossed the bridge, they looked out over the river. Watching the skaters weave gracefully or dart with spirit about the ice, Mantie wished she had skate blades. Her childhood blades on which Jenny now skated were too small for Mantie.

Lane seemed to recognize her thoughts. "You enjoy watching the skaters. Why don't you buy blades?"

"I'd love to skate again, but spending money on skate blades seems frivolous. I haven't much money beyond the little I earned helping at school last month. Walter never complains about supporting me, but I try to buy as many of my personal needs as possible. Then, too, there are Christmas gifts to consider. I make most myself. They don't cost much, but when money is in short supply, each penny counts."

When they reached the house, Lane lit a kerosene light against the encroaching evening darkness while Mantie stirred up the embers in the kitchen stove and added wood to hurry the heat along. A pot of beans that had been baking since morning would soon be warm enough for supper.

She put apple cider on to heat. Cinnamon sticks filled the

air with a spicy aroma.

A sense of pleasant familiarity in performing simple home tasks together heightened Mantie's awareness of Lane. It made her feel good and uncomfortable at the same time, and she pushed the feelings away.

From the small pantry, she brought a plate of sugar cookies and placed it on the table before sitting down across from Lane. "You're receiving company treatment. The family eats only broken cookies before Christmas."

Lane chuckled. "My mother did the same with our family."

"You've never told us about your family."

He told briefly of his parents and life growing up in Pennsylvania, of moving to Wisconsin, of his parents' death after he'd returned from the war, and his decision to move to Peace along with Abe.

"With the war, the move from Pennsylvania, and my parents' death, I felt Nate and I had lost enough people in our lives. I didn't want to lose another friend if I could avoid it. Some people, when they lose someone they love, draw away from others. The risk of losing someone again is too painful to face, I guess. I do the opposite. I figure since it's inevitable we lose people we love—not everyone, but some of them—the only thing that makes it bearable is to love them as much as we can while we're here."

"Yes." Mantie touched the cameo locket pinned at her shoulder. "I don't know what I would have done without Walter, Jesse, and Jenny when my brother and Colin died."

"Was Colin the man you told me about, the man you loved?" His tone was soft, almost apologetic.

"Yes."

151

"Walter said Colin died in the war."

Mantie stared at him, shocked.

"I wasn't asking him about you," Lane hurried to assure her. "He said he lost his brother in the war and that your beau died in the same battle. War's been over four years. That's a long time to love someone." His voice gentled.

"Is it? Love doesn't end because someone isn't with us anymore. Love is too strong. Once it's born, it just goes on forever, don't you think? We don't stop loving people just because we can't see them." She kept her gaze on his, allowing him to search her eyes. She wasn't ashamed of loving Colin, even if most people would have set aside the love after so many years. "When Nate goes off to school, you don't stop loving him until he gets home in the evening."

Lane didn't respond for a minute. "I was going to say it isn't the same, and it's not, in most ways. But maybe in a sense you're right. We expect children to come home from school at the end of the day. In the same way, at the end of our life here, God is waiting for us to come home." He smiled.

"Have you lost a woman you loved?" Mantie asked the question gently, a bit uncertain whether it was appropriate. Would he think the question too personal, too invasive?

"No. I never loved a woman the way you speak of loving. Colin was an especially blessed man to know a love like yours. Tell me about him, will you?"

She began haltingly. Lane listened, attentive, smiling, nodding. The words came more easily as his interest appeared genuine. She told how she and Colin met, of his love for life, the way he brought laughter into her quiet world.

"I've heard people say they began to forget what the person

they loved looked like after awhile."

Lane nodded.

"I never forget. I remember everything. He was short, with wide shoulders." She held out her arms. "Like so. He was stocky and strong. He had wide cheekbones and laughing blue eyes and black hair with curls that fell over his forehead. I remember the sound of his laughter and the way he threw his head back and laughed robustly, loud and uninhibited. I remember—"

The sound of feet stamping on the porch and laughter outside the door cut off her reminiscences.

Mantie pushed her chair back. "I'd best get cups out for everyone. Will you and Nate join us for a supper of baked beans and bread?"

"And broken cookies for dessert?" Lane's eyes danced.

"Or maybe a whole cookie if you behave very well."

Happy chatter filled the kitchen as the family entered. Mantie smiled and nodded as they spoke, but her mind remained on her memories of Colin.

I remember the timbre of his voice, the way it dropped and grew husky when he said, "I love you." Most of all, I remember that.

The next afternoon, Mantie stopped at the general store for crochet thread. She was eager to get started on the collars she planned for Jenny and Alice for Christmas. The clerk was busy helping Lane when she entered the store. She looked in surprise at the large order of red ribbon the clerk was cutting for him. She lifted her eyebrows in curiosity. "Are you planning to dress up the horses at the livery with red bows for Christmas?"

His face turned almost as crimson as the ribbon. "It's a surprise. I mean, what I plan to use the ribbon for is a surprise."

"I see." She didn't, of course. What use could a man possibly find for red ribbon? If he had a sweetheart, she'd suspect the ribbon was for the woman's hair. But no woman needed the yards of ribbon he was purchasing. She was certain he wasn't buying it to trim an outfit. She refused to pursue her rampant curiosity with more questions.

The clerk completed measuring the ribbon for Lane. "Anything else, Sir?"

"Some red paint if you have it. Otherwise, brown will do. And candles. I need a lot of candles. A couple dozen, I'd guess."

Red ribbon, red paint, candles. It was a riddle to Mantie.

While the clerk wrapped the candles and ribbon in brown paper and tied the package with cheerful red twine, Mantie waited beside Lane.

"Beautiful weather today," Lane said. "Crisp air, no wind, no clouds, not too cold but cold enough to keep the snow and ice from melting."

"Yes, beautiful." Weather was always a safe conversational item.

"Would you like to go sleighing?"

It was on the tip of her tongue to refuse. A negative response to a man's invitation was habitual. He spoke again before she could answer.

"It would be a shame to waste an evening like this. I have a great sleigh at the livery."

A smile tugged at her lips. "Red, I suppose."

"How did you know?"

"Oh, just a suspicion." What could it hurt to accept his invitation? After all, he acted almost like a brother toward her. "I haven't been sleighing in years. It might be fun."

"Wonderful. I'll come by with the sleigh about eight. Late, but we want the benefit of the moon."

Mantie watched him as he left the shop, still wondering about his strange combination of purchases.

The clerk discreetly cleared his throat.

She turned about with a bright smile, embarrassed to have been caught watching Lane. She selected her threads and left the shop.

Lane was right. The weather was perfect for sleighing. Her spirits lightened at the prospect.

Chapter 8

Lane hung lanterns at the front of the sleigh and walked around the vehicle for a last check. He'd taken time to polish it this afternoon after Mantie's unexpected agreement to go sleighing. It didn't matter that by the time he got to her house the polish would be smudged. It didn't matter that it was night and Mantie wouldn't see his effort. He'd wanted to polish it; a symbol, he supposed, of how important this evening was to him.

A buffalo robe covered the leather seats. Another robe was folded and lying on the seat. The metal foot warmer filled with warm coals sat on the floor. Was he forgetting anything?

He patted the dapple gray and adjusted its blanket, making sure it was secure and wouldn't fall off or get tangled in the harness as they traveled. He'd selected his favorite, most trustworthy horse for this duty. "You ready, Jeremiah? Be on your best behavior tonight. You'll be pulling precious cargo."

The horse snorted and shook its mane, setting the sleigh bells a-jingling.

Lane chuckled. "You're right. I'd better be on my best behavior, too. Knowing Mantie Clark, I won't have a second chance to put my best foot forward."

His thoughts raced to the evening ahead as he drove toward the bridge over the river and the road to Mantie's house. He could barely believe she'd said yes. From the day less than a month ago when he'd met her at the school, he'd had the impression this was the woman God intended for him. This was the woman who was the answer to his prayers for a wife.

"Is this faith, God?" he spoke into the winter night. "Or am I deluding myself because I'm tired of living without someone to love and someone to love me? The way she talked of Colin yesterday, it's hard to imagine she might ever love anyone else." Even if she was a little interested, he'd need to take it slow and easy, building up to keeping steady company with her.

But she said yes to going sleighing tonight.

Maybe it's sleighing she likes and not the company. Maybe it's best not to get my hopes up.

But they were up, no denying; they were up high.

"Don't forget, you and Nate and Abe are spending Christmas Eve with us," Alice reminded Lane as he and Mantie headed out the door. "Don't you let Abe sit home, you hear?"

"Yes, Ma'am." Lane grinned. "I'll make sure he's here, if it means carrying him myself. Thank you for the invitation."

Mantie waited while he placed the foot warmer she'd prepared next to his own on the floor of sleigh. He helped her up and climbed in beside her, then settled a thick buffalo robe over their laps. With her gloved hands in her fur muff and the fur-trimmed hood of her cape covering her ears, she felt snuggled in warmth.

"Ready?"

She nodded. "I'm excited. I haven't gone sleighing in years." They started slowly, for the road led downhill to the river.

Jeremiah's hooves crunched in the snow. The lanterns danced from their brass hooks on either side of the sleigh, sending golden streams of light shimmering across the snow to banish blue shadows cast by the moon. An owl hooted overhead, startling Mantie and Lane, and they laughed together at themselves. Lantern light briefly silhouetted a deer at the forest's edge. It stood as if frozen, staring toward them, then turned and darted away.

Skaters moved like shadows along the river as the sleigh passed over the bridge. With the cloudless sky, the moon's light made the skaters' way clear. Flames from a small warming fire on the riverbank waved orange and welcoming.

Here the road became flat as it headed into the village. Lane urged Jeremiah to a faster pace. The runners hissed against the snow and the bells' song quickened. The sleigh slipped into a gentle rocking motion.

They passed other sleighers and called and received cheerful greetings. Lamplit windows added a friendly sense of welcome to the town. The crisp air carried the scent of wood smoke, which rose in straight columns from every chimney.

The wood smoke was left behind when they headed out of town, down the road that ran along the river where the land was flat. Only the moonlight and their lanterns lit the road here, but that was sufficient. The silence was broken only by the bells, the singing runners, and Jeremiah's hooves.

Mantie remembered the feel of the cool breeze created by the ride and the way it tugged at her hood. She remembered the way her cheeks felt chilled even while the rest of her body was snug and warm beneath the lap robe. She remembered the sounds and the pleasant rocking.

She'd forgotten how sweetly intimate it felt to ride through the beauty of a quiet, moonlit night with her shoulder rubbing against a man's.

Lane's conversation didn't tend toward romantic intimacy. He asked about the town's short history and queried about her childhood and her life in New York. He shared stories of his own childhood, some which made her laugh, some which made her wish it were possible to hold and comfort him without his misinterpreting her concern.

Sleigh bells announced another sleigh coming up behind them. When it drew alongside, Mantie saw the occupants were red-haired Torey and her new husband.

"How about a race?" the recent groom challenged.

"No, thanks," Lane called back.

"More important things to do?" The challenger and his wife grinned.

Embarrassment swept through Mantie, but Lane only smiled and waved.

The other sleigh picked up speed and was soon out of sight around a bend.

Lane looked at her. "I hope you didn't want to race. I don't cotton much to racing, especially at night. A horse could take a nasty spill."

"I don't like racing, either." She did like the way he cared for his horse; liked that he kept it blanketed against the cold; liked that he didn't use a whip.

There wasn't much she didn't like about Lane Powell, she realized.

She was enjoying the evening so much that a sliver of disappointment ran through her when Lane turned the sleigh around and headed back toward town. Her gaze fell on his gloved hands, which held the reins firmly but gently. What would it feel like to be held by this man?

The image shocked her. She hadn't thought in such terms about any man but Colin. What was happening to her that an evening in a sleigh could make her so unfaithful to Colin's memory?

Lane kept up a friendly but impersonal conversation, and before they reached town, Mantie's emotions relaxed once again.

Lane pulled Jeremiah to a stop on the bridge. "Still a few skaters braving the chill," he observed. The sound of blades scratching against ice was audible in the winter quiet.

"The scene is beautiful in the moonlight, isn't it?"

"There's something about bridges that appeals to me. During the war, one bridge in particular became special to me."

She studied his profile. "You haven't spoken about your war experiences before."

He shrugged, still watching the skaters. "Not much to tell. Not much different than the experiences of other soldiers. Too much blood. Too much death. Too much sorrow." He breathed in a deep, shaky sigh.

Mantie rested a hand over his. "I'm sorry." She slid her hand away.

"It seemed too much for awhile. One summer night when the moon was full, I stood on a bridge like this talking to God. I told Him how weary I was of the fighting. I asked how man could be so evil to his own kind." He shook his head.

"Did He give you an answer?" She didn't blame God for the deaths of Colin and her brother, but no answer ever seemed sufficient for the war and evil that caused their deaths.

He nodded. "In a way. I carried two books with me through the war. One was the Bible. The other was poems by Longfellow."

Mantie still found his love of poetry unusual. She smiled but didn't interrupt him.

"Standing on that bridge, the words of Longfellow's poem 'The Bridge' came to me. Do you know it?"

"No."

"It ends like this:

"And forever and forever,
As long as the river flows,
As long as the heart has passions,
As long as life has woes;

The moon and its broken reflection,
And its shadows shall appear,
As the symbol of love in heaven,
And its wavering image here."

Mantie swallowed the lump that swelled in her throat at his words. "That's beautiful."

"When I remembered those words, it was like I understood them for the first time. They gave me hope. Man isn't perfect; that's no secret. The best love we're capable of is only a 'wavering image' of God's love, a symbol of His love. And I suddenly realized that both God's love and man's love is always around us."

"Even in war? Even on a battlefield?"

"Even there: soldiers risking their lives for each other, women who needn't be there at all coming to help wounded soldiers, soldiers sharing the last of their food with each other." He turned toward her, and their gazes met. "Then there are people like you."

"Me?" Mantie blinked in surprise.

"Yes, you. You and all the other people who raise children orphaned by the war."

"I never thought of that as anything special. How can a person not love the children?"

"That's the answer God gave me on the bridge that night." He smiled at her and lifted his hand to her cheek. "As awful as war is, it hasn't the power to destroy love."

It seemed the most natural thing in the world when his lips touched hers in a kiss that was gentle and warm and filled with reverence. When it ended, he pressed his lips against her forehead. His voice was gruff with emotion when he said, "I'd best get you home."

He slid his arm about her shoulders. She allowed herself to be pulled closer until her head rested against his shoulder. She was glad Jeremiah walked the rest of the way, pulling the sleigh up the winding road. She was glad, too, for the time to spend close in Lane's embrace, without the need to look into his eyes. What would she see there, and what would he see in hers?

Amazement filled her that she'd welcomed a man's kiss. She wanted to push away questions and doubts and relax in the beauty of the moment. Of one thing she was certain. Only Lane Powell could have broken through her defenses. She would never have allowed another man such intimacies.

Lane pulled Jeremiah to a stop in front of the house and wrapped the reins around the terret to keep Jeremiah still. All the while Lane's arm remained around Mantie's shoulder. Her heart raced, but she stayed in his embrace. His lips brushed her cheek, and when he tentatively kissed her lips, she yielded completely and joyfully.

Neither of them spoke while he helped her out of the carriage and walked with her to the door, his arm around her waist. At the door he set the foot warmer on the porch. Then he kissed her again, and she wondered at how right and safe and good it felt to be in his arms.

"Good night, sweet Mantie," he whispered.

Their gazes met. Mantie dropped hers after a brief instant. It was still all too new. She knew her eyes shone with joy and awe and was afraid they were making promises her heart wasn't ready to keep.

She was torn between relief and yearning when the door closed between her and Lane Powell.

Lane's thoughts were a jumble as he climbed back into the sleigh and started down the hill. He hardly dared examine the evening. Mantie had let him kiss her. More than that, she'd seemed to welcome his kiss, had rested in his embrace.

His heart soared with joy. He lifted his gaze to the sky. Was it possible the Lord was answering his prayer so quickly? He wanted to stand up and yell out his thanks.

Yet one small corner of his heart warned him to wait, warned him that Mantie Clark's heart would not be so soon and easily won.

He didn't want to listen.

Instead he wrapped himself in the memory of the feel of her lips, warm and yielding and sweet beneath his own. And he hoped.

Chapter 9

Mantie went to sleep remembering the enchantment of Lane's arms. His arms were her first thought on waking.

The chill set in to her bones and her heart as soon as she stepped out of bed and onto the cold bedroom floor. How could she have been so foolish? A little moonlight, a kind man, and she allowed herself to enjoy his kisses. No matter how much she liked Lane Powell, she couldn't love him. It simply wasn't possible to love anyone as much as she loved Colin. Of course kisses and hugs felt good to a woman who'd lived without the kisses and hugs of the man she loved for over five years. That didn't mean she was ready to give her heart away to another.

At breakfast, she avoided the family's teasing questions as best she could. With a smile firmly in place, she told them she'd enjoyed the ride and scolded them for trying to make something romantic of it. "You know Lane and I are friends."

The children and Walter let it go with a laugh, but Alice's expression made it clear she wasn't certain Mantie was being entirely forthcoming.

That afternoon Mantie and Alice collected pine boughs and cones from the surrounding woods. They piled the collection on the kitchen table and worked together to form garlands. It was fun hanging swags around the parlor and kitchen walls. They tucked fragrant boughs behind the tortoiseshell-framed portraits of Alice's parents in the parlor and the print on the kitchen wall by Currier and Ives titled "Skating Scene—Moonlight." The picture brought tears to Mantie's eyes. She'd always loved it. Now it raised memories she didn't dare face.

Mantie wasn't happy to discover Lane and Nate were again invited to supper. "Really, Alice, do you think that's necessary? They'll be here tomorrow night for Christmas Eve, after all."

Alice's eyes registered surprise. "That's not at all like you, Mantie. Did you and Lane argue last night?"

"No. I just think our family should be able to spend a few nights by ourselves."

"We do."

The truth of Alice's reply only sparked Mantie's impatience. "Lane and Nate shouldn't depend so much on our family. They can't spend their evenings here for the rest of their lives."

Alice shook her head. "I hope you never go for another sleigh ride. Sleighing obviously doesn't agree with you." She tied a strip of red patterned calico about the bottom of the kerosene lamp in the middle of the kitchen table. "There. Doesn't that look festive?"

The red bow reminded Mantie of Lane's purchase of red ribbon. *Isn't there anything that won't remind me of that man?* she wondered. She headed for the stairs and the sanctuary of her room. "I still have some Christmas gifts to finish."

That evening when Lane arrived, Mantie saw his gaze

immediately seek her out. She recognized the thinly veiled joy at seeing her. She shifted her gaze away and answered his warm greeting with a cool hello.

During the meal she continued to avoid his gaze and responded to his attempts at conversation with stiff politeness. She could feel his confusion at her attitude but did nothing to dispel it. Speaking frankly in front of the family wasn't to be considered.

After the meal, as Mantie gathered dishes into the wash pan, Alice whispered, "Brrr. I can feel the blizzard is back."

Mantie shot her an angry look. "It was never gone."

"Wasn't it? My mistake."

Across the room, Lane cleared his throat. "Nate and I will be heading home now. Thank you kindly for supper, ladies. It was delicious as always."

"Aw, Lane, can't we stay awhile?" Nate pleaded. "You and Walt haven't even played checkers yet."

"Big night tomorrow, Nate. Christmas Eve. You want to be rested up."

Mantie kept her back to the door and her hands busy, all the while listening to the good-byes. She tried to forget the hurt, pleading look she'd seen in Lane's gray eyes in the last glance of him she'd allowed herself.

Later, when the others were in bed, Mantie sat beside the kitchen table, a soft warm shawl about her shoulders, putting the finishing touches on the collar she was crocheting for Alice's Christmas gift. Her thoughts stubbornly refused to stay on her work. They drifted instead to Lane.

When the last stitch was made, she studied the collar. In spite of her wandering thoughts, the collar looked just as it should. Mantie rested her head against the back of the rocking chair and closed her eyes.

Why am I letting this man slip into my heart, Lord? I don't want to stop loving Colin. I never want to forget the beautiful love we shared.

Abe's face appeared in her mind.

She frowned. Why had she thought of him? Alice had accused her of being as cold toward men as Abe was toward women. Yet she certainly hadn't been cold toward Lane. That was the problem.

But Lane had said something else about Abe. She struggled to clear the memory in her tired mind. Lane had said when some people lose people they love, they try to stop loving people so they won't risk the pain of loss again.

Is that what I've done, Lord?

No. She wouldn't believe it. She wouldn't believe her love for Colin was an illusion she'd clung to in order to keep at bay the possibility of loving and losing again. Her love for Colin had been real and strong.

But he was gone, and Lane Powell was here. Last night her heart had been light and filled with wonder and joy. It had felt good to be happy again because a man liked her. All day she'd fought that happiness and her guilt. Tonight, she was tired, weary to her very bones.

Lane lay awake long into the night. His heart felt bruised by Mantie's cold rebuff.

How could I have been such a fool, Lord? I knew I needed to work up slow to asking her to keep steady company. To kiss her, to actually kiss her. . . Lane groaned and buried his face in his pillow. Her kisses had been wonderful, and she'd offered them willingly, he had no doubt of that. But he knew her heart still belonged to Colin.

Will she ever allow me another chance, Lord, or have I destroyed any opportunity that she might grow to love me?

Chapter 10

Mantie and Alice banked the fire in the kitchen stove before leaving for church the next evening. They'd eat supper following the service. Pots and kettles and roasting pans covered the top of the stove and filled the oven. The food would stay relatively warm even with the fire banked. It wouldn't take too long to have the meal ready when they returned.

Jesse and Jenny could barely contain their excitement. Gifts wouldn't be opened until the morning, but Christmas Eve was still special. Their excitement was contagious. Mantie's spirits lifted, even knowing Lane would be spending the evening with them.

Alice spoke of that point while she and Mantie put on their capes and gloves. "I hope you can find it in your heart to be kinder to Lane tonight than last night. After all, it is Christmas. You might make an effort not to take the joy out of the evening for him."

Her words stung, but Mantie was in no mood to let down her defenses. What if she couldn't build them up again?

The early evening was crisp, but the family was too excited

169

to mind. There were no skaters to watch as they crossed the bridge. Everyone in town would be at church. Even Peace's three saloons were closed in honor of Christ's birth.

The road was filled with sleighs, wagons on runners, and people walking. Every group carried lanterns, the light swinging in merry golden squares on the snow. Cheerful greetings of "Blessed Christmas to you" were offered and received again and again.

The school bell was bonging when the family arrived at the schoolhouse, reminding stragglers the service would soon begin. They were among the last to find room to sit down, but those who stood didn't complain. Like many people, the Clarks extinguished their lantern lights upon entering the church. A few lanterns remained burning, but there was no need for everyone to waste their candles.

Mantie's gaze swept the crowd. She saw Lane and Nate seated near the front on the opposite side of the room and felt a tug at her heart. Frightened by the attraction she felt for Lane, she looked away.

What is happening to me, Lord? she prayed silently. *If I truly loved Colin, how can that love be swept away so suddenly?*

The service began with a hymn. Mantie turned her mind to God's gift. She wished there were a piano to accompany the group but was grateful for the reverend's fiddle. Certainly the lack of a piano didn't dampen the joy in the congregation's hearts and voices.

The reverend led everyone in prayer, then read the beautiful Christmas story, telling of Christ's birth.

"A new member of our community has a gift for you tonight," he announced after the reading. "Mr. Lane Powell told me of a Christmas Eve tradition in a church back in Pennsylvania where he grew up. He asked if he might share it with you tonight. I was pleased to say yes. Would everyone extinguish their lanterns, please? And all the children under twelve please come to the front."

Whispers and shifting feet filled the room with a sense of confusion. Lanterns were extinguished. Only one lantern, on the teacher's table at the front of the room, remained lit. Children made their way to the front. An occasional "Ouch" and "Sorry" marked their paths.

Lane reached into a basket near the lit lantern and took out a candle. Lifting a window of the lantern with a candlesnuffer, he lit the candle, then extinguished the lantern. The candle he held cast light on his hand and his chin, but not much else.

A little light emanated from the stove in the middle of the room. The drapeless windows were pale gray, as the moon wasn't yet shining in its glory.

"When Christ came to earth as a little baby," Lane began, "He was like this little candle flame. This one candle doesn't cast a very big light, does it?"

The children answered with a chorus of timid no's.

"What do you think Christ's light was?" Lane asked.

None of the children ventured a guess.

"I'm sure you know," Lane encouraged. "What did Christ bring us?"

"Forgiveness," Nate suggested.

"Why did He bring us forgiveness?"

"Because He loves us," another boy replied.

"Why does He love us?"

Silence. Then Jenny piped up. "Because He's God's Son,

and God is love."

"That's right. So what do you suppose is the light baby Jesus brought to the world?"

"Love. God's love," the children eagerly answered.

"How did the little light of God's love, which the baby Jesus brought, grow large enough to light the world?" Lane touched another candlewick to the flame. It flared into light. He held the candle out. "Here, take it."

One of the children held the candle.

"How did the little light grow?" he asked again.

"He gave it away," Jenny answered.

"He shared it," another said.

"That's right," Lane agreed. "Jesus said, 'This is my commandment, That ye love one another, as I have loved you.' "

In the candlelight, Mantie could just make out Lane picking up the basket from the table and holding it out toward the children. "Nate, would you pass these out?"

From the movement and shadows, it was obvious Nate did as he was asked.

Lane whispered something Mantie couldn't hear. In a moment another candle flamed. Then another. Soon all the children held lighted tapers.

"See how bright the light shines when we share it with another?" Lane asked. "Take your candles back to your families, and light your families' lanterns."

The children did as he asked. As they returned to their seats, the light that had been concentrated around the teacher's desk spread throughout the room. When the lanterns were lit, few shadows remained.

Wavering image. The phrase from Longfellow's poem flickered through Mantie's mind as she looked about the room at the many candle flames—wavering images symbolizing God's love.

Mantie glanced down at Jenny's candle. A smile tugged at Mantie's lips. A red ribbon tied low around the candle in a bow protected Jenny's fingers from dripping wax.

Thank You, Lord. Mantie's heart swelled in gratitude. Her prayer was answered.

Lane, Abe, and Nate walked to the Clarks' house with the family. Mantie was anxious to speak with Lane but not with the family around. She did walk beside him long enough to say without the others hearing, "I'm sorry I acted so snobbish last night. I hope you can forgive me."

He looked wary but nodded.

Relieved, she fell into step beside Jenny. Lane's cautious look made Mantie a little uneasy. Perhaps he wouldn't find it possible to forgive her to the extent he'd trust her enough to keep company with her, but at least things should be more comfortable between them among the family this evening. All she could do was offer that bridge of peace and trust the Lord to work the rest out as He saw best.

The scent of pine from the decorations mixed with the cooking aromas as the family entered the house. Mantie, Alice, and Jenny bustled to get supper ready. The women donned their best aprons. The fire in the kitchen stove was stirred. The table was set with the best china and napkins.

Walter had milked the cow and checked on the horses before leaving for church, so there was no need to change out of his church suit. Alice shooed the men into the parlor, where Walter lit the stove to warm the room for family gathering later.

So many serving platters and bowls filled the table that

Walter observed as he sat down, "Hardly room for our plates." Oyster stew started the meal. Roast turkey with oyster stuffing centered the main course. Sweet potatoes, carrots in cream sauce, boiled onions, ruby jelly, and sweet rolls filled it out.

Mantie was disappointed to find herself seated on the same side of the table as Lane, with Nate between them. It afforded her no opportunity to show him by her smiles that she wished to return to friendlier times.

"Where do oysters come from?" Nate asked.

"The ocean," Lane told him.

Nate gave Lane a look of disgust. "No, they don't. The ocean is far away."

His observation brought a chuckle from the adults.

"You're right," Mantie assured him. "The ocean is far away. The oysters are sent to Minnesota by boats on the Mississippi River or the Great Lakes, or across land on the railroad. Some are packed in buckets with ice on top so they don't spoil. Others are canned. It takes a lot of work to get oysters to Minnesota."

"Do you believe Mantie?" Jenny challenged.

Nate heaved a sigh. "I guess so. Even though she isn't a real teacher, she teaches sometimes, so she must be pretty smart."

His comment set the others laughing again, but beneath the laughter, Mantie heard Lane murmur, "That she is, Nate." She missed much of the rest of the conversation. Her mind was filled with arguments for and against allowing Lane into her life as a suitor.

Fruitcake and apple pie left everyone content at meal's end. "We'll serve coffee and cookies in the parlor," Alice informed everyone.

The children's coffee was liberally doctored with milk and

sugar. Jenny sat on the edge of her chair in the parlor, balancing her china cup and saucer in a masterful attempt at imitating a lady. At Jenny's urging, Alice shared stories of her childhood Christmases. Then the children insisted on Lane's Christmas stories, and Abe's and Mantie's and finally Walter's.

While Walter regaled the children, Mantie took the almost empty china cookie platter to the kitchen to replenish it. When she came out of the pantry, Lane was waiting for her beside the kitchen table.

"Alice sent me out here to help you." His voice was more guarded than usual.

She set the platter down on the table, hoping he wouldn't see how her hands trembled. Her smile trembled, too, as she looked up at him. "I don't need your help, but would you wait here for me a moment?"

His brows drew together in a mystified frown, but he nodded.

Mantie hurried up to her room, retrieved a small package, and hurried back down. Her heart pounded wildly. Would he think her unseemly in offering him this gift?

"Since you won't be here tomorrow, I'd like you to have this now." She handed him the package. It was about as long as her hand, thin, and wrapped in a piece of the emerald-green silk from her favorite dress. A length of black ribbon tied it closed.

Light kindled in his gray eyes. For a moment Mantie thought he was going to hug her, but he didn't.

His wide fingers struggled with the ribbon, but eventually he freed the package and unfolded the material carefully. Inside was a crocheted ivory bookmark. His gaze examined it carefully, then shifted to meet hers. Wonder shone from his eyes. "You made this for me?"

She nodded, feeling shier now than before he'd opened it. "It's for your Bible. Or your poetry."

"I'll cherish it. Thank you."

The sincerity in his voice warmed her.

He grinned. "I've something for you, too." He removed a leather bag from the pegs beside the door and pulled a package from it. The package was wrapped in brown paper and tied with red twine. "Not wrapped so fancy as the gift you gave me, but that doesn't diminish the thought."

She knew from the weight and feel what it was as soon as she took the package. Excitement sparked through her. She couldn't hold back a grin. She pulled off the paper with such speed that it brought a laugh from Lane. "Skate blades. Oh, they're the perfect gift. Thank you, Lane. Thank you."

"What do you say we try them out? I brought my own blades along, just in case I could convince you."

Mantie glanced at the door to the parlor. "We probably shouldn't go right now." Everything within her hungered to leave immediately for the river.

"They won't miss us much."

That was all it took to convince her. They hurried into their outer garments, giggling like children. They were just leaving when Mantie heard Alice say, "Mantie, are the cookies ready yet? Mantie? Lane? Where are you going?"

"Skating," Lane called and closed the door firmly behind them.

Only half a dozen other skaters were enjoying the crisp night on the river. Mantie and Lane sat on a fallen log and strapped on their skate blades. When they were ready, Lane stood and held out his hand toward her. She placed her hand in his, smiling, and slid her other hand into her muff.

"Let's try a few laps around the millpond first, where the ice is smoother," Lane suggested.

She stepped onto the ice with caution. Her first strokes wobbled. Her grip on his hand tightened. "It's been such a long time."

"We'll take it slow. You'll get the feel of it again before long."

"It might not be much fun for you skating with me. If you'd rather go off by yourself for awhile, I won't mind."

He slid an arm around her waist. "I'm not going anywhere. We have all the time in the world."

She wondered whether he was referring to skating or romance.

She forced her mind away from his nearness and concentrated on leaning into the outside edges of her skates and keeping her balance over the ball of her foot. Before long her strokes were easy and smooth alongside Lane's.

"There, see? You haven't forgotten how," he encouraged.

Their blades sang in unison as he matched his strokes to hers. They moved well and easily together. "Ready to try the river?"

"Yes."

They skated beneath the arch of the stone bridge. The moon lay a golden path before them. Trees cast blue shadows across the snow-covered banks. Stars burned brightly in the sky overhead. Mantie sighed in contentment.

He grinned. "Your eyes are shining with excitement."

"It's more perfect than I remember. Thank you so much for the blades."

"You are so welcome." He shifted his weight slightly, drawing her nearer to his side.

Her heart picked up its beat. She heard him clear his throat. "Mantie, when you asked me to forgive you earlier. . ."

"Yes?"

"I'm the one who should be asking your forgiveness."

"Mine?" Surprise poured through her.

He nodded. "You told me how devoted you are to Colin. I had no right kissing you."

Was he sorry he'd kissed her? Mantie's thoughts and emotions tumbled into a mess. Surely he must have realized how she'd welcomed his kisses. But he'd properly interpreted her coldness last night. Now what was she going to do? "I liked your gift to the church tonight."

He didn't say anything for a few strokes. "Aren't you changing the subject?"

"Not exactly. I liked what you said about Christ's love being like a candle flame, how it grows when it's shared."

Lane chuckled. "I can't exactly take credit for the idea."

"I've been hanging onto my love for Colin like. . .like it was a shield. I didn't realize it until last night. I was using my love for him to keep the risk of loving someone else away. It's not that I didn't love him," she rushed to explain. "I did love him, truly."

"I know that." His voice was quiet and low.

"During your candle parable tonight, I understood. . .oh, I don't know if I can make it clear to you, but. . .when a person lights one candle and then blows the original candle out, the second candle still burns."

"Yes."

"I know the sermon was about God's love, but. . .it's like that with Colin." It was terrifying to share this. What if Lane thought her a fool? But she didn't know any other way to tell him. "Colin's love touched my life deeply. When he died, what I learned about love from him remained. Tonight it was as if God were showing me it's time to take what I learned about love from Colin and share it." Her chest hurt from fear Lane would reject what she was offering.

Lane's skates hissed against the ice as he stopped. He gripped her shoulders and looked into her face. "Mantie Clark, are you saying you might be willing to share what you've learned about loving with me?"

She swallowed hard. "If. . .if you want it."

"If I want it?" He caught her in a hug that pushed her hood back on her shoulders. "My dear girl, I assure you I want nothing more."

She slid her arms around his neck and laughed softly. "It's not perfect, you know. Only a 'wavering image.' "

He pulled back just far enough to look into her eyes. "It's all I have to offer, too."

"That's enough."

"You dear girl." He lifted her about the waist and swung her around.

"One more thing."

He set her back on her blades, keeping her within his arms. "Anything it's in my power to give."

Mantie's cheeks heated. "About that apology for your kisses. . ."

He chuckled and whispered close to her ear, "May I trade it for more of the same?"

"I was hoping you would."

In the moonlight's golden path, he joyously complied.

His kiss felt as beautiful and right as the first one. With a little sigh, she leaned against him. He touched his lips to her temple, then kissed her dimple before claiming her lips again. "Blessed Christmas, precious one."

A flame leaped within her heart, wavered slightly, then settled into a steady glow. "Blessed Christmas, Lane."

JOANN A. GROTE

JoAnn lives in Minnesota, where she grew up. She uses the state
for most of her story settings, and like her characters, JoAnn
seeks to serve Christ in her work. She believes that readers of
novels can receive a message of salvation and encouragement
from well-crafted fiction. An award-winning author, she has had
over thirty-five books published, including several novels published with Barbour Publishing in the **Heartsong Presents** line,
as well as in the **American Adventure** series for kids.

DREAMS AND SECRETS

by DiAnn Mills

Every good gift and every perfect gift is from above,
and cometh down from the Father of lights,
with whom is no variableness, neither shadow of turning.

JAMES 1:17

Chapter 1

November 1851, near Philadelphia

Falling always came easy for Emma Leigh, especially when she had her mind on other matters. She smoothed the skirt of her worn, brown-and-pink-flowered dress, lifted her chin, and marched toward her employer's office at the Jones Inn. Abruptly, she slammed headlong into Thad Benson's armload of firewood.

The smell of freshly cut wood enveloped her senses mere seconds before the impact knocked her to the floor. Thad's bundle fell with a crash, but thankfully, none of the pieces hit her. Emma Leigh's hoop skirt, however, soared upward in a less than dignified manner.

"Oh, my," she cried, her cheeks aflame with embarrassment. She scrambled to push down her heap of snowy white petticoats and restore some semblance of balance and poise.

A calloused hand reached for hers overtop her hoop skirt and righted her to her feet.

"Thank you, Thad," she mumbled, unable to look at him. He should have seen her coming. A combination of ruffled feelings and a bruised backside produced an untimely bit of irritation.

"Are you hurt?" he asked, shoving aside the pieces of wood. "I'm really sorry, Emma Leigh."

Forcing herself to stare into his face lined with concern, she swallowed a stinging remark and braved a smile. After all, sweet Thad, the young man in charge of the stables and all the outside grounds, would never intentionally harm anyone.

From the office came the sound of someone clearing his throat. Emma turned and looked. Towering in the doorway, Alexander Jones, the owner of the inn, looked formidable. "What's all the racket?" he bellowed.

Thad whirled around. "Sir, I collided with Miss Carter. I do apologize for the incident."

"Is the young lady injured?" Mr. Jones asked, crossing his arms over his narrow chest and leaning in Emma Leigh's direction.

She met the owner's gaze, feeling more humiliated than before. "No, Sir." *Only my pride.*

Mr. Jones pressed his lips tightly, but his mustache and beard jiggled, betraying his gruff reaction. The scene must have looked amusing, further intensifying her embarrassment. "Gather up the firewood, Thad. You are dismissed." Nodding to Emma Leigh, he stepped aside from the doorway. "Miss Carter, I'll see you now."

Emma Leigh followed him into his office. She'd felt nervous before the fall, but now every part of her trembled. For a moment she feared toppling over his desk.

"Are you certain you are uninjured?" he asked, peering down over his long, pointed nose.

"Yes, Sir." She hoped her voice sounded stronger than the

weak reply rising in her ears.

Mr. Jones, impeccably dressed in a black suit, eased into his chair. She'd heard some of the staff refer to him as Old Match Stick. Although Emma Leigh didn't comment on his skeletal frame, she did wonder if he'd blow away on a blustery day. He smiled on occasion and greeted those who graced his inn with the utmost of hospitality and respect, but he insisted upon a meticulous establishment. Most of the staff feared him. He had the type of voice that carried—rather rolled—like thunder. Perhaps his mannerisms had something to do with his military background; but in any event, Emma Leigh had been summoned to his office.

"Sit down, Miss Carter." He gestured to an empty chair in front of his desk. His booming voice, devoid of passion, further alarmed her. "I've been observing you as you interact with the guests, and there's a matter we need to discuss."

The lump in her throat grew to boulder-sized proportions, and she rubbed her clammy hands together. A dozen grievances flashed across her mind, all of which bore discussion. *He must believe I'm shirking in my duties.* She lowered herself onto the chair, sitting stiffly on the edge, and gave him her attention.

"Christmas will be here before we're prepared," he said. The grandfather clock in the main entrance struck ten times to punctuate his words as he continued. "In the past, the staff has engaged in merriment, which I believe is appropriate for the celebration of our Lord's birth. This year—" Mr. Jones cleared his throat. "This year I'd like for us to partake in something different, and I believe you can be of assistance."

Emma Leigh squeezed her fingers together. "In what way, Sir?"

He drew out a sheet of paper from his drawer and placed his spectacles on his nose. Picking up his quill, he dipped it into the inkwell. "Miss Carter, you have a way of exhibiting excellent social skills in your duties as the inn's hostess—however, you do at times overindulge." He scrutinized her over his spectacles.

"Yes, Sir. I mean, I'm sorry, Sir."

He paused. "Very well. I'm assigning you the task of organizing a frugal yet highly enjoyable Christmas party for the staff. In the past, too much emphasis has been placed on an abundance of gift giving. This year, I'd like to see the holiday made more simple and meaningful." He painstakingly wrote something on the paper, then handed it to her. "This is your budget and your orders. Mrs. Weares will be notified of your extra duties and that you will be assisting her in selecting the menu for the Christmas dinner."

Emma Leigh hastily read her new directives. "Thank you, Mr. Jones. When would you like for me to have this completed?"

"Ten days hence," he replied. "I plan to call a holiday meeting to appoint those who will be decorating the inn and such. You can present your findings then. Of course, I need to approve them beforehand."

Humility washed over Emma Leigh. "Yes, Sir, I. . .I am greatly honored."

His eyes widened. "Goodness, Girl. I don't bite. Calm yourself and go on about your business." A slight smile tugged at his mustache. "After all, we're talking about a Christmas celebration. Just remember I want a memorable holiday." With those words, Mr. Jones dismissed her with a perfunctory nod.

Ah, he's not so fearsome after all. Stepping into the entranceway of the inn, Emma Leigh saw the polished floor had been swept spotless. Not a trace of bark or splinter remained to tell of the collision. For the first time, she realized she could have been badly hurt with the firewood flying in all directions. Poor, shy Thad. He must feel terrible. At her first opportunity, she'd reassure him that the happening was indeed an accident and as much her fault as anyone's. She'd been so caught up in meeting with Mr. Jones that she hadn't paid attention to anything else.

Clutching the paper outlining her new duties, Emma Leigh took her position at the front desk where she greeted guests, showed them to their rooms, and helped them in any way she could. Today, however, during the moments when her services were not needed, her thoughts and prayers would be engrossed in providing a memorable Christmas for the staff at the Jones Inn.

Thad lifted the axe high above his head and sent it crashing into the log. Sawdust and splinters flew every which way. Tossing aside the split wood, he set another log in its place.

Craaack. He should have seen Emma Leigh coming.

Craaack. He'd been thinking about those large doe eyes and the sound of her sweet voice when he sent her sprawling to the floor.

Craaack. And right in front of Mr. Jones. The owner had just spoken to him about raising his pay and extending his duties to include inside maintenance of the inn. Thad grimaced. He'd left such a good impression.

Most likely Emma Leigh would never speak to him again, and Mr. Jones would forget about elevating Thad to a new position. Both probabilities ended his dreams of saving additional money and someday inviting Emma Leigh to spend the

189

rest of her life with him.

Thad lifted the axe and rested it on his right shoulder. He'd known Emma Leigh since they were children in school. Back then his parents were living. Those were happier days, when laughter swept through their clapboard country home like a breeze on a hot day. His father, a country doctor, and his devoted mother never said no to a single person in need—whether that need be medical or financial. But all their goodness ended when his parents drowned in a tragic buggy accident.

Thad had spent the first three years since their deaths living alone in Boston, but then he had returned to his home village and moved in with his uncle and Swedish-born aunt. It wasn't that he couldn't fend for himself in his parents' home. He simply chose not to spend time alone. Sometimes he visited the homestead and tidied up a bit, often reflecting on more pleasant times, but he didn't allow his thoughts to be consumed with bitterness or regret. God had taken his parents for a reason, and they had left a legacy of unselfish giving. In their memory and with the peace God had given him, Thad chose to live his life just as his parents had: serving the Lord with all his might. Like his father, Thad had committed his life to medicine.

Kicking aside the split wood, he set the last piece in place and sank the axe all the way through. The chunk divided into two separate pieces, just like Emma Leigh and him.

His favorite memory of her occurred when she was about nine and he nearly eleven. George, one of the older boys, had insisted upon bullying a younger one, and Emma Leigh must have had her fill. She marched over to the children watching the badgering and pushed her way through. She stomped her feet and shook her fist in the bully's face, her light brown pig-tails bouncing with her denunciation of the ignoble deed.

"Jesus doesn't want us hurting other people," she'd said. "When you do, it hurts Him!"

Thad still recalled the way Emma Leigh's turned-up nose wrinkled when she concentrated on something—like poor George that day. Oddly enough, George had released the younger boy.

Even then, Emma Leigh had possessed the ability to make folks see the error of their ways, yet she always did so in a tender fashion. After confronting George, she had turned around and shared her noon meal with him. Years later, George had become a preacher—a good one, too.

Back then, Thad had cared for the little girl, and now he found himself hopelessly in love with her. But she needed an outgoing man, one who could give her a good life and show off her grand beauty. Because of her father's long illness, she knew nothing but poverty, and Thad had medical school to complete. He couldn't ask her to marry him until he had something more to offer.

Thad needed to apologize. And he must speak with her today.

Evening shadows danced across the quiet yard of the inn before he finished his chores. Already the ground beneath him crunched in anticipation of another frost. Glancing back at the barn, he saw the moonlight reflecting in a silvery glow from the weathered side of the structure. Beauty in simple things. Perfection in God's creation. They simply served to remind him of Emma Leigh.

He entered the inn through the back near the kitchen and

stomped his feet until no trace of debris could be tracked inside. His gaze noted the cook, Sarah, placing the finishing touches on a platter of beef, garnished in potatoes, carrots, and onions. Her white bonnet accented her red hair, and the warm glow of the fire spiced her cheeks like red apples. The woman smiled.

"Aye, Thad. Working late, are ye?"

"Yes, Ma'am. Mr. Jones is expecting a large party tomorrow from Philadelphia, and I wanted the harnesses shined before I fetched them in the morning."

"Good boy. Are ye a-needin' something?"

Thad felt his cheeks warm and his toes tingle in his boots. "I needed to speak with Miss Carter."

Sarah tilted her head and gave him a sad smile. *Could she read his heart?* "Her father already came by."

Determined to hide his disappointment, Thad thanked her kindly and trekked outside. Emma Leigh lived about three miles from the inn. He'd gladly walk the distance to ease his conscience. There'd be no resting for him tonight until he knew she'd forgiven him for the fall.

Chapter 2

Emma Leigh chatted with Papa all during the wagon ride home from the inn. The cooler air caused her to wrap her arms about her as she told him about the meeting with Mr. Jones and her new assignment. Of course, she bent poor Papa's ear until she knew he must be ready for her to hush.

"I'm sorry, Papa. I'm talking on and not bothering to ask about your day."

Papa reached to give her shoulders a squeeze. "I daresay the happenings at home were not as exciting as yours. With the grain harvested, my hours are starting to slow a bit. We have good apples this year—I believe plenty for the months ahead."

"They will taste good when the wind is blowing and the snow is piled high," Emma Leigh replied.

For the past year and a half, neither Papa's crops nor his health had done well. Emma Leigh had taken the job at the inn to help her family, despite her father's protests. Her duties at the inn interested her, and she'd stayed on. The extra money provided additional food and clothing for her family.

"You ask your mother about the inn's Christmas. I'm sure

she can help you much better than I."

Once home, Emma Leigh greeted her five brothers and sister before helping Mama ladle tender chunks of rabbit, potatoes, and a few scant carrots into mismatched pieces of cracked crockery for dinner. The enticing aroma of apples and spices slowly simmering over the fire and transforming into thick, dark apple butter tantalized her senses. The wind whistled around the meager cabin, ushering a draft through the cracks in the rough-sawn logs. She glanced at the children and saw they were warmly dressed, but patches were worn thin. A shiver raced up her spine from fear for her siblings in the winter ahead.

Oh, Lord, keep them healthy. We've already lost three to putrid fever. Charles is still not well. Help me not to complain but be a humble servant.

Emma Leigh roused the dog and ordered him to play next to the younger children where the animal's heat would keep them warm. Taking a deep breath, she turned her attention to Mama and explained her dilemma about the inn's Christmas celebration.

"What can I do?" Emma Leigh asked. She accidentally stuck her finger in the hot stew and yanked it back. Poking the finger in her mouth, then rubbing it vigorously, she glanced up at her mother expectantly.

Mama wiped her hands on a clean apron and silently examined Emma Leigh's finger. Hearing a howl, she cast a disapproving glance at one of her sons, who had pulled his brother's hair. "It's Emma Leigh's turn for your mama's attention. Mind your manners." She lifted a crusty brown loaf of bread from the hearth. "Emma Leigh, I think you need to pray about the matter. I will say those fine people at the inn want a holiday that knits their hearts with friendship and love. Simple joys and laughter are the best gifts of all, especially when they are tied with a ribbon of love."

Emma Leigh always paid attention to her mother's wisdom. *Simple joys and laughter.* "How can one give joy and laughter? They can't be wrapped and tied with a colorful piece of yarn."

"But those things are everlasting, the kind of treasures from which memories are made." Her mother snapped her fingers in the direction of the children. "Joseph, do not tease your brother again or you will forfeit your supper."

"I'm confused." Emma sighed and picked up baby Charles, who had crawled to her feet and tugged at her skirts. His little shirt and drawers bore knee marks from the day's adventures.

"Emma Leigh, you will find a way." Mama smiled and planted a kiss on Charles's cheek before motioning for the other children and Papa to gather around the table.

As soon as Papa had asked the blessing, Emma Leigh buried herself in thought. The hum of children's voices rose and fell in the wake of contemplating Mr. Jones's request. The stew tasted delicious, and the hot bread thinly coated with freshly churned butter filled the empty spot in her stomach, but she still had no idea how the staff should celebrate Christmas.

Midway through the meal, a pounding at the door seized her attention. Papa rose from his chair and answered it. The heavy wooden door with its leather hinges squeaked open.

"Evenin', Thad. Come on in. You haven't visited us in a long time." Papa shook his hand. "You're just in time for supper."

Emma Leigh couldn't believe Thad stood before her. Whatever could he need from them? He looked a bit troubled. She hoped nothing terrible had happened to his aunt or uncle.

"Evenin' to you, too, Mr. Carter." Thad removed his cap and nodded at Mama. "Hope everything is well with you, Ma'am. Sorry to disturb your supper, but I will only be a minute."

Emma Leigh noted how broad his shoulders had become. Since they were in school together, he'd grown to quite a handsome man. She felt herself blush. She shouldn't be thinking such thoughts, but Thad had always captured a soft spot in her heart.

"If you don't mind, Sir, I'd like a word with Miss Emma Leigh." Thad's clear blue gaze bore into hers as though he'd read her earlier thoughts.

She felt her skin tingle and knew a bright shade of red glistened on her cheeks.

"You have a fine-looking family, Mr. Carter. I know you must be proud."

Thad's kind mannerisms and carefully chosen words told of his Christian upbringing. If he weren't so shy, Emma Leigh would set her cap for him.

Papa glanced at Emma Leigh. "Daughter, this gentleman would like a word with you."

"Certainly, Papa." She rose from her spot on the well-worn bench and snatched up her shawl from a peg near the door.

"Thank you," Thad said to Papa.

Thad stepped aside from the door, allowing her to pass. Emma Leigh caught a glimpse of his reddened face and assumed the color came from the dipping temperatures. Once again she smelled the rich scent of wood, so much a part of him and his position at the Jones Inn.

Once the door shut, she whirled around in the twilight to

face him. "Is something wrong?"

"I believe so." He replaced his woolen cap. "Emma Leigh, I wanted to make sure you were all right after I knocked you down this morning."

He's walked all this way to check on me? How very much like his father. "Thad, how very sweet of you. I'm fine, perfectly fine. I never gave the matter another thought."

He nodded slowly. "Good, I worried you might be hurt, and I needed to apologize again."

"And I looked for you before I left because I feared I was rude to you earlier in the day."

His eyes widened, and a slow smile spread across his thin face. Thad had been a frail-looking child, but it seemed as though he'd suddenly filled out the hollow places. Those deepset robin's-egg blue eyes and wide smile were now those of a man.

Oh my, what is wrong with me?

"You tried to find me?" he asked, jamming his hands into his pockets. His breath puffed into an icy cloud, giving evidence of the plummeting temperatures.

"Of course. Thad, we're friends—have been since we sat next to each other in school. I always welcome a conversation with you."

He shrugged. "Thank you, but Emma Leigh, you have a knack of being able to talk to people easier than I do. I wouldn't want to embarrass you."

"Never! Oh my, have I turned into some dreadful person? I certainly hope I haven't given you the impression we should be friends in secret." The horror of being rude to him curdled her stomach.

"No, not at all. It's. . .it's simply I can't always think of clever things to say."

Emma Leigh lifted her chin. "Nonsense," she said as gently as possible. "You have always found plenty to say to me." Suddenly her mind began to race. "Thad, you have given me a wonderful idea."

"I have?" He raised a brow.

"Yes." Excitement danced across her mind. "Mr. Jones gave me an assignment today. He wants me to come up with a memorable way for the staff to celebrate Christmas. I couldn't think of a thing until now." She touched his arm. "Oh, thank you. Thank you ever so much."

"For what?" He clearly looked baffled.

She laughed. "Secret friends. Don't you see? We can all be secret friends for Christmas." She placed a finger to her lips as she considered the particulars. "All the staff could place their names into a basket, then each of us would draw a name. The person whose name we get will be a secret friend for. . .for about ten days before Christmas. On Christmas Eve when we have our dinner, we'll find out who's our secret friend!"

He chuckled, and she liked the sound of it. "Emma Leigh, your idea sounds like fun."

"Do you really think so?"

"Absolutely. Mr. Jones will be pleased, I'm sure."

She clapped her hands. "I can't wait to tell him. Oh, Thad, thank you so much. And I will tell him it was your idea."

"But it isn't."

"But it is. You deserve the credit. After all, you're an answer to prayer."

A sudden gust of wind chilled her, and from Thad's stance,

she gathered he must be cold, too, for his face looked rather pinched.

"You need to come inside and warm yourself before heading home." She offered a genuine smile. "I'm sure Papa would hitch up the wagon and take you."

"It's not necessary. Once I start walking, I'll get plenty warm." He glanced toward the road and shifted.

"Are you certain? At least let me make you a hot cup of tea." He'd been so good to walk all this way, and now she had the perfect plan to propose to Mr. Jones.

"I appreciate your thoughtfulness, but I must be going. Please give my best to your parents." A gust of wind caught his scarf and he paused. "I will see you tomorrow."

"Tomorrow it is." Emma Leigh felt a sudden twinge of timidity. Certainly a new emotion for her.

His familiar smile, the one she'd grown up with, now caused a flutter in her stomach. What had happened to the skinny little boy, Dr. Horatio Benson's only child?

He plodded across the barnyard on his way to the road. Emma Leigh watched him curiously, her mind recalling the many lazy hours they'd played together as children.

He'd chased rabbits scampering into the brush. She'd raced after butterflies.

He'd fished in the lazy creek in the back corner of his parents' small farm. She'd waded in the cool stream, allowing her toes to sink into the soft mud.

He'd carved their names into an old oak. She'd picked wildflowers. And when Emma Leigh had tried to make friends with the neighbor's bull, Thad had pulled her beneath a fence just in time.

Then a tragic accident took the lives of his parents. For the next three years, Thad had lived in Boston. Emma Leigh hadn't seen him until she began working at the Jones Inn and discovered he had sought employment at the same establishment.

"Thad," Emma Leigh called out.

He whirled around, and she waved. An unexplainable impulse caused her to hurry in his direction. "I'm so rude, please forgive me, but how are you doing?"

He waited until she caught up with him. "Fairly well. I'm able to help my aunt and uncle with their farm and still keep up my parents' place."

"I'm surprised you're not living at your parents' home."

"I thought about it long and hard, but this seemed the best way for me to put aside money to attend medical school and help out my aunt and uncle at the same time."

Her heart raced. "Thad, you're going to be a doctor?"

He scuffed at the hard ground before lifting a smiling face. "Yes, just like my father. Once I'm finished with my schooling at the medical school in Boston, I'd like to tend the same folks here as he did."

Her heart felt a certain comfort. "I'm proud of you. And you'll make a fine doctor. You've always been so gentle and caring."

He massaged his hands. She wished she had gloves to offer him. Maybe next winter she'd have some of her own.

"I appreciate your encouragement, Emma Leigh. You have a real gift with words and making folks feel good about themselves. God willing, I'll do my best. My father gave his life to the people of this community, and I can do no less."

She felt chills mounting on her arms. "I won't keep you any longer. Good-bye and Godspeed."

As she trudged toward the cabin and the firelight flickering in the window, she had a sudden urge to turn around.

Thad Benson stood in the same place she'd left him. He lifted a hand and waved. Perhaps they'd collide again. . .real soon.

Chapter 3

T had walked the six miles home in the dark and cold, but his heart felt as light as a spring day. No matter that snow dusted the road before him and the wind attempted to find solace inside his coat. He had reasons to rejoice. Emma Leigh was neither hurt nor upset with him.

He'd even seen a blush on her cheeks. How he'd like to think he might have put the color there. Thad's mind danced with pictures of Emma Leigh—her hair as dark and rich as the soil on his parents' farm and her skin as fair as thick cream. To him she looked like a queen, from her sweet ways to her lovely features. He envied the lucky man who won her heart.

The cold dissipated with more warm thoughts of Emma Leigh, and only when he lifted the latch on his aunt and uncle's wooden door did he notice the frigid temperatures.

"Thad, I've been so worried," Aunt Klara said, rushing from a chair at her spinning wheel to the door to meet him. Her Swedish accent soothed him, and he stepped into her motherly embrace. "Warm yourself by the fire, and I'll get you something to eat. I have beef stew." She released him but not before patting him on the back.

"I'm sorry to have alarmed you. I needed to pay a visit to the Carter family, and it took longer than I expected."

Uncle Albert lifted his gaze from his Bible. A concerned look etched additional wrinkles into his leathered face. "Is everything all right there?"

"Yes. I–I accidentally caused Miss Emma Leigh to take a spill today and wanted to make sure she escaped unharmed." He grasped his uncle's hand. "I apologize if I caused you any unnecessary discomfort. I'll do the evening chores now rather than after I eat."

"They're finished. You're home now, and the load is lifted from my mind." Uncle Albert offered a reassuring smile.

Thad scraped a chair across the wooden floor and sat at the table. "Thank you, but I could have done them." Weariness suddenly settled in his bones, and for the first time that day he relaxed. The aroma of Aunt Klara's *kalops,* Swedish beef stew with special spices, caused his stomach to rumble. She dished out a hearty bowl and sliced a thick piece of rye bread to go with it.

The comforts of home kept him at his aunt and uncle's. Perhaps selfishness ruled a part of his heart, but he despised being alone—and knew he'd starve with his cooking.

"The health of the Carters could be better. Mr. Carter is still pale, and the younger children have runny noses," Thad announced after quietly blessing his food. "Looks like two new additions to their family since I was there, too."

"Elizabeth and Charles," Aunt Klara replied. "Nearly lost the boy that first year, but he's getting stronger."

The thought troubled Thad. "Makes me wish I already practiced medicine."

Uncle Albert closed his Bible. "You'll be a fine doctor when the time comes."

Emma Leigh made the same comment earlier.

"God is with you," Uncle Albert added. "He's given you a sound mind and a gift for wanting to heal. I saw the same attributes in your father."

"Thank you, Uncle. I'm anxious to begin my studies. If I can be half as good a doctor as my father, I will be pleased."

His uncle chuckled. "The young—anxious to be about their business."

"I have enough money saved for the fall session," Thad said, "although I will miss both of you. All I need to put aside now is money to live on and to purchase my books."

"I heartily approve of your frugal ways," his uncle replied. He turned back to his Bible reading.

Thad turned to Aunt Klara and thanked her for the stew. When he first came to live with his aunt and uncle, her Swedish mannerisms and traditions often confused him. He hadn't always been pleasant. Later when he apologized, Aunt Klara quickly forgave. "It would have been easier if I'd been more like your mother," she'd said and tilted her head as though she understood the grief plaguing his heart.

Often he wondered why God had not blessed Uncle Albert and Aunt Klara with children. They gave so much of themselves.

She poured him a cold glass of buttermilk. "I keep thinking the sooner you leave for school, the sooner you'll return. This time for good."

Uncle Albert stood and tucked his Bible under his arm. "Mornin' comes early. I'm heading to bed."

He dutifully kissed Aunt Klara's cheek and ruffled Thad's hair as though he were but a boy.

"Good night, Uncle. Sleep well."

Uncle Albert disappeared into a darkened room and closed the door behind him.

"You need your rest, too," Thad said to his aunt. "I'm fine, and I'll be ready for bed as soon as I finish eating."

She pulled a chair closer to him, folded her hands in her lap, and took a deep breath. "Thad, is there a matter plaguing you?"

"I don't think so." *Unless you consider my useless feelings for Emma Leigh.*

"Are you working too hard with the farm and at the inn? Every day you do chores at your parents' home and then here." She leaned closer.

"Not at all. I enjoy hard work."

Silence crept between them. The fire crackled, and the dog snored.

"Is your heart hurting for Miss Emma Leigh?"

Thad closed his eyes. Did it really show?

"Love can be a painful thing," she continued, gray tendrils framing her oval face.

He nodded. "She's a fine lady."

"And you're a fine man."

He shrugged. "If I had my schooling done, perhaps I could think about. . .well, consider the possibilities. I could make a few repairs on my parents' home and clean things up proper-like."

Aunt Klara touched his arm. "Sounds to me like you have done a lot of thinking about the matter."

Thad never lied, but offering information he deemed another matter.

"Well, you finish your supper, and I'll leave you to your thoughts." She rose from her chair and bade him good night.

If Aunt Klara read his heart so easily, did others know, too?

Monday, November 17, 1851

"I'd like the inn ready for Christmas by Monday, December 1," Mr. Jones announced at the morning staff meeting. He dug his hands into his trousers' pockets, and the motion revealed a festive plaid vest of red, green, and gold. He teetered back and forth on his heels, grinning broadly. "This is our favorite time of the year. Don't you agree?"

Thad glanced about at the staff of eleven—seven women and four men—nodding and voicing their approval. The spirit of Christmas had arrived at the Jones Inn. The excitement would mount until it seemed the walls would burst with laughter and merriment. He'd joined the staff a little more than a year ago, and he well remembered last year's joy in celebrating the Lord's birth. Guests loved the atmosphere of the inn during this special time, and the staff took pains to make their stay memorable. The mirth could not be equaled at any other season of the year.

Mr. Jones cleared his throat. "Thad, you are in charge of finding the tree—a tall, full one for the entranceway. Make sure you take someone to help you. Mrs. Jones and I will decorate it. We rather enjoy that part of Christmas. Mrs. Weares, as in years before, your responsibilities are to oversee the overall trimming of the entire inn. I'd like every room to hold a bit of Christmas cheer."

Mrs. Weares nodded, her thin face breaking forth into an enthusiastic smile.

"Sarah, as head cook, I want you to provide the guests with the best of food. Spare nothing when it comes to their pleasure." Mr. Jones nodded at Emma Leigh. "Miss Carter, are you ready to explain the details of how all of us will spread good-will-towards-men amongst each other?"

Ah, so this year Mr. and Mrs. Jones plan to be included in the excitement. Thad stole a glimpse at Emma Leigh. Her rosy cheeks brightened, and as always when she was excited, her big brown eyes seemed to sparkle.

"Yes, Sir," she replied, rising from her chair.

"Come along then. We're all ready to hear your plan."

Emma Leigh grasped a small basket and made her way to Mr. Jones's side. He stepped back, making a formal gesture for her to begin. The staff laughed. For certain, the holiday season reigned in their bones.

Emma Leigh moistened her lips. "This year, our Christmas party will be slightly different. Oh, we'll have a marvelous meal on Christmas Eve, but there will be one addition." She took a deep breath. "In just a moment, all of us will write our names on a piece of paper and place them in this basket. Then we will take turns drawing out a name. The one you select is your secret friend from December 15 until Christmas Eve. As often as you like, you may select something for your secret friend and leave it on the wooden table in the kitchen for him or her to pick up. The items are to be small, a sweet treat or a note—or anything you feel appropriate. The idea is to spread love and cheer in ways that don't involve a great deal of money. We simply want everyone to be remembered. On

Christmas Eve, we all find out who our secret friends are. Is this fine with everyone?"

From the sounds of the women clapping, Thad surmised the secret friend proposal suited all of them, although the men looked a little less pleased. To him, it really didn't matter. He merely wanted to see the joy on Emma Leigh's face.

"Oh my," Sarah said and covered her mouth to stifle a giggle. "I hope I get one of you skinny maids so I can fatten you up."

Mr. Jones held up his hand. "Nonsense. I've been trying to add a little meat to my bones for years. I hope you draw my name!"

The hum of the staff's chatter rose like pealing bells. Thad suddenly remembered the days before Christmas when his parents were alive. His father loved to tease, and his mother always pretended mock indignation. On Christmas Eve, she'd take the time to bake an apple pie to have after they'd selected a tree. Father would declare it sour. "You're a fine doctor's wife," he'd say, "but at Christmas I need a woman who can bake a sugary crusted pie." Of course, he always chuckled with his words and ate every bite.

Thad missed those days.

One by one each member of the staff dropped his or her name into Emma Leigh's basket. Closing her eyes, she waded her fingers through the pieces of paper. "Mr. Jones, would you like to be the first one to select your secret friend?"

He dutifully stepped forward and made a grand production of inserting his hand into the basket. He winked at his wife, a quiet, gentle woman who never spoke ill of anyone. Mr. Jones pulled out a name. He lifted his chin and read the paper. "This is grand," he said. "I believe I have the best name of all."

His wife or Sarah, Thad speculated.

One by one the staff filed up to select a name. One of the stable boys drew his own, causing much laughter until he replaced it and reached down into the basket for another. Thad watched the expressions on their faces—and on Emma Leigh's. Surprise. Elation. He waited until the end of the line. How grand if one dark-haired beauty became his secret friend for an entire ten days.

"You have the last name, Thad," Mr. Jones called out.

Thad felt the others study him. They all knew him to be a shy sort. Forcing a faint grin, he reached inside the basket for the lone slip of paper.

Emma Leigh Carter.

Chapter 4

Emma Leigh finished her work promptly before Papa came with the wagon to drive her home. She could very well walk the three miles and did when Papa had a full day in the fields. But now a nip of winter tugged at her heels, and he took her each morning and came by every afternoon. Emma Leigh understood his need to do all he could for her. Ever since he took ill, Papa had troubled himself with her working. Emma Leigh realized he felt inadequate as provider for his family, but in truth she loved her position at the inn. Greeting guests and making sure they were comfortable suited her fine. Admittedly, she loved the Jones Inn.

Glancing about, she looked for signs of Thad. Odd, he'd been on her mind since last night, more so than she deemed proper. Emma Leigh hoped he'd drawn an easy name for the Christmas celebration. In fact, she'd hoped all the men found her plan easy. The secret friend project should be fun for everyone, or it wouldn't suit Mr. Jones's idea of a memorable holiday.

Taking a peek into the kitchen, she didn't see signs of Thad there, either.

"Can I help ya, Emma Leigh?" Sarah asked, giving her a

quick smile. Her sleeves were rolled to her elbows, revealing forearms dusted with flour. She took both hands to the dough and kneaded it again, putting all of her strength into the white mound.

"Have you seen Thad?" Emma Leigh asked, sensing embarrassment for inquiring about the man.

"Not in the past hour. He's probably in the carriage house or the stables at this time of day."

"Thank you. I'll try those places," she replied, avoiding the curious look on Sarah's face.

The moment Emma Leigh closed the outside door, she regretted leaving her shawl behind. But she'd only be a moment with Thad, just long enough to see if he was content with the name he'd drawn. After all, he'd given her the idea of a secret friend.

She spotted him instructing a stable boy on how to properly escort the guests to and from the carriage. Emma Leigh listened, wondering why she'd never heard the deep timbre of Thad's voice before. After all, they'd worked together for more than a year and grown up together on neighboring farms.

She tilted her head and smiled at the scene before her. A few days ago, a pine bough had been draped across the shiny back of the carriage, adding a festive touch.

"If you are in the position of assisting the lady into the carriage, always offer your hand and address her appropriately. Think of her as a royal queen. Greet the men as though they were kings, and you will never disappoint the guests or Mr. Jones."

The young man nodded in Emma Leigh's direction. "Good afternoon, Miss Emma Leigh."

She stifled a giggle, knowing his mannerly words came as a result of Thad's careful instruction. "Hello, Baxter. I see you are having an excellent lesson."

Thad turned and grinned broadly. He bent low and offered her his hand. "My lady."

This is the Thad I remember, the fun-loving boy who played make-believe with me. With a deep curtsy, she reached for his outstretched hand and allowed him to lead her to the carriage door. He opened it wide and assisted her inside.

"Have a pleasant and safe journey, Miss Carter," Thad said. "We look forward to having you return as a guest of the Jones Inn." He closed the door and tipped his woolen cap as though he wore a top hat.

"Bravo." Emma Leigh clapped her hands. "I shall recommend you to the owner of this excellent establishment," she said, no longer able to contain her laughter. "Your manners are exquisite."

"I appreciate your generous compliments," he replied, opening the carriage door and taking her hand as she stepped to the ground.

She caught his gaze, and its warmth branded her heart. *Oh dear, Thad will be able to see I'm clearly flustered.*

"I understand the formalities now," Baxter said with a laugh. "Thank you for helping me."

Thad shook the young man's hand. "You won't have any problems. You have a quick mind."

Baxter disappeared from the stable, leaving Emma Leigh and Thad alone.

"You were very kind to him," she said, willing her heart to cease its incessant pounding.

"He's a fine lad." Thad leaned against the carriage and rubbed a dull spot on the carriage door.

"You reminded me of when we were children." Emma Leigh shook her head at the memories. "You were always so good about playing the games I suggested."

"Oh, but you never refused climbing trees or marching to my soldier's drum."

Laughing with Thad came easily. She sighed happily and relaxed a bit. Suddenly she recalled her errand. "Are you satisfied with the name you drew today?"

"I'll manage," he replied. "It's a challenge, but your idea was excellent."

"You inspired it."

A rooster strutted past them with two hens trailing behind. "Best you watch your manners," he said to the chickens. "Sarah will have you for dinner tomorrow if you venture too close to the kitchen."

Emma Leigh joined him in laughter and realized she needed to get back inside. Papa would be coming soon, and she didn't want to detain him. "Please give your aunt and uncle my regards." She turned to leave. "And my parents said you were welcome to stop by anytime."

Immediately she felt the color tinge her cheeks. What had happened to her?

Thad set the pail of milk inside the front door of his aunt and uncle's frame home. He smelled dinner, and his stomach rumbled.

"Hungry?" Aunt Klara asked, wiping her hands on her apron.

"Enough to eat a horse," Thad replied. He washed his hands

in a basin, all the while thinking about the Christmas happenings at the inn. *Thank You, Lord, for allowing me to draw Emma Leigh's name. Now, if I can only come up with the right gifts.*

"I sure could use your help, Aunt Klara," Thad said, drying his hands. "Can we talk later?"

When Aunt Klara smiled, her whole face radiated, reminding him of how an angel must look. "You can have all the time you need."

He hugged her waist, and Uncle Albert wrinkled his brow in mocked annoyance. "Find your own wife, Thad," he grumbled. "Klara is mine, and I've seen you looking at her—especially at mealtime." He winked and stuck his pipe into his mouth.

I know the wife I want, but I'll never have her.

As they ate, Thad reflected on the past year with his aunt and uncle. He'd still been grieving for his parents when he arrived from Boston, and often he'd lashed out at Aunt Klara when she tried to comfort him. Praise God he had finally come to his senses and realized this precious woman was a gift. Every day he thanked God for Aunt Klara's love and wisdom.

Once they'd completed the meal, Thad read the Scripture aloud while Uncle Albert listened and Aunt Klara bustled about tidying up the kitchen. He made certain she heard his voice in the next room, clear and strong. Tonight he chose Psalm 37. Verse four seized him as though God had lifted the words from the page: "Delight thyself also in the Lord; and He shall give thee the desires of thine heart."

God knew how Thad's heart longed for Emma Leigh. Dare he ask for so great a blessing as to have her always? Thad took a deep breath and continued reading. Still, Emma Leigh should have a husband who had mastered witty conversation.

She'd be bored with the likes of him. What could he possibly be thinking? Medical school lay in the near future, and he had little money to support a wife.

Soon after, Aunt Klara joined them for prayers. Once Uncle Albert concluded with a hearty "Amen," he stood and yawned. "I'm in need of some sleep."

"Are you going to bed because I want to talk to Aunt Klara?" Thad asked.

"Of course not," his uncle replied and chuckled. "Mind you, don't be making plans to run off with my wife, hear me?"

Thad returned the chuckle and bid his uncle good night. He pulled an extra chair around the cozy fire. He loved this house and the many ways Aunt Klara had graced the room with touches of beauty. She'd brought countless reminders of her homeland from Sweden. Near the fireplace rested a huge, hand-painted wooden chest. The top and sides were bordered in a deep blue vinelike pattern. Yellow outlined lighter blue flowers in the middle. The chest held many treasures from her native land. Every box, tool, and dish had been intricately painted. Shades of blue, green, dull reds, and oranges made up the background colors while greens, reds, whites, yellows, and different shades of blue formed the designs.

Thad remembered the first time Aunt Klara had opened the box to show him her handsomely carved distaff called a scotching knife, and her mangle, used to smooth the wrinkles from wet clothing. Both were painted in green and orange-red. She called the colorful technique rosemaling, and on long winter nights she busied herself in painting plates, chests, and even some of Uncle Albert's tools with the beautiful designs. The chest also contained a Swedish hymnal and a pair of hand-painted gloves.

Thad glanced up at the ceiling beam near Aunt Klara and Uncle Albert's bedroom. Aunt Klara had bordered some of the walls with flowers and leaves. A beam was draped with a hand-woven blanket in green and orange. Upstairs in his loft-like room hung another blanket in blue-green, light green, and red.

"How can I help you?" Aunt Klara asked, interrupting his reverie.

He rubbed the legs of his breeches. His carefully chosen words had slipped his mind. He might as well leap into it all. "Today at the inn, everyone drew a name for a secret friend. We're supposed to give this person a token of friendship as often as we desire. On Christmas Eve we all find out who has our name. Mr. Jones wants this Christmas to be memorable, and the gifts are to be more from the heart than the purse."

Aunt Klara nodded. "And whose name did you receive?"

Thad took a deep breath. "Emma Leigh's."

Aunt Klara tilted her head, and her clear blue eyes peered up into his. "My dear boy, are you happy about this?"

He sighed. "I think so, but I only have a few ideas. That's where I need help."

Aunt Klara touched her finger to the dimple in her chin. "In Sweden, we celebrate Christmas for a whole month. Perhaps I can help you with some of the gifts."

He felt himself smile.

"What are your thoughts?" she asked.

Thad swallowed hard. "I can write a little, but not fancy words. I can whittle some. Candy would be nice. She doesn't have any gloves, and I don't remember her having any last winter, either." He shrugged. "Maybe a pretty ribbon for her hair. And I know her family is so very poor, so maybe I could give her food to share. I know the things I have in mind will cost a little, but there are so many things she needs." He remembered the small pot of stew on their table the night he visited her. They were all thin. . .too slight to fight the cold of winter.

"Those all sound like fine ideas."

He forced a hesitant smile. "I also wondered if you could show me how to do the rosemaling—I mean a few simple strokes that I could add to a small box."

Her eyes moistened. "I'd be honored, but when will you have the time? Your days and evenings are so full."

"I'll simply stay up later."

She seemed to ponder his words. "We could work on the painting together. You can learn, and we both can add touches to it in our spare moments."

Thad took a deep breath. "I don't want you to have added work."

She patted his arm in her familiar affectionate manner. "It's not work when you use your hands for someone you love."

"I love you," he whispered, then grinned. "I dare not say those words too loud. Uncle Albert may come out of his bed with a gun after me!"

"Ah, I believe I know where your heart lies, and the young woman is most lucky indeed."

He hesitated. "Aunt Klara, she is a beautiful woman inside and out. Look at what she's doing for her family, and she is always happy."

Aunt Klara caressed his cheek with her hand. "I pray God grants you the same as in the psalm you read this night."

The desires of my heart. Great, heavenly Father, should I dare even ask such a thing?

Chapter 5

Emma Leigh took a peek into Mama's cooking pot to see if she could ladle a few more beans and broth into her bowl. The day had been long and busy, and for some reason the excitement about introducing the Christmas celebration had made her hungrier than usual.

"Would you get us some more, please?" eight-year-old Simon asked, holding up his empty bowl.

She gazed into the eyes of her younger brother and then at the other children who looked up expectantly. Such sad, hungry eyes. Would life ever get better? *How could I be so selfish and not think of them? God, forgive me.*

"I'd be happy to," she said cheerfully.

"And bread, too," Simon added.

Emma Leigh held her breath. Not a crumb remained.

"The bread's gone," Papa said, a bit harshly.

"Here, take the rest of mine," Mama quickly added, placing her remaining quarter piece of bread into Simon's palm.

Emma Leigh fought the overwhelming urge to weep. The wooden spoon scraped across the bottom of the pot as she placed every bean she could find in the empty bowls. She hated this constant turmoil over food. At least she could get a good meal at the inn. That fact alone made her feel guilty when the pangs of hunger tugged at her siblings' empty stomachs. Sometimes Mr. Jones asked Sarah to send the day's leftovers home with Emma Leigh. Papa disliked the charity, grumbled about being able to care for his family, but he took the food nonetheless.

Mama cleared her throat. "How was your day, Emma Leigh? Did everyone like your idea for Christmas?"

Nodding, Emma Leigh set the food before her brothers before taking her place on the bench. "Everyone seemed excited and talked about it most of the day. Even Mr. Jones and his wife participated in the drawing."

"Whose name did you receive?" Mama asked, reaching across the table and taking Emma's hand into hers. Mama's thin hands felt comforting despite the sadness that constantly threatened the family.

"Sarah, the cook."

Papa raised his brow. "What do you plan to give her over the next ten days?"

"I'm thinking of Scripture, and I already have paper."

"Excellent choice," he said quietly. He sat straighter in his chair. "I think tonight would be the perfect evening for me to bring out my fiddle. Anyone feel like singing?"

Mama smiled, and the children clapped. Christmas would be celebrated in spirit only at the Carter cabin, but they had enough love to fill a large house.

Later on that night, Emma Leigh snuggled Charles and Elizabeth close to her, wrapping her arms around their little bodies in an effort to keep these two youngest members of the household warm. She allowed delicious thoughts about the day to occupy her mind.

Spending time with Thad in the stables had kindled something in her heart. Something she dared not allow herself to dwell upon except in moments like these. His lighthearted antics with Baxter carried her back to those wonderful days when they played together as children without cares or worries.

The desire to have a home of her own one day tore at her heart, especially when many of her friends were already married. But how could she desert Mama and Papa when they needed her income? Papa had borrowed money to help through the frightening period when he nearly died, but he must pay his debts. God had blessed him with renewed strength, and this year's harvest had been better than the preceding year's. Yet the scant supply of food on the table proved that her destiny, for now anyway, was at home helping her family.

Those working at the inn must surely know of her destitute situation, but she'd never spoken of it. Although she wore the same thin dress day after day, she refused to complain about her poverty. After all, God did supply her needs.

Emma Leigh clung to the hope of a better life for her family. Perhaps then she might meet a man as fine and godly as Thad. Until life proved easier, she'd keep smiling and giving, just as the Lord wanted.

Thad woke before dawn, excited about his gift for the first day of the Christmas celebration. He'd gotten the idea just before falling asleep last night—or rather God had given him the answer to his prayers.

"My, you're bustling about early this morning," Aunt Klara

said, once she opened her bedroom door and saw Thad had already stoked the fire and added wood to the embers. It crackled like a welcoming old friend.

"I needed to talk to you this morning," he replied, rising from the rug by the hearth.

She laughed. "Seems like you are needing to do a lot of that lately."

He couldn't stop the smile. "Uncle Albert worried again?"

"Never know," she remarked candidly. "So how can I help you?"

"I'd like to buy a dozen eggs."

"Certainly not."

Thad lifted a brow in a silent question.

"I know you want those eggs for Emma Leigh and her family. God be my witness, I would never sell food meant for a hungry family."

"But I'm the one doing the purchasing." Thad felt somewhere between helpless and frustrated.

Aunt Klara pointed her finger at him. " 'Tis your uncle and I who owe you for all your hard work. Now, you take those eggs and don't say another word about it. Hear me?"

Later, Thad chuckled all the way to the inn. Aunt Klara had scolded him until he'd agreed to take the eggs. He'd carefully printed Emma Leigh's name on a piece of paper and slipped it between two large brown eggs, and he'd left early so he could set the small basket on the wooden table in the kitchen before Emma Leigh arrived.

⁓

Laughter from the inn's kitchen nabbed Emma Leigh's attention. Part of her wanted to see if her secret friend had left a token of the season, and the other part didn't really care.

All morning Emma Leigh had tended to guests and helped the maids change bed linens. She'd feigned excitement in hopes no one would see her fatigue. Shortly after she'd fallen asleep the night before, Emma Leigh had been awakened by little Charles coughing uncontrollably. His flesh seared hers. She roused Mama, and they prepared a hot mustard plaster for his chest and gave him chamomile tea mixed with honey. When she noticed Mama felt feverish, too, Emma Leigh offered to stay up with her brother. Mama reluctantly agreed to go back to bed when Emma Leigh pointed out that the children needed a healthy mother. Throughout the long night, Emma Leigh prayed for her family.

Poor little Charles didn't sleep until nearly dawn, and his fever didn't diminish by the time she hurried to the inn. She'd managed to carefully write out the Twenty-third Psalm on a piece of paper and place it on the wooden table in the kitchen before Sarah arrived.

The scent of pine filled the air, and although Emma Leigh did not feel like celebrating, the aura of Christmas cascaded around her like a rushing waterfall. Emma Lee forced a cordial greeting to Mrs. Weares as the older woman descended the stairs, her heels clipping on the wood flooring and her lips humming "Silent Night." The gangly woman looked a bit manly with her severe hair pulled back sharply. The style accented her long nose.

"I received the best gift today," Mrs. Weares said, fanning herself as though the excitement might cause her to faint.

"And what did your secret friend leave for you?" Emma Leigh asked, pleased to see the woman happy.

"Oh. . ." The older woman turned her head and laughed lightly. "A peppermint stick. Can you imagine enjoying candy at my age?" She fanned her face, the wrinkles around her eyes deepening with each precious giggle. "And I see your gift is still on the table."

Emma Leigh's eyes widened. "Mine?"

"Why, yes!" Mrs. Weares leaned closer. "I couldn't help but see your name sticking out from it."

Glancing toward the door, Emma Leigh suddenly had an urge to see for herself.

"Run along, now. I'll mind things while you see the pleasant surprise in store for you."

Emma Leigh scurried off to the kitchen. In all of the worries about her family, should she rejoice in a gift left for her?

As she reached the kitchen, Emma Leigh greeted the cook. "Hello, Sarah. How are you today?" The red-haired woman was busily peeling potatoes, but she had time to offer Emma Leigh a wink.

"Aye, perfectly wonderful, Lass. I've had a beautiful psalm to keep me content all this morning long."

"I'm glad for you," Emma Leigh said, her heart warming at Sarah's words.

"Indeed! I have a secret friend who knew exactly what I needed today. Yes, indeed, the Lord is my Shepherd."

Emma Leigh advanced across the room to hug Sarah and hide her own tears that threatened to spill over. She fretted so much about her family, although the Bible said not to worry but trust God. Constantly, she asked the Lord for healing and a way for her family to receive their basic needs.

"And your secret friend blessed you," Sarah said, when the

two ended their sweet embrace.

Emma Leigh's gaze flew to the wooden table where a small basket rested. She stole a look inside. Several lovely light brown eggs nestled together like delicate rolls. Catching her breath in her throat, Emma Leigh nearly cried. "Eggs. Little Charles's favorite." *Bless you, my secret friend. Whoever you may be.*

Chapter 6

E mma Leigh forgot her aching body for the remainder of the day. She couldn't wait to get home. Surely the eggs were a sign of God's healing for Charles and Mama, as well as for Papa's continued strength.

She spotted Thad in the entranceway just before Papa came by. Her heart lifted at the sight of him. *I can only be his childhood friend. Nothing more. He'll be a fine doctor one day and need a wife who is much smarter than I am.* But her logic didn't stop the yearning in her heart.

He smiled, but a guest requested his attention and the two disappeared outside. Tomorrow perhaps she and Thad might have an opportunity to visit.

~

Thad regretted not talking to Emma Leigh before she went home, but he treasured her response to the eggs. He'd been standing behind the door when she discovered them, and he found it difficult to remain hiding once she shared her enthusiasm with Sarah.

Later that evening, Aunt Klara began instructing him in rosemaling by demonstrating a few simple strokes. At first he believed the art impossible to grasp, but as he persevered, he found success.

"Are you taking Miss Emma Leigh a gift tomorrow?" Aunt Klara asked as he practiced two brush strokes—C and S curves.

"I think so," he replied, concentrating on the task at hand.

"Do you need any help selecting something?" Aunt Klara leaned closer, a habit when she wanted to make sure she was heard.

"Not this time. I kept one of the cinnamon sticks from my last trip to Philadelphia." He arched his back, which felt a bit stiff from bending over his work. "And late tomorrow afternoon I need to drive some guests to the city. Mr. Jones said for me to take my time in returning, so I plan to purchase a few things."

"What a lovely idea."

The following day Thad drove two fine chestnut mares along the brick streets of Philadelphia. The rhythmic clopping of the horse hooves mesmerized him as he listened to the sights and sounds of one of the nation's largest cities, the birthplace of America. He drove the carriage down Chestnut Street to view Independence Hall. Thad never tired of this sight. A mere glimpse filled him with pride. The Georgian-style edifice stood as a symbol of liberty and freedom for all Americans.

He reined the horses right onto Fifth Street and on toward Market Street where he could view Christ Church. Many wonderful stories surrounded this beautiful building that silently commemorated those who had worshiped within its sacred walls and was rich in history. The Second Continental Congress had attended its services, as had Benjamin Franklin and George Washington.

Thad took a moment to reflect on the beautiful landmark

before gathering up the reins and urging the horses onto Third Street and on south.

Outside Philadelphia, he passed through a small community that held a sizable dry goods and general store. He pulled alongside, secured the horses and carriage, and made his way through the establishment. Thad knew exactly what he wanted for Uncle Albert and Aunt Klara, but his Emma Leigh proved the most difficult.

When had he begun to think of her as his? Pressing his lips together firmly in contemplation, he realized she'd always been his—nestled somewhere in a treasured part of his heart. But this time next year, he'd be in Boston attending medical school. Asking her to wait for him didn't seem fair, but he selfishly admitted he didn't want to tell her good-bye in a few months. He simply must enjoy the time with Emma Leigh now and leave the rest up to God.

Thad found a warm, woolen scarf for Uncle Albert and a new shawl for Aunt Klara. He felt like being extravagant, mostly because he had the money saved for his education and he didn't know what his circumstances might be next Christmas—or even if he would be able to come home. So this year he would give his dear aunt and uncle the best gifts possible. A trace of nostalgia for Christmases past when his parents were alive passed through his mind. He allowed a few pleasant thoughts, but when sadness ushered in painful memories, he shoved them all aside.

Practicality ruled a large portion of Thad's life, and he believed a gift should be something the recipient needed. Glancing about, he saw many things Emma Leigh and her entire family could use. Poverty and indebtedness hammered at their door, and until Mr. Carter repaid all he owed, the family would continue to suffer. Nothing would give Thad more pleasure than to give all of the Carters a splendid holiday. Just to see a spark of joy in those children's eyes would make him extremely happy, but the Carters were a proud sort.

An idea began to form, and while he meandered through the store, peering at and examining the many items upon the shelves, he prayed for guidance and wisdom.

"Do you need some assistance?" a gentleman asked, his face akin to a dried apple.

Thad stopped and considered the question. "I'm looking for a few small gifts for a young lady, something useful. I definitely want a ribbon for her hair."

The man offered a smile. "Right this way, Sir." The storekeeper led the way to where bolts of beautiful fabric and notions rested on shelves and a long table. "Would this do?" He held up two spools of ribbon in red and green.

"The red one, please." Already Thad could envision the bright color woven in Emma Leigh's dark curls.

"Do you see anything else here that catches your fancy?" the man asked.

Thad studied the notions, buttons, and other sewing items. If she were his wife. . . *What am I thinking?* Anyway, Emma Leigh did need a new dress, but fabric didn't fall within his responsibility, nor was it proper.

"A thimble?" Thad lifted his gaze questioningly to the storekeeper.

"Excellent idea."

Together they selected one. Thad remembered the night he'd walked to the Carter home and the chill permeating the air.

"The lady needs gloves and a thick scarf," he said aloud.

By the time Thad finished, he'd found a beeswax candle and enough penny candy to give to each of Emma Leigh's siblings on Christmas Day. By then she'd know he'd been the one to draw her name. A flutter arose in his stomach, and the fear of her shunning his gifts settled like a gray cloud.

Emma Leigh's not pretentious!

As Thad drove the carriage back to the Jones Inn, he added up the gifts and the nine days remaining: the hair ribbon, cinnamon stick, thimble, candle, the deep green gloves, matching scarf, the small box that he planned to paint with the rosemaling technique, perhaps some freshly churned butter, and perhaps a piece of bobbin lace that his aunt Klara had made. He counted nine, and the eggs he'd already given made ten. Except he wanted to do more.

Truth be known, he must surely be courting. The thought scared him, especially with the uncertainty of the future. Still, he couldn't put the idea out of his mind. Poetic words began to form in his mind, slowly at first, then more freely as thoughts of Emma Leigh wrapped around him like a thick quilt.

A candle's flicker in the darkness,
A fire's warmth to greet the weary,
Only Jesus shines more brightly
Than my lovely Emma Leigh.

Would she think him foolish? Laugh at his attempt of showing his affections through verse? Thad's stomach twisted into a painful knot. Giving a poem to her required more courage than venturing to medical school. At least he knew how to study.

But with Emma Leigh, he didn't know what kind of reaction to expect.

Emma Leigh balled her fists and dug her fingernails into her palms in an effort to keep her hands warm. Soon she'd be at the inn where a toasty fire would stop the ache in her hands and feet. But what of the little ones left at home? Last night's snowfall only made her feel more dismal about the long winter ahead.

"Papa, why don't you and I patch the walls after I'm finished this afternoon?" she asked, willing her teeth to cease chattering.

"The drafts are making the others sick," he said, his voice echoing with despair.

From the corner of her eye, she saw his pallor. He looked so old and beaten.

"You and I could have the chore done in no time. And Simon, he's able to help, don't you think?" She tried to sound cheerful, optimistic about the work that should have been completed more than six weeks ago when a heavy rain and windstorm dislodged much of the mud and straw used to chink their cabin.

"You work too hard," Papa said gravely. He coughed, a deep gut-wrenching sound that seemed to originate in the soles of his feet. Once he gained control, he continued. "I'll see to it today."

"Papa, why don't you rest and let us attempt it together?"

He shook his head, and from the determined look upon his face, Emma Leigh knew not to argue. His pride dug at his grave.

At the inn, she kissed him good-bye and hurried into the warm building. How dreadful of her to prefer the atmosphere of this fine place to her own home.

The staff bustled about their work, eager to find out if their secret friend had remembered them. Whoever held her name had been most generous, for two days ago she'd received a delicious cinnamon stick that she had shared with the younger children at home, and yesterday she'd received a lovely red ribbon for her hair. She had no idea who had drawn her name, but it didn't matter. Thad occupied her thoughts more than any plan devised to celebrate Christmas. She wondered if she appeared ungrateful to her benefactor and quickly asked God to forgive her. But a few words from Thad or his cheery smile meant more to her than material things.

As if knowing her feelings, he called her name from the kitchen. "Emma Leigh, your secret friend left you something."

She glanced up at his face, seemingly brilliant in his wide smile. How incredible that each time she saw him, he became more handsome. . .and more dear.

"Again? Oh my, I'm not worthy to receive yet another gift."

"Why not?" he asked, opening the kitchen door for her to step inside.

"I didn't mean for others to become extravagant." Trouble loomed over her. She never wanted to cause problems.

"Nonsense. Today I received a peppermint, and I do enjoy sweets."

She made her way the short distance to the table. Her eyes widened, and she gasped. "Surely Mr. or Mrs. Jones have my name, for the giver is most generous." She picked up the gloves with tears in her eyes and slipped them on. Her fingers were still cold from the morning ride. "I can't accept this," she murmured. "It's too much."

Thad moved to her side. "Why don't you let the one who gave you the gift decide what is appropriate?"

She lifted her gaze to meet his. "I simply feel uncomfortable. . .when I can't do for my secret friend what is being done for me."

His eyes reflected a certain tenderness, or did she simply wish they saw only her? Her bold thoughts brought a flush to her cheeks.

"God requires we give our best, whatever that may be," he said.

"Thank you, Thad. You always have a way of making me see things differently."

The smile lingered on his lips, and she memorized it for later when the burdens of home threatened to overwhelm her.

"How is your family?" Thad asked.

Melancholy crept across her heart, but she masked it as best she could. "Little Charles has been ill, but he's doing much better. The others have coughs and are feeling a bit poorly with runny noses and such. I'm so glad we grew herbs to help them through the winter."

"I'm sorry."

"Oh, it will be remedied soon. Papa and I are going to patch the outside walls this evening."

"Tonight?" He frowned, looking disconcerted.

"Yes," she said, forcing a smile.

"Would you like some help?"

Emma Leigh shook her head. "Papa doesn't approve of charity."

Thad appeared to ponder the matter. "What if I came by for a visit? I could help while I talked to your father."

Oh, Thad, you are so good to do this. "I suppose he'd agree, but are you sure you want to work in the cold?"

"Of course. I'll send a note to my aunt and uncle, explaining where I'll be." He pointed to the gloves. "Please, wear these so whoever got them for you will know you are pleased."

She nodded happily.

"Would you like to go ice skating on Sunday afternoon? I believe a few from church are planning a Christmas party."

"Yes. . .why, yes; I'd love to." How good of God to give her such a fine friend as Thad Benson.

Chapter 7

That knew mixing mud with straw to patch the Carter cabin meant a tedious task. The hard ground and frigid temperatures combined with working at dusk didn't appeal to him at all, but the thought of helping Emma Leigh and her family set well in his spirit. He remembered when high winds and a thunderstorm did tremendous damage to nearby homes and barns. Obviously those hit included the Carters, and Mr. Carter had barely enough strength to harvest the fall crops, much less repair the cabin.

Within an hour after Emma Leigh departed from the inn, Thad made the trek after them, thankful that he'd ridden his horse to work that day. Taking a quick look at the sky, he realized they'd most likely be working by kerosene light long before they finished the job. Anger swept over him as he considered the arduous task ahead for Emma Leigh. He wanted to ask her father why the rest of the family hadn't patched the cabin instead of leaving it all for his precious lady.

But Mr. Carter has been ill. I've no right to judge.

He spotted Mr. Carter and Emma Leigh along with two of the boys daubing the north side of the small structure. As he grew closer, he saw the east side had already been completed. The sight pleased him; Emma Leigh need not carry all of the work on her frail shoulders.

"Good evening," Thad called heartily.

Mr. Carter looked up and waved. "Good to see you, Thad."

"I dropped by to say hello. Looks like you're busy." He secured his horse and advanced at a sharp pace. The wind blew at a brisk speed, inviting a nasty chill up his spine. If he felt the cold, how badly did the others feel? "Evening, Emma Leigh." He glanced at the other two boys but couldn't remember their names.

Emma caught his gaze and smiled knowingly. "The one beside me is Simon, and by Papa is Joseph."

Thad rubbed his hands together. "You folks got yourself a big job here."

Mr. Carter continued to work, the mud dropping from his fingers onto the cold ground. He'd mixed straw with it for durability. Normally moss and clay made the mud harder. "Yes, we do. I started earlier today, and I think we'll finish tonight."

"Can I offer a hand?" Thad asked.

"It's not necessary," her father said. His voice sounded raspy, and he coughed as though consumption nailed at his chest. Thad prayed not.

"I'd like to talk to you, and I can say my words just as easily working."

Mr. Carter appeared to deliberate the matter. His pale skin alarmed Thad. The older man didn't need to be in the cold.

"I guess that will be fine," Mr. Carter replied.

Thad peeled off his gloves and bent to stick his hands into a pile of dirt already dampened by water. Ice cold. All of them would be sick. Adding a little straw, Thad worked the mud, then slapped it up against a bare spot. He reached down and did the same thing again. . .and again.

"So what did you want to talk about?" Mr. Carter asked after another series of coughs.

Thad figured Mr. Carter thought he'd come to ask about courting Emma Leigh, and the truth of the matter was the older man probably guessed correctly.

"Well, Sir. The matter is rather delicate."

"I see." He rubbed his nose. "Emma Leigh, you and your brothers go get us some more straw from the barn."

She nodded, but before she turned in the direction of the barn, a slow blush ascended her cheeks.

After daubing another hole and making sure they were alone, Thad began. "Mr. Carter, I'd like permission to stop by now and then."

"For what reason?"

Slaaap. Another handful of ice-cold mud hit against the wall. "To visit you and your family."

"I'm not so certain you're being honest here."

"What do you mean?"

Mr. Carter dipped into the mud and grabbed a handful of straw. "I mean I believe you want to court Emma Leigh, but you don't want to ask me for permission because you're leaving for school."

Slaaap.

The sting of Mr. Carter's words held more truth than Thad cared to admit. "I hadn't considered the situation in that way," he replied. He attempted to give the impression of studying the patched wall while he pondered Mr. Carter's observations.

"And how do you view it?" the older man asked, taking a deep breath.

Thad shrugged. "Friendship."

"Do you care about my daughter?" the man blurted out before he broke into another coughing spell.

"Yes, Sir. We grew up together."

The coughing ceased. "Do you care for her in such a way that you'd expect her to wait while you're studying to be a doctor?"

For an ailing man, Mr. Carter didn't mince words when speaking his mind. "I don't know, Sir."

"Well, as her father, I'm saying you'd better decide about the future before talking to me about Emma Leigh."

Thad felt his face redden. "Are you telling me no?"

"I'm saying I care too much for my little girl to have some fellow break her heart."

"I'd never hurt Emma Leigh!"

"What do you think would happen if I give my permission for you to come visiting, then you up and left for Boston?"

Thad realized how selfish he'd become. Bringing Emma Leigh gifts as a secret friend was a ruse for her affections. How despicable of him!

"Mr. Carter, I apologize for not considering her feelings. I will not see her again unless I am prepared to make a decision about my future. I'd asked her to go skating with me on Sunday, but I see an afternoon together is not considerate of her feelings."

The older man neither smiled not frowned. "I see the way she looks at you. The damage may already be done. I'll tell her she can't attend on Sunday."

Emma Leigh approached Papa and Thad with the straw.

Neither looked happy; neither conversed with the other. What had happened? She'd so hoped Thad wanted to ask Papa if he could come courting. Lately she and Thad had found plenty to talk about, and her mind often wandered to dreams about him. Oh yes, she knew he needed to leave in the spring for Boston. But if they truly cared for each other and God meant for them to enjoy the special gift of love, then He'd show the way.

Or am I acting foolishly?

Why would Thad be interested in a poor girl with nothing to offer? And her family. Who would take care of them if Emma Leigh no longer had a job to help support them? She shouldn't think about such things. Her life—everything about it—lay in God's hands. Taking a cleansing breath, she lifted her head to the dark blue sky and smiled in the direction of Papa and Thad.

"We have straw," she announced. "My, we're already working on the final wall."

"Yes, we'll be finished here shortly," Papa said as he continued to daub the holes.

"How good of you to help," she said to Thad.

He didn't acknowledge her.

"Thad needs to get home," Papa said firmly. "Darkness is upon us, and we're taking advantage of a good neighbor."

Slaaap. "Sir, I don't mind seeing this to completion," Thad replied. "My aunt and uncle are not expecting me until late."

"And I would not want to abuse our good friendship with Albert and Klara by keeping you any later." Papa stopped long enough to give Thad a steely glance. "Thank you, and may God bless your endeavors."

Emma Leigh watched Thad head down the road until he

disappeared from sight. He'd been cordial when he left and taken the time to bid a proper good-bye to Mama and the younger ones, but something terrible must have happened between Papa and Thad.

By kerosene light, she stole a glance at her father. She could tell by the determined set of his jaw she dare not interrupt his thoughts with questions. He coughed and spurted, the effort obviously draining his strength.

"Papa, let Simon, Joseph, and me finish this," she urged, wanting to embrace him. He'd be angry if she touched him; she'd tried in times past and failed.

"Not when we are this close to having the job done."

Emma Leigh chose not to respond. Most likely Papa would spend tomorrow in bed, and she intended to talk to Thad about this evening.

Later on, Papa pulled her aside. "It's not a good idea for you to attend any skating events with Thad Benson."

Her heart cried out for an explanation, but she must not be disrespectful.

The next day she walked to work. Papa had a fever and his cough worsened. She trudged through the snow, praying to keep her mind from the cold and despair. At least she had gloves to keep her hands warm. Papa simply had to get better. She didn't dare think of anything else.

At the inn Thad avoided her, or so she thought. In the afternoon she stepped into the carriage house in hopes of finding him there, but he walked out with Baxter as soon as she entered. He greeted her kindly, but his gaze never met hers.

Her secret friend once again remembered her. In the kitchen she found freshly churned butter. Although her spirits sank with thoughts of home, she praised God for the food.

The next day, she spied Thad with Sarah in the kitchen.

"Do you have a moment to talk?" she asked. Her hands trembled, and she instantly thrust them behind her back.

"I can't right now, Emma Leigh. Perhaps later when my duties are completed. The Christmas guests are keeping me extremely busy." Thad shifted from one foot to the other. He excused himself and stepped out into the cold wind.

She swallowed her disappointment and glanced at the gift table. There sat a thimble. She remembered patching a shirt for Joseph without one and how her thumb had bled. The thought of anyone caring enough to give such useful gifts had brought tears to her eyes on more than one occasion. But the gifts didn't ease the aching in her heart.

Chapter 8

On Saturday, Thad gave Emma Leigh the green wool scarf to match her gloves. Sarah had discovered he had Emma Leigh's name, so the cook reported the young woman's reaction to his gifts.

"Aye, she cried," Sarah said, wiping her eyes with the corner of her apron. "I don't believe she has ever been given such fine things."

"She has needed everything I've given her," Thad added, genuinely pleased at Emma Leigh's sentiment, even if he couldn't talk to her like he wanted.

"Your heart longs for her?" Rather than irritate, Sarah's question soothed Thad's turmoil over Mr. Carter's ultimatum.

He shrugged, not sure how to pose his reply.

"Have ye talked to her father?"

Thad nodded slowly and gazed up into her round face. "I can't talk about it, Sarah, but I know you mean well."

She smiled sadly, and he believed she really understood. He pulled the beeswax candle from inside his jacket. "Would you make sure she finds this tomorrow? I shan't be here until Monday."

Sarah agreed. "A prayer for your Miss Emma Leigh might help."

"I keep asking God for wisdom. Perhaps tomorrow, the Lord's Day, He will give me some answers."

The next evening by firelight, Thad toiled over the small box where he'd begun a reddish orange chrysanthemum. Aunt Klara had instructed him to outline the flowers in white and add leaves around it. The finishing touch would be a leaflike scroll outlined in the same reddish orange. All the while he worked at the painting, his mind spun with thoughts of Emma Leigh, his plans as a doctor, and what God intended for his life.

"My dear boy, you look so troubled," Aunt Klara said. She placed a comforting hand upon his shoulder. "Has something happened?"

He glanced up into the wrinkled face he'd grown to love. "I spoke with Mr. Carter the night I helped patch their cabin."

"About Emma Leigh?"

"Yes, Ma'am. He doesn't want me seeing her until I make a decision about my future." Thad sighed and bent back over the box. "He doesn't believe it fair for me to see her now and leave in a few months for school."

"I see," Aunt Klara murmured.

"Unfortunately, I agree with him."

She pulled a chair beside him close to the fire. "Do you love her?"

"Yes, I most certainly do."

"God gives us the gift of love to glorify Him. He will help you find an answer."

Shaking his head, Thad released a pent-up sigh. "I listened very hard to the sermon this morning but heard nothing about what I must do. I'm spending extra time pondering over the Scriptures and in prayer. Still, I'm confused."

"What is your dream?"

He peered into the fire, listened to the cheerful sound of its crackle. "I would like to marry her and take her with me to Boston." Simply speaking his secret longings aloud made him feel as though they threatened to vanish into ashes.

Uncle Albert joined them by the fire, pulling a rocker near his wife. "Forgive me for listening, but Thad, why is this not possible?"

For the first time, Thad realized how much his uncle resembled his father. Even his uncle's deep voice and the gentleness reflected in his eyes reminded Thad of the man he sorely missed.

"I have enough money saved for my tuition and to live meagerly—but certainly not with the lifestyle Emma Leigh deserves."

Uncle Albert cleared his throat. "What does the dear child have now? She works all day and goes home to take care of her family. Surely you could offer her more than she now receives."

Thad considered his uncle's words. True, in being his wife, she would not exhaust herself day after day. Another realization saddened him. "Her father may refuse me because she supports the family."

"Surely not!" Aunt Klara said. "He is an honorable man."

Uncle Albert studied Thad. "Isn't Mr. Carter improving?"

"Slowly, but I believe he's harboring a hard cough."

"Do any of us have anything we could offer to make their lives easier until he regains his strength?" Aunt Klara asked.

Thad straightened. A warm sensation spread through him. "I have no need for the seven cows and bull on my parents' farm. Do you think if I offered them to Mr. Carter in return for him keeping a watchful eye on my land, it would help?"

"An excellent idea," Uncle Albert replied and chuckled. "You and I tire of keeping them milked, and I was going to suggest you sell them before you left for Boston."

"Perhaps the Carters could grow a season of crops there, too," Thad continued. "Enough for them to eat and to sell."

Aunt Klara smiled, and her eyes moistened. " 'Tis an answer to prayer, Thad. See, God did hear your heart."

"I believe so," he said, his heart picking up pace to match his new hope. "I'll talk to Mr. Carter tomorrow."

Emma Leigh spotted Thad heading her way Sunday morning after church. For the first time since he'd helped patch her home, he smiled at her freely. She'd never learned what transpired that night, except Mama said it was best not speak of it to Papa.

To her dismay, as soon as church dismissed, she needed to help Mrs. Weares at the inn. Oh, for a day to help Mama with the children and not have to spend herself between responsibilities at work and at home. Mama said she felt fine and didn't need an extra hand, but Emma Leigh still longed to give her mother a rest.

The next morning she spotted Thad as she made her way into the inn.

"Good morning," Thad called with a wave.

"Yes, it's a beautiful morning," Emma Leigh replied. She allowed herself one long look at him. The thought of his leaving in a few months for school grieved her—not because she regretted his desires to be a doctor. She'd simply miss him.

"Are you excited about tomorrow's Christmas Eve celebration?" he asked, rubbing his gloved hands together.

"For certain. I want to find out who my secret friend is so I can thank the person properly for all of my treasures." She felt the familiar trembling that so often came these days whenever Thad was near. "But I do believe it is Mr. or Mrs. Jones. Who do you think has your name?"

He laughed. "I've had sweet treats nearly everyday. I'm convinced my secret friend is Sarah." Thad's gaze seemed to search her face. "You look very nice this morning."

She grew warm with his compliment. "Why, thank you. I feel wonderful on the inside."

"It shows," he whispered.

"Did you have a grand time skating?" At once, she wished she hadn't brought up the canceled Sunday afternoon activity. No matter that Mr. Jones had asked her to work; she simply wished she could have been there with Thad.

"I didn't go."

"Why?" *Do I dare think you wanted my company?*

He shuffled and dug his hands into his coat pockets. "Emma Leigh, I didn't want to attend without you."

She gasped, unable to believe her ears. What had brought about the change in him?

Silence prevailed, and for a rare moment, Emma Leigh couldn't think of a single thing to say.

Thad broke the silence. "Shall we see if we have anything in the kitchen?" Before she had an opportunity to respond, he offered her his arm, and they walked up the back wooden steps of the inn.

Inside the cozy kitchen where Sarah and her helper fried

thick pieces of bacon and broke eggs into a huge wooden bowl, other staff members bustled about the gift table.

"Ah, sweet bread," Thad said, inhaling the tantalizing scent of apples and cinnamon. "Sarah, I know you must have my name—trying to fatten me up like a Christmas goose."

Sarah said nothing, but a smile caressed her lips.

Emma Leigh glanced down to see a piece of delicately made bobbin lace, finer than anything she'd ever seen. "This is beautiful. I don't know how I will ever be able to thank my secret friend."

"I imagine the smile on your face will be enough," Thad said.

She heard something in his voice, more tenderness than before. Could she hope for more than friendship?

"Emma Leigh," he began softly. "Do you have a moment?"

Startled and pleased all in one breath, she agreed. "Of course. Would you like to walk with me to Mr. Jones's office? I need to see him about the dinner tomorrow."

Thad opened the kitchen door, and the two stepped out into the huge front entrance of the inn. A floor-to-ceiling pine tree was decorated with crystal stars and angels, some of Mrs. Jones's heirlooms from England. Neatly tied gold and red satin bows adorned its limbs. The scent—the fragrance of Christmas—swirled through the air.

"I'd like to visit your father this evening, if you don't have any objection," Thad said.

"I'm sure he will be pleased to see you." Her heart fluttered against her chest, especially when she remembered Papa and Thad's parting the last time.

Thad glanced about. "I want to ask him if I can come courting."

Holding her breath, she feared she'd heard incorrectly.

"I want to make sure this is something you want before I seek permission," he said, his gaze fixed on the floor.

Heat raced through her veins. "I think that is a most pleasant idea."

"You do?" He looked up, and his robin's-egg blue eyes sparkled. "I'm deeply honored, Emma Leigh."

By this time they had reached the front of Mr. Jones's office. Emma Leigh remembered the moment, just a short time ago, when she had collided with Thad in that very spot.

"I hope we have time to talk this evening," Thad added, "providing your father approves of me."

She wanted to shout her delight for all to hear, but at that instant Mrs. Weares made her way across the wooden floor. She frowned disapprovingly. "Is there a problem?"

"Not at all, Mrs. Weares," Thad replied. He nodded to Emma Leigh and turned on his heel to leave before she could offer him a reassuring smile. Emma Leigh was certain her father would approve.

Chapter 9

No matter what consolation Thad offered himself, the fact remained he feared speaking with Emma Leigh's father. Once Thad had decided to ask permission to come courting, anxiety took a strangling hold of him. By now, Mr. Carter might have concluded Thad was not suitable for Emma Leigh or that her family needed her to help support them.

Lord God, I pray Your will be accomplished in this endeavor—whatever that may be.

Once he finished his work, Thad saddled his horse. He'd ridden to work because of his planned visit at the Carters on his way home. Now, he wished he'd walked so he could clear his mind.

A startling revelation occurred to him. He was embarking upon what was, next to accepting the Lord as his Savior, the most important step of his life. God had given him a peace about the future, but Thad felt ill prepared to converse with Emma Leigh's father.

A wisp of smoke from the chimney of the Carter cabin came much too quickly. Thad's stomach tightened as he recalled his last encounter with Mr. Carter.

As Thad dismounted, Simon and Joseph rushed from the barn to greet him. "Hello, Thad," they chorused. He noted Simon didn't have a coat, and the sight made him want to give the boy his own.

"Hello, boys. Finishing up your chores?"

Simon nodded. He and Joseph were both shivering. "We're done now," Simon stated.

"Your father at home?"

Simon motioned to the cabin. "He's inside."

With a deep breath and a prayer, Thad crunched through the snow to knock at the door. Emma Leigh answered. Her face radiated an ethereal glow, giving him courage to take on a dozen difficult fathers who might protest his courting her.

"Is your father at home?" he asked softly.

She nodded shyly. "Papa, Thad Benson is here to see you. Won't you come in?"

"I'd rather wait outside for your father," he replied. He smelled chicken and remembered Sarah giving Emma Leigh the remains from dinner at the inn.

As soon as Mr. Carter stood in the doorway, Thad stuck out his hand and eyed him squarely. "Good evening, Sir. May I have a word with you?"

Not a trace of emotion settled upon the older man's face. He nodded and snatched a coat from a peg. "Let's talk in the barn away from the wind." He caught sight of Simon and Joseph. "You boys head inside now. Your mama has food nearly ready."

Thad tried to think of something clever to say, but the only thing bursting from his mouth sounded more like a snort about the weather than polite conversation.

"I remember the last time we talked," Mr. Carter stated, sauntering into the barn.

The scent of fresh hay, sweet and clean, met Thad's nostrils. The horse whinnied, and a single chicken scurried past them. "I'd like to continue our discussion," he replied.

Mr. Carter leaned against a horse stall. "I thought as much."

Thad cleared his throat. "Sir, again I apologize for sounding selfish the last time when I talked to you about Emma Leigh."

The man nodded. Still no emotion. Mr. Carter would not make this easy.

"I don't want to request permission to come courting Emma Leigh."

The older man's features hardened.

Thad braved his way forward. "I want to ask for her hand in marriage." His heart thumped like a scared rabbit. "I have the money saved for my schooling and some besides to live on. While I'm learning to be a doctor, I can't give her fine things like she deserves, but I can take care of her."

"Hmmm," Mr. Carter replied, his face stoical.

"With this in mind and providing I get your blessing, I'd like to ask you a favor, one that might help both of us."

"And what might it be, providing I approve of your marrying my daughter?"

"Uncle Albert and I have been tending to seven cows and a bull on my parents' farm. It's more than my aunt and uncle need once I'm gone, and they are getting on in years as well. Since my land borders yours, I'm wondering if you would take care of the cattle for me during my absence, and in return you could have all the milk you needed and any calves born while

I'm away at school. I do need to sell one of the cows, though."

"Sounds like charity to me," Mr. Carter grumbled.

"We'd be family," Thad replied. "I also wondered if you'd help me out by tending to my apple trees. You might want to use some of the land to grow a few crops."

"Still sounds like charity."

"Not if we split the sale of the crops. I could use the extra money to take care of Emma Leigh."

Mr. Carter rubbed a bristled chin. "Not once have you told me your feelings for my daughter."

Where are my thoughts? "Mr. Carter, I do love Emma Leigh. I want to take care of her always. Why, we grew up together, and I can't imagine any woman in my life but your fine daughter."

Mr. Carter said nothing, and Thad believed the man just might order him to leave. He prayed as Emma Leigh's father slowly paced the length of the barn.

"Emma Leigh works much too hard," he finally said. "She never stops to rest, always wanting to do more. We'd be lost without her, but it's not a good reason to stop my daughter from having a life of her own. She deserves more than waiting on all of us like a servant." Mr. Carter shook his head and wiped a single tear from his cheek. "I am getting better. The good Lord has seen fit to restore my health. You've given me a generous offer—one by which I could pay my debts and take care of my family proper. But more importantly, you've offered a way for my precious Emma Leigh to do better for herself."

Thad swallowed hard. *Is this a yes?*

"I misjudged you, and I'm the one who owes you an apology. If Emma Leigh will have you, then I give my blessing for her to wed."

Thad reached for his hand, a smile bursting through his face from deep within his heart. "Thank you, Sir. I'm deeply grateful."

Mr. Carter held on to Thad's hand. "You'll be a fine husband and doctor. I see much of your father in you, and I'm sure he'd be proud." He glanced about the barn. "Would you like me to get Emma Leigh for you?"

"I'd rather this be a surprise," Thad said, tripping over his words like a schoolboy. "So I don't want her to have any idea of what we've discussed until tomorrow night."

Mr. Carter chuckled. "I understand." He released his grip and nodded toward the house. "I imagine she's in a tizzy wanting to know what's going on out here, but I'll not say a word."

"I appreciate that. You see, I drew her name in the secret friend celebration at the inn. I have an idea for tomorrow, something special."

Mr. Carter smiled broadly. "You're going to make her very happy."

They walked toward Thad's tethered horse. "Sir, may I come by tomorrow night and escort Emma Leigh to church?"

"By all means," Mr. Carter whispered. "She will have the best Christmas ever."

Thank You, Lord. I'll not disappoint You. Thank You for showing me the way.

Emma Leigh found it nearly impossible to mask her disappointment when Papa entered without Thad. "Where's Thad?" she asked, searching her father's face. "I thought he might want to stay for dinner."

Papa hung his thin coat on the peg and moved toward the

fire. "He's gone home."

Emma Leigh hastily blinked back the tears. What had gone wrong? Why didn't Papa want Thad to come courting?

Thad sang all the way home, making use of every Christmas carol he could remember. Neither the darkness wrapping its blanket around him nor the cold air nipping at his fingers and toes could chill him tonight. Thad understood God's plan for his life and was confident that God intended him to marry Emma Leigh. They'd have a rich life together, rich with the blessings that come only from the heavenly Father.

He stopped at his parents' farm and tended the cattle. Odd, he always referred to it as his parents' when, in fact, the house and land belonged to him. *Emma Leigh's and mine.*

Once at his aunt and uncle's, Thad took care of his horse and hurried in to tell them the good news.

"I plan to ask Emma Leigh to marry me tomorrow night," he said. "I'm not worried in the least about it. God has brought me this far, and I know His hand rests in this."

"She won't refuse such a handsome, caring man," Aunt Klara said, unable to conceal her excitement.

"Or a godly man," Uncle Albert added.

"Simply pray for me," Thad said. The seriousness of asking Emma Leigh to marry him weighed heavily upon him. What had he just done?

"Delight thyself also in the Lord; and He shall give thee the desires of thine heart."

Chapter 10

Emma Leigh dutifully kissed her father good-bye at the inn. She didn't feel much affection, though. Tears were ready to surface each time she thought about Papa refusing to let Thad see her.

Either Papa doesn't like Thad, and I don't know why, or he needs me to give all my attention to the Jones Inn and home.

No matter what the reason, Emma Leigh felt it unfair. Christmas was tomorrow, the inn staff's celebration this afternoon, and she should be rejoicing in the Lord's birth. But how could she when her heart threatened to break into irreparable pieces?

"But I must," she whispered. "Mr. Jones expects me to be cheerful for the guests and the activities planned for today." She stiffened her spine. *The Lord will help me.*

Opening the back kitchen door, Emma Leigh pasted on a smile and greeted Sarah with a hug. "Merry Christmas, Sarah. Are you excited about today?"

"Oh yes. I want to find out who's been sending me such sweet Scripture messages. One day last week, I came in to work and found the eggs, bacon, and potatoes all ready for me to cook."

Emma Leigh smiled. Sarah's face glowed as though she'd just seen Jesus, and indeed she had through all those excited about celebrating His birth.

All morning Emma Leigh looked to see Thad, but Mr. Jones obviously kept him busy—or perhaps Thad was avoiding her. In any event, his absence made it even harder for her to wish Merry Christmas to the guests and staff.

While Emma Leigh set the extra long table with Mrs. Jones's fine English china and silver in the main dining room for the guests, the smell of turkey basted in herbs and butter wafted around her. What a splendid dinner the guests and the staff would enjoy with an array of vegetables, bread, and sweet treats. The thought made Emma Leigh a bit sad. How she longed for her family to partake in such a fine meal. She could only imagine the sparkle in her siblings' eyes at the sight of such wonderful food.

"Are you ill, Emma Leigh?" Mrs. Weares asked, staring into her face.

Snapped from her thoughts, Emma Leigh produced a smile. "Of course not. Merely thinking about our Christmas party this afternoon."

"Very well. Let's not dawdle about our duties then," Mrs. Weares said with her typical firmness. "We all want to enjoy Sarah's cooking." She fanned herself furiously. "Oh my, I forgot to tell Thad about the guests wishing a sleigh ride as soon as dinner is completed."

Will he not be here for the staff celebration?

The hours passed swiftly in a flurry of joy and Christmas carols. The time came for the staff to eat. Sarah prepared the same menu as she had provided for the guests, but she put aside a plate for Thad since he'd not returned from the sleigh ride. All were in attendance, except the man Emma Leigh longed to see. The man to whom she longed to give her heart.

I know I'm selfish and Papa needs me, but oh, I love Thad.

At the completion of the meal, Mr. Jones rose from the table. "I see we have gifts to be opened from our secret friends. Miss Carter, would you do us the honor of presenting the final mementos?"

The items were brought into the dining room and set on the walnut sideboard. Mr. Jones motioned for Emma Leigh to come forward. *I'm so tired of smiling. Thad isn't here for any of this, and he gave me the idea.*

One by one she picked up the small notes and tokens and distributed them to each staff member, setting aside a brown paper wrapping with her name and another small parcel for Thad. She'd open hers at the end.

Ooh's and *ah*'s rose from the group as each one discovered their secret friend. Sarah hugged her soundly. "Such a blessing you've been to me. Thank you."

From the corner of her eye, Emma Leigh saw Thad slip into the dining room. Mr. Jones greeted him and presented him with his gift. Emma Leigh watched Thad open a small prayer book and note that identified the item as being from Mrs. Jones. Thad caught Emma Leigh's attention and their gazes met. She saw tenderness, and her heart nearly burst.

"Now, it is your turn, Emma Leigh," Mr. Jones announced, handing her the gift.

"I am excited to learn who has my name," she admitted softly. For the first time, she sensed a lilt in the celebration. Now she could properly thank the giver.

Mr. Jones handed her the brown parcel, and she sat to open it. Pulling away the wrapping, she gasped at the small wooden box embellished in red-orange flowers and an ornate border. "How beautiful," she murmured, tracing the flowers with her fingertips. Curiously, she lifted the lid and saw a piece of paper inside. Now she'd learn for sure that Mr. Jones had indeed drawn her name. How she appreciated his generosity.

Unfolding the paper, she read:

> *A candle's flicker in the darkness,*
> *A fire's warmth to greet the weary,*
> *Only Jesus shines more brightly*
> *Than my lovely Emma Leigh.*
>
> > *Love,*
> > *Thad*

Tears brimmed her eyes, and her gaze flew to his face. "You," she whispered. "I never thought. . . I never imagined."

Suddenly it seemed she and Thad were the only two people in the crowded dining room. He stood before her and bent to one knee.

"Then you are pleased?" he whispered.

"Oh, Thad, all the things you gave me—so extravagant, so generous. I don't deserve your goodness, but I do thank you."

A smile spread over his face, and she saw an image of herself in his blue eyes. "Good. I'm pleased. Tonight we can talk, for your father has given me permission to come calling."

A tear trickled over her cheek. Emma Leigh quickly wiped it away. "This is the best Christmas I've ever had." Her cheeks flushed warm, and joy abounded through every inch of her.

Thad rose to his feet; his adoring look promised what her heart felt. Never had she known such contentment.

Thad counted the hours until he could leave the inn and ride to the Carter home. Once Mr. Jones had learned about Thad's plans for the evening, he'd given him use of a carriage to escort Emma Leigh to church. He could return it later when he came by the inn to get his horse.

Too excited to think, his stomach toying with a game of leapfrog, Thad drove to the Carter home. In his pocket, he had his mother's ivory cameo brooch as a token of his love and devotion to Emma Leigh.

Once he caught sight of the cabin, he believed the firelight from the windows shone more cheerfully than usual. Tonight, he'd ask Emma Leigh to marry him and later escort her to Christmas Eve services.

Mr. Carter answered the door as soon as Thad's gloved knuckles tapped against the wood. "Welcome, Thad, and merry Christmas to you."

"And the blessings of Christmas to you, too, Sir."

Mr. Carter stepped back to usher Thad inside. The older man winked; surely the good-will-toward-men sentiments had taken hold. "Emma Leigh, Thad is here to see you."

Thad's gaze flew to her face and took in the sight of her. She'd woven a red ribbon through her dark hair, and the bobbin lace decorated her throat, but their beauty did not compare to the love he saw in her eyes—eyes reminding him so much of an innocent doe. For a moment he couldn't speak until the sound of the children's laughter shook him to his senses.

"Hush, children," Mrs. Carter said. Her face blushed nearly

as radiantly as Emma Leigh's. "Good to see you, Thad."

"Good evening, Mrs. Carter." Thad swung his attention to Emma Leigh. "Would you like to take a ride with me before going to church?"

She glanced at her father, and he nodded. "You have my permission."

Once she gathered her scarf and gloves, Thad offered his arm, much to the giggling of Simon and Joseph, and stepped out into the cold, crisp night.

"Oh," she breathed. "You have one of the inn's carriages."

"Only the best for my Emma Leigh," he said, glad for the darkness settling around them so she wouldn't see his reddened face.

"I don't know what to say except thank you."

He assisted her up onto the seat, marveling at her lightness, then lit the kerosene lanterns on both sides of the carriage.

Soon they were on their way down the road leading to his parents' farm. Thad had so much to say, but the words simply wouldn't form on his lips. He'd thought of little else but this moment for the past twenty-four hours.

"Are we going past your land?" Emma Leigh asked. The wind whistled, and she snuggled against his shoulder.

"Most assuredly. Remember all the winter days we skated on the pond behind the barn?"

She laughed. "And all the times we fell until we learned?"

We'll have many more times to skate together—years of memories. "I remember the time you threw a snowball and bloodied my nose." He laughed heartily in remembrance, causing him to relax a bit.

She shuddered. "Dare you remind me? I ran all the way

home and hid in Papa's barn for fear I'd get thrashed." She sighed in a mellow sort of way. "You never told anyone."

He pulled the horse in front of the house, his and Emma Leigh's future home. "Would you like to come by here tomorrow?" he asked, taking her hand. "I'd like to walk through the rooms and remember Christmases past."

"Of course. Is everything there as before?"

He nodded and smiled, recalling every piece of furniture and handmade item from his mother. "But tonight, I have something else on my mind." His heart began to pound furiously. *Lord, help me to do this right.*

"Is everything all right?" she asked, staring into his face. "You seem distressed."

The overwhelming urge to kiss her nearly drove him to distraction, but not yet. Soon enough he'd claim her lips. Taking her hand, he began. "Last night I talked to your father about more things than courting you."

Her eyes widened, but she said nothing.

"We discussed matters about the future."

Emma Leigh was always chatting away. Having her say something, anything, would help his scattered nerves.

Taking a deep breath, Thad forged on. "Emma Leigh, I love you. I can't remember ever loving anyone but you. So I'm asking you to marry me. Now, we might have a difficult time while I'm in school, but one day I'll be a doctor, and things will be easier."

In the faint light, she quivered. "I love you, too, Thad, but I can't marry you. I simply can't."

"Why?" he blurted out. *Did I not feel God wanted Emma Leigh as my wife?*

Tears fell swiftly from her eyes, and she did nothing to stop them. "Papa and Mama need me to help them take care of the family."

He removed his glove and with his thumb brushed the wetness from her cheeks. His heart swelled with love for his precious Emma Leigh. "No, my darling. Your father and I have an agreement. He is going to take care of my cattle, and in return he will have the milk to use and sell. He will also have any calves to start his own herd."

She held her breath as though unbelieving of his words.

"Come spring," Thad continued, "he's going to take care of my apple orchard and till the land to plant crops. We'll split the difference come harvest time."

"But his health?"

Thad lifted her chin. "Granted, he had a deep cough less than ten days ago, but look how he's doing now. God is healing him, Emma Leigh. By spring he'll have his strength, and by midsummer, you and I can be married. If you will have me."

She continued to cry.

Desperate and confused, Thad couldn't even pray. "What is it? Do you not care for me?"

She stiffened and shook her head. Then she took a deep breath. "No, I do love you. I'm crying. . .I'm crying because I'm happy."

He gathered her into his arms and held her close. Slowly he bent to kiss away her salty tears now chilling against her soft cheeks. His lips trailed to hers and tasted their sweetness. "You will marry me in midsummer?" he whispered.

"Maybe sooner, if you would like," she replied, standing back and offering a smile.

Reaching into his coat pocket, he pulled his mother's brooch into his palm. "I'd like for you to have this," he said. "I know you can't see it very well in the darkness, but it's a cameo that belonged to my mother." He slipped it into her hand.

"Thank you," she said breathlessly. "I'll take such good care of the brooch—just as I will of you."

"No," he said. "I'm taking care of you, and God will do the rest."

Before dawn on Christmas morning, Thad and Uncle Albert quietly unloaded the wagon and set its contents by the Carter door. Two smoked hams large enough to feed a family of growing children for much more than one meal, flour, potatoes, red cabbage and bacon, squash, turnips, green beans harvested from the summer, stewed apples, and Aunt Klara's delicious rice pudding—all ready for the family inside. Atop the food, Thad placed six cinnamon candy sticks, one for each of his soon-to-be brothers and sister. In a bundle, he'd placed warm coats for each member of the family—the result of selling one of his cows and taking a small portion from his savings.

As he and Uncle Albert drove away, Thad looked back to see the cabin door open and Emma Leigh wave and blow him a kiss. God had indeed given him the desires of his heart.

DIANN MILLS

DiAnn lives in Houston, Texas, with her husband, Dean. They have four adult sons. She wrote from the time she could hold a pencil, but not seriously until God made it clear that she should write for Him. After three years of serious writing, her first book, *Rehoboth*, won favorite **Heartsong Presents** historical for 1998. Other publishing credits include magazine articles and short stories, devotionals, poetry, and internal writing for her church. She is an active church choir member, leads a ladies' Bible study, and is a church librarian. She is also an advisory board member for American Christian Romance Writers.

CIRCLE OF BLESSINGS

by Deborah Raney

Dedication

In memory of my beloved grandmothers,
Dorothy Teeter and Helen Reed,
and my dear great-grandmother, Stella Rankin.

Thy righteousness also, O God, is very high,
who hast done great things: O God, who is like unto thee!
Thou, which hast shewed me great and sore troubles,
shalt quicken me again, and shalt bring me up
again from the depths of the earth.
PSALM 71:19–20

Prologue

Dakota Territory, 1864

It was almost closing time, and in all of his seventeen years, James Collingwood could not remember being so bone-weary as he felt tonight. It seemed almost more than he could do to trudge one more time across the large dining room to the hotel's kitchen and lift yet another pot of coffee.

The Christmas crowd had kept all the staff hopping this week. He had put in more than ten hours himself today—and that with only five hours of sleep last night. Of course it was no one's fault but his own that he'd chosen to keep the candle burning and his nose in a book into the wee hours of the morning.

He ran a hand through his hair and mentally shook off the self-pity that threatened to take up residence in his mind. He knew all too well that he was lucky to be here, fortunate to be working long hours. If not for the mercy his employer had shown him, he might well be sitting under lock and key in the jailhouse across the street. He owed Mr. Browne more than restitution for his foolish offense. He owed him his life. Still, in spite of his gratitude that he was a free man able to provide for the needs of his mother and sister, his deep-held desire to continue his education consumed him. He wanted to attend the university and make something more of his life. He had begun to set aside a minuscule portion of his wages—after paying Mr. Browne the sum they'd agreed upon for restitution, of course. But he'd already missed the deadline for the new term at St. Bartholomew's Academy over in Clairemore, and if his savings didn't multiply any faster in the months ahead, it was doubtful he'd get in for the following term, either.

"Dear Lord," he prayed, weaving his way through the queue of waiters lined up for their orders, "if You desire for me to attend the university, I know You'll supply my needs. Help me to leave it in Your hands." It was not a new prayer. He'd bothered the Almighty with those words a dozen times in the past week. And he intended to bother Him as many times as it took to receive an answer. If that answer was no, he would accept it with grace; but until he heard otherwise, he would pray.

He took a steaming granite pot from the stove and carried it back out to the dining room.

"Care for more coffee, Sir?" he asked the gentleman seated at the head of a small corner table."

"Why, yes," the diner said, "I believe I will have one last cup. Thank you."

The family at this table was pleasant and undemanding. Unlike some of the hotel's patrons, who treated him like a lowly serf, this man and his wife had engaged him in polite conversation and had even inquired about his family. Throughout the evening, James had enjoyed watching their interaction. The couple chatted quietly yet were attentive to their children—an infant, who slept in a basket at their feet, and a talkative little girl of ten or eleven.

Yet something about watching the little family caused a deep ache in the region of James's heart. He could scarcely remember what it was like to be part of a real family. His father had died when he was a tot, and his mother could hardly *be* a mother when all her time was taken up being a nurse to his sister. He didn't fault Mama—or Sylvia. He'd lived long enough to know that they hadn't chosen their lots in life. And in spite of everything, he knew Mama loved him.

He poured coffee for the man's wife, checked on his other tables, and went back to the kitchen. Mr. Browne met him at the door.

"James, are you still here?"

"Yes, Sir."

The older man put a hand on James's shoulder. "Go on home. I'll finish up for you here. You've been putting in some long days."

"I don't mind, Sir."

Mr. Browne smiled and clapped him on the shoulder. "Go on now. I'll hold your gratuities for you."

"Oh, I'm not worried about the tips, Sir. They never amount to much anyway." He tried to make a joke of it, but the truth was, every copper that was laid on the table put him that much closer to the academy.

Ten minutes later, as James shoved his arms into the ragged sleeves of his coat, Mr. Browne came into the cloak-room and held out an envelope to him.

James questioned him with knit brows. But Mr. Browne merely thrust the envelope into his hands. James opened the loose flap and peered inside. A crisp bill with the likeness of Christopher Columbus engraved on its front stared back at him. It was a five-dollar note—one of the newly issued bank notes that James had seen pass through the hotel's cash register on occasion. In fact, there had been several of the bills in the till the night he'd foolishly helped himself to its contents.

He shook off the memory. "It's not payday, is it, Sir?" Even with the extra hours he'd put in, this was far more than he was owed.

"No, James, it's not payday. But this is yours. It has your name on it."

James turned the envelope over in his hands. Sure enough, his name was inked boldly on the front. "I don't understand," he told his employer. "What is this for?"

"One of your patrons left it on the table."

"Are you sure?" He inspected the envelope again. "There's no last name. There must be some mistake, Mr. Browne. I—I can't accept this."

"You can and you will, Mr. Collingwood. Apparently someone feels you offered exceptional service tonight."

"But. . ." He looked from the envelope to his employer and back. "Five dollars, Mr. Browne! My service couldn't have possibly been *that* exceptional. Do you know who left it?"

"I couldn't say, James. I couldn't say. But it could not be more rightfully yours. You take it and have a Merry Christmas. Go on home and get some rest now." Mr. Browne turned and disappeared into the dining room.

James stared after the man in stunned silence as realization washed over him. The envelope he held in his hands was the answer to the prayer with which he had long hounded heaven. Added to the small amount he had saved already, he was only a few dollars short of making tuition for next term.

It was all he could do not to sink to his knees on the cloak-room floor in humble gratitude.

And that was exactly what he *would* do the moment he arrived home.

Chapter 1

Dakota Territory, 1871

Stella Bradford hurried across the campus of St. Bartholomew's Academy, a stack of textbooks in her arms and a bulging drawstring bag looped over one shoulder. The petticoat beneath her long-sleeved cotton dress clung to her legs, and with her free hand she dabbed beads of moisture from her brow with a crumpled handkerchief. *One should not have to perspire in October!* If she didn't hurry, she was going to be late for class, and it would be the second time this week. She was having enough trouble with this infernal English grammar class as it was. It certainly wouldn't help matters to be late again.

The tower clock in the center of the campus quadrangle began to chime the hour, and Stella lifted her skirts above her ankles and broke into a very unladylike trot. She rounded the ivy-draped corner of Andrews Hall at top speed but was halted in her tracks when she bumped headlong into a broad masculine chest. The only thing that kept her from stumbling to the brick walk beneath her feet was the strong pair of hands that reached out to grab her by the shoulders.

"Whoa, Miss! Watch where you're going there." The voice was as deep as the brown eyes that looked down into hers.

"Oh, p—pardon me," she stuttered, "but I'm about to be late for class." She took a step back, out of the man's grasp.

The last chime of the carillon clock died away on the still autumn air, and Stella gave a little gasp of dismay.

"It looks to me as though you *are* late," the gentleman told her. "And at the reckless speed you were going, I'd venture to say you would have arrived so out of breath that you might as well not have bothered going at all."

"Please," she pled impatiently. "Let me pass. I simply can't miss this class again."

"Oh, I see," he said, a rather wicked gleam in his eyes. "So you make a habit of tardiness? And let me guess—you are not exactly a candidate for honors in this particular class?"

She stamped her foot and took another step back. *Of all the impudent—*

She did not have time for this. Donning her most patronizing smile, she told him, "I do appreciate your concern, Mister. . ."

"Collingwood," he supplied, tipping an imaginary hat. "James Collingwood."

"I appreciate your concern, Mr. Collingwood, but I cannot waste my time standing here arguing about either my habits nor my grades—as if it were any of your business!"

"Or," he said.

"I beg your pardon?"

"The correct word is 'or.' *Either* my habits *or* my grades. It's 'either, or' and 'neither, nor.'"

Of all the nerve! How dare this complete stranger stand here and correct my grammar!

He folded his arms across a broad chest and stepped back to gaze at her. "And let me guess," he said. "English Grammar is the class you're tardy for?"

"For which you are tardy," she shot back.

He raised an eyebrow. "Pardon me?"

"The correct phrase is 'the class for which you are tardy.' It is not proper to end a sentence in a preposition." She bobbed her chin for emphasis, crossed her arms, and glared at him, pleased beyond words to have beat him at his own game.

The corners of his lips curled in a slow smile. "Touché, Miss. I stand corrected."

Recognizing his deference to her, Stella's smile became genuine. She turned, ready to continue on to class, but remembering her manners, she tossed an apology over her shoulder. "I *am* sorry to have bumped into you. And thank you for. . .for catching me."

Stella hurried on her way, her face flushed and warm—and from more, she feared, than the warm sun of an Indian summer.

The campus was nearly empty, and Mr. Collingwood's winsome smile still lingered in her mind when she stepped inside Voorhaven Hall a few minutes later. The heels of her shoes clicked on the tiled floor and echoed through the spacious corridor, tattling on her tardiness to anyone who was listening. Both doors to the classroom were closed, but Stella heard noisy chattering inside. Behind the frosted beveled glass in the front door, boisterous, flitting shadows testified that the session had not yet been called to order. She opened the door and was relieved to see that Dr. Whitestone had not arrived. She quickly made her way to her assigned desk at the back of the room. She slipped into her seat, pulled the drawstring bag open, and rummaged inside for her fountain pen and notebook.

A few minutes later, the door swung open and the class quieted immediately. Stella followed the other students' collective gaze to the door, but it was not Dr. Whitestone's profile she saw behind the frosted pane. Instead, the shadowy silhouette behind the door looked vaguely familiar. Recently familiar. She took in a sharp breath as the man she'd nearly bowled over on campus a few minutes ago stepped into the room and placed his small valise on the oak desk at the front of the room. Without looking up, he unfastened the latch on the case and took out a bulky textbook, then stepped behind the podium.

Clearing his throat loudly, he looked over the room, waiting until he had their undivided attention. "Good afternoon," he said. "Dr. Whitestone took ill suddenly, so I'll be substituting for him this hour. My name is Mr. Collingwood and I'm new to the English department here at the academy."

His gaze moved from student to student in the large classroom, and Stella thought she saw an amused glimmer of recognition when he noticed her shrinking in her seat at the back of the room. He turned and picked up a stubby length of chalk from the lip of the blackboard. "Please open your texts to page ninety-two, and copy the three sentences at the top of the page into your notebooks."

As they worked, the studious sounds of chalk on slate and pen nub on pad filled the otherwise quiet room. When the substitute had finished chalking the sentences on the board, the students went to work diagramming them.

Once nouns and verbs had been labeled, Stella was completely lost. She was far more concerned with the dangling hang-nail on her left pinkie finger than with the dangling participle

Mr. Collingwood was so intent on identifying. *Why does it matter?* she thought, allowing herself to be carried away on a daydream. She wanted to be an architect, not a grammarian. She loved the logic and precision of mathematics. She couldn't care less about the structure of the sentences on the board. But let her study the structural design of the historic buildings on campus. Now *there* was an interesting and worthwhile pursuit.

"Isn't that right, Miss Bradford?" a bass voice broke into her reverie.

"Um. . .I–I'm sorry. Could you repeat the question, please?"

The other students tittered like grammar school children, and Stella felt the blood rise to her cheeks.

Mr. Collingwood chose to ignore her and turned to another student who was waving his hand madly. "Yes, Mr. . ." The instructor referred quickly to his seating chart. "Mr. Granger?"

Peter Granger smugly answered the question—something about noun-verb agreement that meant absolutely nothing to Stella. She slunk a little lower in her seat. After forty interminable minutes, during which Stella prayed fervently that she would not be called upon again, the bell in the hallway finally sounded, and Mr. Collingwood dismissed them.

Stella attempted to blend in with the flow of students and sneak out the back door, but she was stopped short. "Miss Bradford?"

She turned to find James Collingwood beckoning her with a slender finger.

"I'd like to see you for a moment, please."

She stepped back and waited for the last student to file out, then wove her way through the labyrinth of desks to the front of the room. "Yes?" she said, forcing her sweetest smile.

He gazed at her thoughtfully. "You don't much want to be here, do you?" he said finally.

"Here at the academy? Why, of course I do! I—"

"No," he interrupted. "I mean in this grammar class."

She had the decency to hang her head. "I'm sorry, Sir. I–I just don't understand it. It makes no sense to me. And frankly—" Suddenly feeling brave, she plunged in with her reasoning, gathering confidence like steam as she went. "Frankly, I see no reason why anyone needs to know whether a verb is active or inactive or whether a noun is proper or not. I mean, really, Mr. Collingwood, when you are on the street, how likely are you to strike up an intriguing conversation on the topic of dangling participles?"

He threw back his head and laughed. For a moment she was inclined to feel that he was laughing *at* her, but the warm gleam in his eyes assured her otherwise.

"Miss Bradford—I do have your name right, don't I?" he asked, running his finger down the seating chart again.

She nodded.

"You may be correct in your observation. However, I have not yet achieved a powerful enough position here at the academy to do away with the grammar requirement, and until such day as that has been accomplished, I'm afraid you shall be compelled to remain in Dr. Whitestone's class and learn enough to earn a passing grade."

She conceded with a slump of her shoulders.

He laughed again. "Oh, come now. It can't be that awful, can it? Dare I remind you that this class is meant to be merely a refresher course? Didn't you learn to diagram a sentence in your high school?"

"I could never make sense of it," she said flatly.

"Ahh... Well, Dr. Whitestone tells me he has suggested that you work with a tutor to get your marks to a more acceptable level in this class."

She nodded slowly, wondering how he could have known this. "Yes. I'm supposed to have my first session tomorrow, though I don't know what good it will do."

James Collingwood took a small appointment book from his inside breast pocket and leafed through it. "I don't know if he has mentioned it to you yet, but I feel it is only fair to inform you that Dr. Whitestone has appointed me to be your tutor."

As if he thought she would require proof, he pointed to a neatly printed notation in the logbook. Sure enough, there, beneath tomorrow's date, on the line reserved for four o'clock, was her name.

She gaped at him. "*You* are the tutor I've been assigned to?"

"I am the tutor *to whom* you have been assigned, yes. And one you are obviously in desperate need of," he said, with a sidewise grin.

Her mind scrambled to think of a comeback. True, he had ended his pathetic quip in a preposition; but she didn't dare argue with him, for she realized with dismay that his words were correct—in substance, if not in grammar.

Chapter 2

James Collingwood locked up the classroom and plodded down the hall, completely drained after a long day of filling in for Arthur Whitestone. As he stepped from the building, he shielded his eyes against the waning afternoon sunlight and started across the campus lawn. Though autumn had begun to paint the campus in its annual array of gold and scarlet and James looked forward to the chill air the season would bring, for now, he savored the warmth of the sun on his face.

He breathed a contented sigh and quickened his step. The ghost of what he had once been sometimes haunted his thoughts; but on days like this, the satisfaction he found in teaching managed to eclipse the unchangeable truth of his past. Working with Dr. Whitestone's students had reminded him all over again how greatly his life had been redeemed, how readily God could remake a worthless sinner into a willing servant.

Upon his graduation from St. Bartholomew's Academy the previous year, James had been offered a job as an assistant to his professor and mentor, Arthur Whitestone, the head of St. Bart's English department.

For this first year, his job mostly entailed grading papers and serving as a secretary of sorts to Dr. Whitestone. The work provided a modest income while he continued postgraduate studies at the academy. His ultimate desire was to become a professor himself. He had discovered the deepest fulfillment whenever he was given an opportunity to preside in the classroom.

And now, at his mentor's request, he'd taken on an additional assignment—one that would test his mind, not to mention his patience. Dr. Whitestone had asked him to tutor a student, the daughter of the department head's longtime friend Marcus Bradford. James had agreed without hesitation. He loved to teach, the extra money would be a blessing, and besides, how difficult could it be to help a first-year student with the basics of English grammar?

He smiled to himself, remembering the two exchanges he'd had with the young woman since then. Had he met Stella Bradford before Dr. Whitestone's proposition, he might have spent a bit more time in prayer before agreeing to the job—and he might have negotiated for a higher wage as well. Yes, he would have all he could handle, attempting to impart a grammatical rule or two into the brain of that little spitfire. But he welcomed a challenge, and the distraction would be good for him. With her halo of sunny curls and that engaging wit, James could see how Stella Bradford might, indeed, become quite a distraction.

Leaving the grounds of St. Bart's, he headed east. His sister's boardinghouse, where he lived, was almost a mile from the college. He didn't relish the thought of making this walk once winter set in. On a day like today, it was difficult to believe that blue skies would soon give way to snow flurries and bitter winds, but it would happen soon enough. This was the Dakota Territory, after all. He walked past the lumber mill on the edge of town. Here, at least, business seemed to be booming in the postwar economy; and James offered up a little prayer of thanksgiving. He knew too well the despair of financial hardship and what it could do to a man.

In front of him, the tattered slate shingles of the three-story boardinghouse rose through the trees, and he quickened his pace. He wondered how Sylvia was feeling. His sister worked far too hard. Since her husband's death two years ago, she hadn't had much choice. He would be glad when his tuition was finally paid and his first wages were in the bank so he could be of more help to her. How he would manage to get her to *allow* him to help, he wasn't sure. He knew Sylvia still felt guilty for the trouble he'd gotten into, though the Lord knew that his sister was no more to blame than God Himself. Why, she'd been a mere girl when it had all happened. Still, he'd committed his crime in an attempt to help her, and Sylvia seemed intent on making it up to him somehow.

As he opened the gate to the yard, he spotted his sister on the wide front porch. Wearing a light cotton dress and wielding a decrepit broom, she beat at the handful of prematurely fallen leaves that skittered across the whitewashed floor. The surface was already clean enough to eat from. She smiled when she noticed James coming up the walk, but Sylvia's smiles never quite reached her eyes.

"Hi, Sis." He bounded up the steps and planted a kiss on her smooth, pale cheek.

"Hi, Jimmy. How was school?"

He laughed. "You make me sound like a little boy just home from grammar school."

"If the shoe fits. . . ," she said wryly.

"And how was your day?" he asked, ignoring her joke. "Did Mr. Graves bring the rent money by?"

"Half of it." She sighed.

He shook his head and grumbled under his breath. "Well, that's something, at least." Unknown to Sylvia, he had delivered a stern lecture to Herbert Graves just last evening. How was his sister supposed to make a living—let alone pay for the medicine she needed—when her tenants refused to pay their rent?

"Well," he brightened, "you go ahead and see the doctor. I took on a tutoring job today. That'll tide us over."

Sylvia shook the broom at him. "There is no 'us' about it, Jimmy. That money should go to your tuition loan," she scolded. "I don't want you spending your hard-earned dollars on me."

Gently, James took the broom from her work-roughened hands and ushered her into the front parlor. "I'll spend my hard-earned dollars however I choose. And if I choose to spend them on my favorite sister, what business is it of yours?"

She rolled her eyes, but he heard the love and gratitude in her voice when she ordered him, "Go wash up for supper. It's just you, me, and old Mrs. Bellingham tonight."

⁓

James sat facing the door of the small study hall in Robinson Library. For the third time in as many minutes, he pulled his watch from his vest pocket and inspected it. She was already five minutes late. Much as he hated to begin their very first tutoring session with a reprimand, he would not tolerate tardiness. Stella Bradford had demonstrated with their very first meeting that she had no regard for punctuality. Well, *his* time was valuable, even if hers was not.

A clatter in the hallway beyond the door interrupted his thoughts, and a few seconds later, as her perky countenance lit up the room, he quickly decided to let her tardiness go unmentioned for this one time. If it happened again, she would hear about it in no uncertain terms.

He rose from his chair. "Good day, Miss Bradford. Please, come in. Have a seat."

"Good afternoon, Mr. Collingwood. I do apologize for being late," she said, her breaths coming in labored, rapid gasps. "I confess, I don't know my way around the library yet."

He pulled out the chair beside his at the table. "Please, sit down. . .unless, of course, you'd like a moment to catch your breath."

She looked at him carefully, as though she were trying to decide if he was angry. He returned her gaze with a smile meant to put her at ease, and she took the chair.

"Thank you. I'm sure you must think that I am forever tardy."

He wasn't sure how to respond to that. What else *was* he to think? But she quickly relieved him of the need to reply.

"Well," she said brightly, opening her textbook decisively and resting her chin on one slender hand. "We'd best get started. I fear you have taken on a hopeless case in me, Mr. Collingwood, but I'm willing to give it a try if you are."

"All right," he said, amused by her brashness. "Let's begin with the sentences we worked on in class yesterday—since you seemed to be a bit lost. That was on page ninety-two, I believe."

While she copied the lines onto her notebook, he scooted his chair back a few inches so he could watch her discreetly. Her unruly curls were fugitives from the hairpins meant to hold them in place, and they formed a becoming halo about her fair face. He watched with amusement as she traced each letter simultaneously with pen and with tongue, like a first grader just learning to write. Surprisingly, the resulting script was elegant and refined.

She glanced up and caught him watching her. "Yes?"

"You—you have lovely penmanship," he finally stuttered.

"Why, thank you. Shall we begin?"

"Of course."

He began to walk her through the process of naming the parts of speech in the sample sentences. But once past the basics of noun and verb, she floundered. He patiently defined adverbs and adjectives, but it seemed obvious from her blank stare that he was not getting through to her.

Finally, with exasperation in her voice, she laid down her pen and turned to him. "Why must we dissect this sentence as though it were a frog in the biology laboratory? I can see quite clearly that it is a frog and that it can jump. Isn't it enough to know that? Why is it also necessary for me to know that the slimy thing has a heart and lungs and muscles and other ghastly parts? Will the frog jump any farther once I know how to label its parts?"

James scrambled to think of a way to counter her charming metaphor, but before he could utter a word, she answered her own question.

"No, it will not jump any farther because the poor creature will be *dead!*"

He burst out laughing. She certainly had a point.

But she ignored his laughter, her voice rising an octave. "Truly, Mr. Collingwood, I see no use whatsoever in tearing apart a perfectly fine sentence when I can understand its meaning quite well *without* taking it apart."

An idea came to him. He placed his fountain pen on the table and leaned back in his chair. "What, might I inquire, is your field of study here at the academy, Miss Bradford?"

"I am going to be an architect." By the resolute tilt of her chin, he suspected that she'd had to defend her ambition on more than one occasion. It *was* a highly unusual aspiration for a young woman.

"An architect, eh? Well, that is a fine goal. But let me ask you: Do you take the same attitude toward the study of architecture that you seem to have taken with the study of the English language?"

"I don't understand."

"Do you believe it unimportant to understand how a building is constructed before you go about designing one yourself? Does it not matter a great deal that you know exactly how the beams and rafters should be secured? That the cornerstone be square and precisely placed?"

"Of course it matters," she said. "But I don't desire to build sentences, Mr. Collingwood. I desire to build buildings."

"Ah. . ." He held up a finger in triumph. "But whether you desire to or not, you *have* been 'building' sentences since you walked in that door"—he indicated the door to the study room with a slight tilt of his head—"and I must inform you that several of those sentences have been quite poorly constructed. Now—"

She opened her mouth, but he cut her off with an upraised hand.

"Please. Hear me out. When you are established in the business of architecture, do you not think it would be to your advantage to be able to communicate with your clientele in a grammatically correct fashion?"

"Certainly, but—"

He sighed and held up a warning hand. "Miss Bradford, I think it is clear that I am not going to convince you of the necessity of knowing how to properly diagram a sentence. But you must concede that passing this grammar class is a requirement for graduation from the academy. You will never become an architect without a passing grade in English grammar. Correct?"

He waited until finally she nodded in defeat.

"Perhaps, then, we should use that fact alone as our motivation for continuing: You must have a passing grade in this class; it is my job to see that you achieve it. Do you think we might be able to get somewhere with such an understanding?"

She thought for a minute, and a slow smile spread across her face. "That makes more sense than anything else I've heard this afternoon."

He returned her smile. "It's decided then. I will do my best to impart the knowledge you need to pass this class, and you will do your best to understand the material, regardless of how useless you believe it to be. Agreed?"

She nodded again, and they set to work.

For the next hour, he wrote sentences, and she struggled to—as she'd so aptly put it—*dissect* them. She was certainly bright enough, with an impressive vocabulary that seemed to expand in direct proportion to her frustration. And she did, indeed, grow frustrated as she struggled to comprehend and label the parts of speech represented in the increasingly complex sentences he invented.

Feeling she had reached her limit, he printed one last string of words on the notepaper in front of him: *Stella Bradford has successfully completed her first grammar lesson under the expert tutelage of James Collingwood*. He slid the pad of paper in front of her.

She read it and let out a little snort of laughter. "Oh, this is an easy one," she said. "Let's see. . ." She took her pen and underlined her name. " 'Stella Bradford' is the noun; 'has completed' is the verb." She glanced up at him with a mischievous gleam in her eyes and continued. " 'Successfully' is a questionable adverb, and 'under the expert tutelage' is a highly fictional qualifying clause."

He laughed. "Now you're making up entire new categories for the parts of speech."

"I'm sorry," she said coyly, "but your ridiculous sentence demanded it."

He gave an exaggerated sigh and closed the notebook. Pushing back his chair, he told her, "I can see that you have had all the expert tutelage you can handle for one day." He pulled the watch from his pocket. "And we've gone over our time as it is."

She stood beside him and gathered her things. "Thank you," she told him, turning serious. "I truly hope you don't feel you've taken on a lost cause."

"Not at all," he said encouragingly. "I believe we've already made some progress."

She left the room with a cheerful "Good day."

He straightened the chairs, closed the door behind him, and went into the main room of the library. As he approached the wide front doors, he saw that his student was just leaving the building also.

He held the door for her, and they walked out into the fresh air together. The sun was low in the west. "It will soon be dark," he said. "Do you live nearby, Miss Bradford?" St. Bart's had only recently opened its doors to women, and the campus housing was for men.

She shook her head. "I live with my parents a couple miles outside of town. But I am going to the mill to meet my father. I usually ride home with him each evening," she explained.

"Ah, Bradford Mills. Of course. I just happen to be going

that direction. I'd be delighted to have your company as far as the mill."

She hesitated for the slightest of moments, then transferred her bag and books to her right arm and placed her left hand around the crook of his offered arm. "Why, thank you, Mr. Collingwood," she said.

They walked in silence for a few moments, and he wondered if he'd made her uncomfortable. After all, in spite of the fact that he was probably only four or five years her senior, he was an employee of St. Bart's—and her instructor.

"So tell me about this desire of yours to design buildings," he said, attempting to make conversation.

She looked up at him from beneath curly lashes, as if to determine whether or not he was teasing. Apparently deciding that his question had been sincere, she launched into her story. "Mama says I've been sketching houses and churches and shops ever since I could hold a crayon in my fist." She clenched creamy, white knuckles to demonstrate.

It was all James could do to resist wrapping that delicate little fist in his own large hands. He forced himself to concentrate on her words.

"Papa has been in the lumber business as long as I can remember, and I've always been fascinated watching houses and buildings arise from the flat earth. I guess you could say I was born to it."

"I suppose so," he conceded.

"Tell me about yourself, Mr. Collingwood."

He turned to her as they strolled along the walk on Main Street. "You know, Miss Bradford, if I'm going to be your tutor, I think you could call me James. Unless I'm teaching Dr. Whitestone's class, of course. A more formal title might be appropriate in front of the other students."

"Of course. Well then, please call me Stella."

"It's a very lovely name."

"Why, thank you. I'm named after my great-great-grand-mother, Stella Mae Bradford."

"She would be proud."

"I'm told that I am a lot like her," Stella confessed. "Like my father, too."

"Oh? And how so?"

She gave an impish grin. "A little stubborn, a little tenacious, more than a little pigheaded, I'm afraid."

He reeled back in feigned surprise. "You? Surely not."

"I hide it well," she said, sounding quite serious.

He didn't have the heart to tell her that she didn't hide it nearly as well as she might think. Instead he said, "Rightly directed, those can be endearing qualities, you know."

"Endearing?"

"Charming, appealing." He defined the word for her.

She smacked his arm with a dainty hand. "I know what it means, Silly. I was challenging the idea itself. I'm afraid not many people find my stubbornness charming."

Little do you know, he thought. "Maybe you are right. Perhaps 'beneficial' is a better word. Sometimes it pays to be stubborn and tenacious."

"I wish you'd tell that to my father," she said, a frown creasing her forehead.

"There are certainly worse qualities a child could have than a little stubborn streak," James replied.

She turned and peered up at him. "You sound as though you speak from experience, Mr. Collingwood. Did you cause your father as much anxiety as I've caused mine?"

"I don't know about fathers, Stella. Mine died when I was very young. But. . .well, let's just say that I gave my mother far more trouble than the good woman deserved."

"And is your mother living?"

"No. She died a few years ago. But I will be forever grateful that she lived long enough to see her son back on the straight and narrow path."

"I'm sure you made her proud," Stella said.

"I had much for which to atone," he told her, surprising himself with his honesty.

Stella looked at him, intense curiosity in her eyes, but she didn't voice the questions that were obviously in her mind. Instead, she asked, "And you live in a boardinghouse, you say?"

"Yes. Since her husband's death, my sister takes in boarders. If it were winter, you'd be able to see Sylvia's rooftop"—he pointed ahead toward a group of homes that rose above the trees in the distance—"just in front of that tallest gray roof to the south."

They chatted pleasantly all the way through town, and as they approached the mill, James fought to think of an excuse to continue their conversation, to see her again. "Have you lived in Clairemore long?" he asked.

"Since I was about twelve," she replied. "We moved here from Barton's Grove after Papa bought the mill."

Stella went on chattering about her family, but at the mention of the neighboring town, James felt his face grow warm and his heart begin to pound in his ears. He struggled to pay attention to what she was saying, but he wondered if there would ever come a day when he could be reminded of his past without flinching.

Chapter 3

Stella didn't know what had caused James Collingwood to turn suddenly sullen, but as the mill came into sight, her concerns shifted in another direction. She released James's arm and turned to him. "This will be fine. Thank you so much for walking with me."

He kept his arm bent, offering it to her again. "Please, let me take you to the door. I don't mind."

"No, truly. I'm fine."

But it was too late for her protests. From the corner of her eye, she saw Papa open the door of the mill office and step outside. He spotted her immediately, and even from a distance, she could see him craning his neck, trying to figure out the identity of this man who was harassing his daughter.

"You go on, Mr. Collingwood," Stella urged. "There's Papa now. I'll be fine."

James seemed to sense her unease and tipped his hat in farewell. "Good day, then. I'll see you for a lesson on Thursday?"

"Yes, of course." Stella was distracted, worrying that her father would try to detain her tutor and grill him without mercy, as was his habit where her suitors were concerned. But once James Collingwood started on his way, she saw that her father had ordered their rig brought around and was standing beside the wagon, waiting for her.

She hurried to meet him, took the hand he offered, and climbed up onto the wagon seat.

"Hello, there," Papa said, climbing up beside her and clicking his tongue at the team. The horses gave a low whicker and turned toward home as though they knew the way by heart.

As they headed west, Papa indicated James's retreating form with a backward flick of his thumb. "You had an escort, I see."

"Yes, Papa."

"A boy from the academy?"

"Yes. He graduated last year, that is. Now he's an assistant in the English department."

"He *teaches* at the school?" Stella heard accusation in his voice.

"He's Dr. Whitestone's new assistant, Papa," she explained. "His name is James Collingwood. He's working toward a professorship at St. Bart's."

"He's Arthur's assistant, you say?"

Stella nodded. "Yes. He's the one Dr. Whitestone assigned to tutor me."

"I see," her father said, stroking his silvered beard, obviously deep in thought.

For a moment, Stella dared to wonder if perhaps James would pass muster with her father simply because of his connection to Arthur Whitestone. Papa had the highest regard for the department head.

But she was mistaken. The interrogation had only begun.

"And just how did this Mr. Collingwood come to walk you home?" Papa demanded.

"I finished my session with him—my tutoring session—and he. . .he noticed that it was beginning to get dark, so he offered to walk me home."

"Home? Did you tell him that you live a good distance in the country?"

It took every ounce of self-control she possessed to keep her voice steady. "I told him, Papa, that I was meeting my father at the mill. Mr. Collingwood lives at his sister's boardinghouse east of town." She pointed back toward the group of older homes beyond the mill. "Since he was going this way already, he offered to accompany me."

Papa grunted as though he didn't buy Mr. Collingwood's story. Stella could barely stifle the sigh that escaped her. For as long as she could remember, her father had scared off every young man who'd dared attempt to court her. Papa was a wonderful, generous, Christian man, and she knew that his intentions were fueled by deep love and a desire to protect his daughter. But if one more log were thrown on the fire of his intentions, she would end up a spinster for eternity. *Perish the thought!*

Until now, there had never been anyone who mattered enough for her to risk her father's ire. But something told her that James Collingwood might just change all that.

They rode the rest of the way in silence. But when the horses slowed and turned up the lane that led to the Bradford farm, Papa turned to her. "I never liked the idea of you going to the academy in the first place, Stella Mae." He shook his head in apparent exasperation, but the hand he laid on her shoulder was gentle. "You and this harebrained notion of yours—an architect! I don't know what you—"

"Papa—"

He hushed her, not unkindly. "All I can say is I hope you won't give me more reasons to regret the fact that I allowed you to go."

She turned to him, struggling to remain calm. "Papa, a very thoughtful gentleman walked me safely to the mill. I should think you would be grateful."

He reined the horses in and stopped the wagon in front of the house. Taking her hand briefly, he gave it an affectionate squeeze. "Go help your mama with supper. Tell her I'll be in shortly."

Stella managed a smile and jumped down from the wagon, dragging her books and bag off the bench behind her. She reached for the gate to the side yard, but before she could unfasten the latch, the back door flew open and her little sister raced into the yard.

"Stella's home! Stella's home!" Helen sang out merrily to no one in particular.

"Hi, there, Shortcake," Stella called, using Papa's nickname for the petite girl.

"We're having roast chicken for supper. Mama needs your help mashing the potatoes."

"I just got home, Helen. Give me a minute, will you?" She cringed inwardly. She hadn't meant to snap like that. It wasn't Helen's fault that Papa was so bullheaded.

"I'm just telling you what Mama said," the little girl pouted. "Was school hard today?"

"A little. How about your day? Did Miss Wickham like your drawing?"

Helen frowned. "She didn't get to see it. Timmy Hardtner tore it up before I got a chance to show it to Teacher."

"Why, that little—"

"Don't tell Papa," Helen breathed, her eyes wide. "He'll just make trouble. Timmy was only teasing."

Stella could scarcely suppress her laughter. Timmy must have fallen hard for Helen. As dark as Stella was fair, Helen was already a beauty. But the poor girl was barely eight years old, and already she was wise to Papa's fatherly sanctions against the masculine gender.

Stella put an arm around Helen and turned her toward the house. "I won't say anything. I promise. But you'll have to learn to stand up to Timmy. He shouldn't have torn your picture, even if he was teasing. That's just plain mean. Such a nice drawing—wasted!"

Helen smiled sheepishly, and love for her little sister welled up in Stella's heart.

"Come on, Shortcake," she said. "Let's go help Mama."

Thursday morning Stella had a full day of classes, but as she sat through her world history lesson and worked the problems in her mathematics course, she realized that she was merely biding her time until her tutoring session with James that afternoon. She had been on pins and needles since Tuesday night, terrified that Papa might forbid her to walk with James again. Fortunately, her father hadn't said another word on the subject of James Collingwood, and Stella fervently hoped James might offer to walk with her again after today's session.

Finally four o'clock approached, and Stella hurried across campus to the library. This time she had no trouble locating the study hall where they'd agreed to meet. But even though she arrived several minutes early, James was waiting for her when she opened the door.

"Am I late again?" she sighed.

"Not at all," he said. "Right on time, in fact. I finished early in Dr. Whitestone's office and thought I could find a few moments of solitude here." He held up the book he'd been reading. *"Uncle Tom's Cabin,"* he explained, though Stella could easily read the embossed title on the book's cover for herself. "A fascinating novel. I hadn't read it before, but when I heard that President Lincoln had credited the author for starting the war, I decided I'd better see what kind of writing this was."

"And *is* Harriet Beecher Stowe a warmonger, in your opinion?" There had been a discussion of the book in one of her classes, though she hadn't read it herself. Papa and Mama didn't put much stock in reading works of fiction.

"Oh, no," James said. "I don't think that's what the president meant. To the contrary, I think his comment was a tribute to the author's skill with words. She managed to stir up some powerful emotions with her fiction."

For the next twenty minutes, she listened intently while James expounded on his impressions of Mrs. Stowe's novel. Stella was much relieved at the confirmation that James was a strong abolitionist. She had assumed so, given his friendship with Dr. Whitestone, who was a well-known supporter of the fight against slavery. But still, seeing this strong yet compassionate side of James's character only made Stella like him more.

Finally James gave her a guilty grin. "I've rattled on long enough. We'd best get on with the lesson."

As Stella opened her notebook and readied her fountain

pen, he glanced at his pocket watch and took in a sharp breath. "Stella, I've cheated you of nearly half your allotted time. I am sorry. I promise to make it up to you. Perhaps you could come ten or fifteen minutes early for the next two sessions?"

"Certainly," she agreed. She looked forward with pleasure to any extra time with him.

They set about diagramming sentences, but each sentence James dictated seemed to remind one of them of a story, and when the clock in the library's entry chimed five o'clock, they were once again far off the subject, laughing and chatting about every topic *except* English grammar.

"I'm ashamed of myself," James told her, as they gathered their belongings and walked through the library stacks to the wide front doors. "I've wasted your time and your father's money."

"Please, James. Don't think anything of it. I did my share of the talking, too. Besides, I enjoyed every minute of our time together." Suddenly she felt rather shy with him. She hadn't meant to wear her feelings quite so obviously on her sleeve. "It was certainly more interesting than those silly grammar problems," she stammered.

"I'm afraid you'll feel differently when you fail your exam," he said solemnly.

"I'll work extra hard next time," she promised.

They reached the front doors and, as Stella had hoped, James issued an invitation.

"If you don't mind waiting while I stop by Dr. Whitestone's office to pick up some papers he asked me to mark, I'd be honored to walk you to the mill again."

"Why, thank you. I'd like that."

They stepped outside and were met by a blast of wintry air. "I believe the temperature has dropped by ten degrees," James said, perusing the sky. "I'm afraid our Indian summer has come to an end."

Stella shivered and pulled her wrap more tightly around her shoulders. She took the arm James offered, and they headed toward the building that housed the English department.

Arthur Whitestone was just locking up when they came down the main corridor of Voorhaven Hall. "Ah, James. There you are." He looked at Stella, an unspoken question in the tight knit of his bushy, snow-white brows. "Good day, Miss Bradford."

"Hello, Dr. Whitestone. We've just finished a tutoring session," she offered, knowing that her father would likely hear about her showing up at the office on James's arm. "James— um, Mr. Collingwood is going to escort me to the mill."

"I see," the professor said.

Stella imagined she saw a knowing glimmer in the older man's eye.

"Well, please give your father my greetings. It's been some time since we took tea together."

"I will tell him."

Dr. Whitestone disappeared into his office and came back with a thick sheaf of papers for his assistant. James secured them in the small valise he carried, and he and Stella waved to the professor and started across campus.

"I still feel awful about taking up all your time with my blather."

"Please, James." She gave him her sweetest smile. "You have nothing to be sorry for."

"Oh, but see there, you've just proven me right."

She raised an eyebrow in question.

"It's apparent that I have much *for which* to be sorry," he said pointedly.

She immediately picked up on the words he'd emphasized and put a hand to her forehead in mock distress. "Oh, I've trampled the English language once again, haven't I?"

He nodded, laughing. "Don't despair, Miss Bradford." He bent his head near hers, and his voice took on a conspiratorial tenor. "In truth, unless you are giving a dissertation before the faculty of the academy, you can often get away with in speech what would be inexcusable in print."

"That is good to know. Otherwise I wouldn't dare speak another word in your presence for fear of making a grammatical fool of myself."

He laughed again. James Collingwood was obviously easily entertained. She was glad, because she loved hearing his easy laughter, loved even more that she was the cause of it.

She barely noticed the chill in the air as they walked along, joking and talking together. As they neared the mill, Stella opened her mouth to insist again that James need not walk her all the way to the door, but before she could get a word out, he stopped abruptly in the street and turned to her. "Do you have classes tomorrow?"

"Yes."

"What if we meet again tomorrow afternoon at the library so I can make up the time I wasted? You wouldn't be charged for the extra session, of course," he added quickly.

She smiled to herself at his transparent excuse to spend time with her again, but she wasn't about to miss the opportunity. "I was going to be studying at the library anyway," she told him, "until Papa gets done at the mill. If you're certain you don't mind, that would be very nice."

She looked up to see Papa's team and wagon appear from behind the mill's warehouse. Stella could tell by her father's alert posture at the reins that he had been watching for her. When Papa spotted her with James, he nudged the horses forward and drove across the mill yard to meet them.

From his perch high up on the wagon seat, Papa tipped his hat politely in James's direction.

James returned the courtesy. "Good day, Sir."

"Papa, this is James Collingwood, the tutor I told you about. James, this is my father, Marcus Bradford."

"Pleasure meeting you, Mr. Bradford," James said.

"Likewise," Papa responded. He turned his gaze on Stella, and she recognized the tight wariness in his voice when he said, "We'd best be on our way, Stella. It looks like there might be a winter storm brewing, and we don't want to worry your mother."

Stella turned to her escort. "Thank you for walking me, James. I'll see you tomorrow."

James helped her into the wagon, and as they drove off, she gave a little wave, hoping that he hadn't noticed Papa's rudeness.

When the horses had trotted out of James's hearing, Papa leveled a one-word accusation at her. "James?"

Not understanding at first, she started to explain. "Yes, Papa. It's James Collingwood."

"And since when are students at St. Bartholomew's on a first-name basis with their professors?"

"Papa, I told you, he's not a professor. He's an assistant. He fills in teaching for Dr. Whitestone once in awhile is all."

"He is your tutor, Stella, and therefore your superior. I don't think it's proper for you to be on a first-name basis with the man."

"He *asked* me to call him James, Papa. It would have been rude to ignore his request."

"Well, I don't like it. And what's this business about tomorrow? Perhaps I should speak to him."

"Papa, no! James—Mr. Collingwood didn't do anything wrong. Please, Papa."

They bumped along the country road in silence, Stella's mind churning. She would be mortified if Papa said anything to James. Suddenly she remembered her exchange with Dr. Whitestone.

"By the way, Papa," she started, trying to keep her tone casual. "I spoke with Dr. Whitestone this afternoon, and he said to tell you 'hello.' He mentioned that it's been some time since the two of you visited."

Papa thought for a moment. "Yes, it has been awhile. I suppose I should remedy that. Perhaps I'll pay Arthur a visit tomorrow."

Stella cringed. She knew exactly why Papa was suddenly so eager to visit with his old friend. Yet the more she thought about it, the more optimistic she grew. Dr. Whitestone knew James well. Perhaps her professor could serve as a liaison between James and her father. Perhaps he could put Papa's mind at ease about James. If anyone might be able to persuade Papa that there was no harm in her and James's friendship, it would be Arthur Whitestone.

Chapter 4

T he encounter with Stella's father at the mill ate at James like a dog gnawing away at a dry bone. At dinner, over Sylvia's succulent roast beef, he barely said a word. Of course with Mrs. Bellingham at the table, one did not need to worry about a lack of conversation. The elderly widow expounded at length on every subject under the sun. Though he could usually tolerate the woman's well-intentioned lectures, tonight her high-pitched voice gave him a headache. He excused himself to his room as soon as he could politely do so.

Then when he should have been marking students' papers, he sat at the cramped desk in the tiny sitting room off his bedchamber and replayed the brusque meeting with Stella's father. He had gotten the distinct impression that Marcus Bradford was not at all happy about seeing James with his daughter. Maybe it wasn't personal. Perhaps Mr. Bradford was simply one of those overprotective fathers who never wanted to turn their daughters over to *any* man. But he worried that it was more than that. He knew that Dr. Whitestone and Marcus Bradford were friends. Was it possible that Dr. Whitestone had told Stella's father about him? And if so, was Marcus Bradford the kind of man who refused to forgive a man his past?

Guilt poured over James. It was one thing to mentally berate the man for having a judgmental spirit. But when Stella didn't know how much there was to forgive, he couldn't very well credit her for having a generous, forgiving spirit.

James knew that he had long ago been forgiven by the only One who mattered. Nevertheless, it wasn't fair to court a woman the way he wanted to court Stella Bradford without telling her the whole story. They could never have an honest friendship until she knew the truth about him and had an opportunity to decide for herself whether she could live with the ugly history that would always be a part of who he was.

He adjusted the wick on the kerosene lamp beside him and forced his attention to the compositions spread in front of him. If he didn't get to work, he would be up past midnight reading mostly dreadful freshman essays.

But before he set to work, he paused to bow his head and offer his worries to heaven. When he lifted his head, the flame in the lamp flickered, and a tender ember of peace glowed within his heart as well.

The Indian summer returned with surprising strength, and for a month and a half of Tuesdays and Thursdays, Stella Bradford spent her afternoons in Robinson Library with a handsome and fascinating tutor who was fast becoming her dearest friend and confidant.

James had taken to walking Stella to the mill each evening, even when he sometimes had to turn around and return to the academy for a meeting or to teach a late class. Papa had not said another word to her about James Collingwood. On the rare occasions when the two men encountered each other in front of the mill, Papa treated James with polite indifference. Stella was happy to leave well enough alone and was merely content that, for once, her father was not interfering.

In the early hours of a late November morning, Old Man Winter finally made his first appearance, dumping half a foot of snow on Clairemore and the surrounding area.

When the Bradford sisters awoke at dawn and discovered the blanket of white outside the farmhouse, young Helen danced around the cozy kitchen in delight. But Stella paced the hallway from front door to back a dozen times, wishing Papa would come in and tell her his decision about going into town. He had gone out to do the morning chores and to hitch the horses to the sleigh; but before he'd left the house, he had warned Stella that he doubted there would be classes at the academy after such a storm.

"Stella Mae, would you stop your pacing?" Dorothy Bradford said from her position at the stove, where she was frying bacon. "I never saw a child so enamored with school. You'd almost think there was another reason you were so anxious to get into town."

Stella looked suspiciously at her mother and detected a twinkle in the soft brown eyes. Though Stella usually confided in her mother, she hadn't yet dared to voice her growing feelings for James Collingwood.

She smiled coyly. "I don't know what you are talking about, Mama."

"Stella, Stella, what have we taught you about telling lies?" Mama teased.

Stella rushed to her mother's side and put an arm around the soft shoulder. "Oh, Mama. You have to make Papa let me go!"

Mama looked at her intently. "What is his name, Child? As if I couldn't guess, since I've heard the words of a certain handsome tutor quoted a dozen times over the past weeks."

Stella knew her smile betrayed her feelings. "Yes, it's James, Mama. Papa met him, you know—at the mill. Oh, Mama, he's wonderful. Did Papa tell you?"

"That James is wonderful?" She shook her head. "Hardly."

Stella smiled at her mother's attempt at a joke, and her heart overflowed with affection for this woman who had always been a buffer between a stubborn father and an equally stubborn daughter. "You have to make him understand, Mama," she begged again. "I'm supposed to meet James in the library this afternoon."

"But I thought your sessions with your tutor were on Tuesdays and Thursdays."

Stella blushed. "That's right. But. . .well, sometimes we meet there just to visit."

Mama walked to the dining-room window and pulled back a corner of the heavy drapes. "My sweet, silly girl, we are in the middle of a frightful storm. If you don't show up, I'm sure your James will understand that the weather detained you. And if he lets a little snowstorm change his mind about the prettiest girl in Clairemore County, then he wasn't worth pining over anyway," Mama declared.

Stella heard the door to the spring room open and the muffled sound of Papa stamping snow from his boots. She ran back to meet him. "How are the roads, Papa? Can we get into town?"

"I am going, Stella, but the snow is quite deep and there

are branches down everywhere. It will be slow going. I don't think there is a chance that the academy will hold classes. And if they do, you won't be the only one absent. I think it's best if you stay home."

"But, Papa, I have an exam in history today. I can't be absent!"

The look he gave her made her feel as though her real reason for not wanting to miss class was written upon her forehead in India ink. She squirmed under his careful scrutiny, but she continued to try to convince him. "If we get there and find they're not having classes, I could come to the mill with you and help out in the office," she said hopefully.

Her father held firm. "Your mother will need your help here today. It will be all the two of you can do to keep the fires going, the snow cleared from the walks, and the animals cared for."

Stella recognized the resolve in his voice and knew that there would be no changing his mind. She went to her room and pouted for awhile, then came downstairs to help her mother. Mama was right. James would understand why she wasn't there. But that wasn't the point. Though she had seen him only hours ago, she realized that she didn't want a day to go by without hearing that deep, gentle voice and that rumbling laughter she could so easily provoke in him.

Another two inches of snow fell that night, and the wind drove the white stuff into drifts as high as horses' backs along the hedgerows. Many of the trees, still heavy with leaves, had broken under the weight, and the countryside was littered with broken limbs and splintered branches.

Even Papa stayed home the next day to deal with the havoc the storm had caused. Stella bundled up and went out to help clean up the mess in the farmyard, but when Papa forced her back inside after an hour, she thought she would go mad. She wondered what James was doing and whether he would go to the library for their regular Thursday session. She wondered if he was as disappointed as she to have lost two opportunities to spend time together.

Finally, on Friday, the sun came out, the winds calmed, and Papa hitched the horses to the sleigh and declared that Stella could accompany him to town. It was as though she'd been lying beneath a load of bricks for the past two days and finally, blessedly, someone had come and removed them from her body.

Papa let her take the reins, and as the horses trotted along the icy road into town, Stella's hands and face felt frozen, but her heart was toasty warm. Though she didn't have an appointment scheduled with James today, she had a feeling that she would see him anyway.

Sure enough, as she crossed the campus in the middle of the morning, carefully minding her footing on the snowy pathways, she heard her name called out. That masculine voice had haunted her dreams more nights than she could count, and as she turned toward the sound, her heart began to thump in her chest.

"Why, hello, James," she said, striving to effect a nonchalant air. "Isn't this something?" Her gaze swept the campus, which looked like a war zone. Though work crews had already picked up many of the limbs, the quadrangle was still littered with smaller branches and ice-encased leaves, and the sidewalks were lined with foot-high snowdrifts.

James had smiled when she'd first turned to greet him, but

he ignored her question. There was a timbre to his voice that she couldn't interpret. "Stella, I—I'd like to speak to you."

She tilted her head, curious. "Right now?"

"Do you have a minute?"

"Well. . ." She turned to glance up at the tower clock behind her. "I have a class at eleven, James. I really can't be tardy again." She flashed him a coy smile at this blatant reminder of their first meeting, but he seemed not to notice. He appeared to be agitated and preoccupied.

"Is something wrong?" she asked, reaching out to put a hand on his arm.

"No. . .no." He shook his head and gave her a smile that didn't seem quite genuine. "It can wait. I—I just need to talk to you sometime. Will you be free after this class? I'd be happy to share my lunch with you."

She patted the bag that hung from her shoulder. "Thank you, James. But I brought my lunch. I'd like to eat with you, though."

"Good." He glanced around the grounds of the academy and pulled the collar of his coat up around his neck. "I guess it's not exactly picnic weather. Why don't we meet at the library at noon? Maybe our study room will be empty."

She nodded her agreement, only slightly reassured by his reference to "our study room."

Stella might as well have not been present in her history class. The professor had allowed them another week to study for the test, and now he droned on and on—something about the repercussions of the French Revolution on the economy. Stella scarcely heard a word he said, wondering why James had seemed so anxious to talk to her.

After her class was dismissed, she hurried to the library and went to reserve the room where they had enjoyed so many hours together. She sat at the little table, daydreaming of James's face, his voice, the sound of his laughter. But when he had not appeared almost an hour later, Stella ate her lunch alone. She finished, but still she waited in the room, getting up every few minutes to peer into the hallway to see if he was coming. Her thoughts were a tangled jumble, wondering why he hadn't shown up. She skipped her afternoon mathematics class, and by then, she didn't know whether to be worried sick or mad as a wet hen. Finally, when the clock in the main hall chimed five o'clock, she gathered her belongings and went to wait at the edge of campus where Papa had promised to collect her in the sleigh.

That night Stella helped her mother and sister clear the dishes from the table while Papa stoked the fire before settling into his big chair in the parlor. At supper, Papa had mentioned that he'd met Dr. Whitestone for tea that morning. She was anxious to find out whether they'd spoken of James. Perhaps Papa could shed some light on why James had failed to make their appointment.

The minute she came into the parlor, Papa put his newspaper down, leaned over, and patted the chair beside him. "Come. Sit for a minute, Stella. There's something we need to discuss."

Stella didn't like the sound of this. She watched her father's face closely as she settled in the chair that Mama usually occupied in the evenings. She heard Helen reading to Mama in the kitchen.

"Yes, Papa. What is it?"

"I had a visit with Arthur Whitestone this morning. He tells me that you and this James Collingwood have been spending a great deal of time together." He gazed into the fire, not looking at her, apparently waiting for a reply.

Stella didn't know how to respond. "You know we have, Papa. He tutors me each Tuesday and Thursday afternoon, and he's been walking me to the mill each evening for some time now. But you know all that."

"Arthur says you've come by his office on Mr. Collingwood's arm on several occasions."

She nodded. "Yes, Papa. I sometimes stop by Dr. White-stone's office with James on our way to the mill. He. . . he offers his arm as any gentleman would."

Her father cleared his throat. "I learned some rather disturbing things about Mr. Collingwood this morning, Stella. I've asked Dr. Whitestone to assign you a new tutor."

"But, Papa, why?" She couldn't imagine what could have possessed her father to do such a thing.

He turned to her and looked her in the eye. "I don't believe an explanation is necessary, Stella, but I know you well enough to know that you will badger me until you find out the truth, so I'm going to do you the courtesy of telling you what I know, with the understanding that this information is to stay in this room."

Stella's curiosity about what Papa had heard almost overwhelmed her anger at his actions.

"Do you understand what I'm saying, Stella Mae?"

"Yes, Papa, but—"

He stopped her with an upraised palm. "I am not a man to judge another by the deeds of his past, Stella, and what I am about to tell you does seem to be in the past. Nevertheless, when it comes to my daughter, I believe a man's past is an important factor."

"Papa! What are you talking about?"

Marcus Bradford leaned forward in his chair, put his elbows on his knees, and tented his fingers beneath his bearded chin. "It seems that James Collingwood got into a bit of trouble a few years ago. The details aren't important, but it involved a serious crime—theft, if you must know. As I understand it, the young man has made restitution, and Arthur believes him to be rehabilitated. I trust Arthur's judgment, and I'm willing to let time prove Mr. Collingwood's sincerity. But until it has been sufficiently proven, I want you to have nothing to do with him."

"Papa! You can't be serious! Theft? James would never do anything like that!"

Her father was silent for a moment, gazing again into the crackling flames. When he finally spoke, his voice was soft, but Stella didn't miss the waver it held when he told her, "Then you have just proven your poor discernment where the man is concerned, Stella, because Arthur heard the story from James Collingwood himself. It seems that Mr. Collingwood was employed for a time at the hotel in Barton's Grove. He was caught stealing from the owner. Quite a large sum of money, as I understand it. I don't mind telling you that the fact that Mr. Collingwood has chosen to keep this information from you offers me no comfort."

Stella's mind was reeling. What Papa said couldn't be true! Yes, James had hinted at a rebellious period of his youth. But the things he had said implied the usual boyish tomfoolery—turning over privies and other harmless pranks, she had imagined. Not criminal activity!

But Papa said Dr. Whitestone had heard it from James himself. It must be true, then. And of course, this explained why James had broken their appointment this morning. Her heart lurched, and her face flushed as she realized what a fool she'd made of herself defending James to Papa. No, she corrected herself, it was *James* who had made a fool of her. Her hands began to tremble, and she wished James were here so she could give him a piece of her mind.

Instead, she stuttered, "Papa, I don't know what to say. I–I assure you, James has been nothing but a gentleman toward me."

Papa reached out and put a warm hand on her arm. "Stella, from what Arthur says, it appears that young Collingwood is making an effort to reform. However, this black mark on his past causes me to feel very cautious, particularly when I learn that my daughter is spending an inordinate amount of time with the man and, in addition, he has told her none of his story." Again, Papa cleared his throat noisily. "I have requested that Arthur assign you a new tutor. I trust that will relieve Mr. Collingwood of the opportunity to accompany you to the mill after your sessions, but should he persist, I want you to let me know immediately and I will see to it that the man leaves you alone."

"But, Papa—"

"I don't intend to discuss the matter further, Stella. If Mr. Collingwood has kept his record untarnished a year or two from now and if he still has an interest in pursuing a respectable courtship with you at that time, we shall revisit the matter. Until such time, I have asked Arthur to see to it that his assistant has no dealings with my daughter." Papa picked up his newspaper and turned his back on her.

Chapter 5

P lease, I'd like to speak to Mr. Collingwood."
The young girl behind the desk in the antechamber of Arthur Whitestone's office in Voorhaven Hall was preoccupied, sorting a stack of what looked like examination papers. She barely glanced up at Stella. "He's teaching this morning, Miss."

"Oh. Do. . .do you know which class he's teaching?"

The girl puffed out her cheeks with annoyance and put her work aside. She opened a drawer of the desk and took out a schedule. Running her finger down the columns, she said, "It looks like he's filling in for Professor Cramer in Room 201 Andrews. That class gets out at half past ten."

"Thank you." Stella hurried from the building and started across campus. Leaving the narrow brick walk, she tromped through the snow, taking a shortcut across the lawn. She paused for an anxious glimpse at the tower clock. Quarter past ten. She should be able to catch him if she waited outside the entrance to Andrews Hall. Brushing off the snow that had blown onto the bench in front of the building, Stella pulled her collar close and sat down to wait.

She stayed there, shivering, for twenty minutes. The carillon clock chimed the half hour, and the campus filled with students. But a few minutes later, the crowd of young people thinned, most of them inside again for the last class of the morning. And still no sign of James.

Stella stood, put her hands on her hips, and spun full circle to scan the pathways that radiated like the spokes of a wagon wheel toward the immense limestone buildings. Laughter drifted from a distance down one walk, and she spotted James Collingwood strolling her way. But Stella tensed as she saw the young woman at his side. The girl was flirting boldly and giggling, as though James were not only the best-looking man on campus but also the funniest.

A streak of jealousy shot through Stella, though she could hardly fault the girl. As the two came closer, Stella recognized Iva Mae Waxler, a first-year student who was in her English Grammar class—the same class in which Stella had met James. She started down the walk to meet them, and James greeted her with something like relief in his eyes.

"Hello," Stella said, looking pointedly at James. She suddenly realized that she had no idea what she would say to him. But she had to talk to him—alone. She forced a smile in Iva Mae's direction. "Hello, Iva Mae."

"Oh. . .hi, Stella," the girl said, as though she'd just noticed Stella's presence.

James gave Stella a look she couldn't interpret and glanced at his watch. "Well, I hope I've answered your questions, Miss Waxler," he said to the student. Then, turning to Stella as though he owed her an explanation, he said, "Iva Mae had some questions about the essay assignment."

Iva Mae bestowed an adoring smile on James. "Mr. Collingwood has been *so* helpful," she gushed, her voice revealing her Atlanta roots. "I don't know what I'd do without his help."

"Just doing my job," he said, tipping his hat and coloring slightly. "Well, good day, Miss Waxler."

The young woman's smile drooped, but she said, "I'll see you this afternoon for our tutoring session, won't I?"

James's color deepened. "Yes. . .yes, of course."

Iva Mae wished them good day and turned to walk slowly up the path toward Andrews Hall.

"How are you, Stella?" James's tone was polite but distant, exactly as it had been with Iva Mae.

"James? What is going on?"

He took a step back, as though he were uncomfortable being so close to her. Looking down at his boots, he said, "I assume your father informed you of his discussion with Dr. Whitestone?"

"Oh, James, it's all mixed up! He's forbade me to see you! Papa heard some things—awful rumors—that make him think you've done something terrible."

James ran his fingers through his hair, and when he looked up, she saw that his face had paled.

"Tell me what he heard, Stella."

His voice was a low monotone, and she almost imagined that he was trembling. Watching him, she knew it couldn't be true. Her James was simply not capable of the things of which he'd been accused.

"Dr. Whitestone told him you'd been arrested for stealing! From the hotel in Barton's Grove. Isn't that preposterous?

You've probably never even *been* to Barton's Grove! I think Papa is just looking for any excuse to keep us apart. He didn't want me going to the academy in the first place, and now he's afraid someone is going to take his precious little girl away—"

James took a step toward her and placed his hands on her shoulders. "Stella, we need to talk."

Something in the tone of his voice frightened her, but she couldn't seem to stop babbling. "He's just an old ogre!" She stamped her foot. "I knew he'd try to keep us apart. I just knew it—"

Again, he spoke the words. "We have to talk, Stella."

"What, James? What is it?" Her heart was beating like a drum. After Papa had told her the news last night, she'd been angry with James. But now, seeing his kind face, hearing his voice, she knew that even if what Papa had said were true, anyone who knew James now knew that he'd straightened out his life. She didn't know a more generous, kind, upstanding gentleman. Perhaps he'd had some trouble in his past. He had told her that he'd been a bit of a rebel in his youth. Granted, he'd never given her the details. But that was all in the past. It didn't matter now. Papa just needed to give him a chance.

Silently, James steered her down a short sidewalk to the stairs that led into Andrews Hall. He slumped onto the top step and pulled her down beside him. "Your father is right, Stella."

"What? What are you talking about, James?"

His Adam's apple bobbed in his throat, and his words came out in a whisper. "I *was* caught stealing. In Barton's Grove. . . just like your father said."

Her breath caught. "But. . .why didn't you tell me, James?"

He tipped her chin, forcing her to look at him. "You must

believe me, Stella. I didn't mean to keep it from you. I've never lied to you. You have to believe that. But neither have I told you everything. And that was wrong of me."

"I–I know you said you'd done some wild things, but James, stealing?"

He pressed his fingertips to his temples. Then as he stared at the ground, the story unfolded. "I was sixteen. Sylvia became ill, and Mother couldn't work any longer. Since I was the oldest, I was expected to provide for them. I took a job at the hotel. It was hard, going to school all day and working till late at night, but it was the only way to put food on our table. Except that Sylvia's medicine took almost every dime I made. I got to eat for free in the hotel's kitchen, and sometimes Mr. Browne—the owner—let me bring home scraps. But Sylvia and Mama were hungry all the time, Stella. It about killed me to see them near-starving like that."

James paused, and she waited in silence for him to continue.

"I–I made a terrible decision, a foolish, stupid mistake—one I'll regret for the rest of my life." He swallowed hard. "One night the cashier accidentally left the cash register open. I was dusting the front desk and the drawer just slid open and there in front of me seemed to be the answer to all my problems. I took the money, Stella. All of it. I know. . .I know how stupid it sounds now. And I intended to pay every cent back, truly I did. But of course I got caught before that could happen."

"Oh, James," she breathed. She didn't know whether to be angry or whether to cry for the foolish, desperate boy he'd been back then. "What happened? Did you. . .did you go to jail?"

"No. The owner of the hotel forgave me. In fact, he gave me a job in the dining room waiting tables at a wage almost twice what I'd made before—on the condition that I pay him half my earnings until I'd repaid what I stole."

"But if he forgave you, how did Papa hear about it after all these years?"

James picked up a clump of snow from the side of the walkway. He formed it into a hard ball and threw it forcefully to the ground. Anger and frustration were revealed in his action, but the look he gave her was one of adoration. "You're so innocent, Stella. Don't you know 'once a thief, always a thief'? The word was all over town about what happened. If Mr. Browne hadn't been willing to keep me on, I guarantee you I would never have worked anywhere in the county again. But God was with me, Stella. You have to believe that. After Mr. Browne forgave me, I dedicated my life to the Lord all over again. I prayed so hard that God would make a way for me to go to university. It seemed as though I were praying for the impossible. Then that Christmas Mr. Browne handed me an envelope—and inside was more money than I had ever dreamed of saving. From that day on, I never doubted God's care for me, and I knew He'd truly given me a second chance."

Stella wanted to offer some comfort, some comment on the things he'd confessed, but she found herself uncharacteristically speechless.

James took her hand in his. "I'm sorry, Stella," he said. "I should have told you before. And I don't blame your father for not wanting you to have anything to do with me. If you were my daughter, I'd feel the same way."

She looked into his eyes, and she could find nothing there that hinted of a thief or a scoundrel. All she saw was her precious James. Papa didn't know him. Papa was making his judgment based on cold, impersonal facts. But she knew her father well enough to know that he'd made up his mind about James, and nothing she could say or do would cause him to change it.

"Stella, I'm so sorry. I—I've grown to care for you deeply. But I can't ask you to go against your father's wishes. He's only doing what he thinks is best for the daughter he loves. I—I shouldn't even be talking to you now, but I couldn't leave things unsettled between us. I wanted you to hear the truth from me."

"Oh, James. I don't hold what you did against you. I know you've changed. From what you say, anyone could see that you had a good reason for what you did."

"Thank you, Stella. That means a great deal to me. But it doesn't change the fact that your father has forbidden you to see me."

She put a hand on his arm. "It's not fair. I have to convince him to get to know you. Can't Dr. Whitestone vouch for you?"

"From what I understand, he already did. But your father isn't thinking about me, Stella. He's thinking about his daughter. And that's only right. I certainly understand his concern."

Somehow she had to convince Papa to get to know James, to see the man she knew. The strong, loving, honest man who sat beside her now, his head bowed in defeat.

"I'll talk to him, James," she cried. "I'll convince him that you've changed. He has to see that—"

"Stop it, Stella." James stood abruptly and backed down the steps away from her. "I think it's best that we leave well enough alone. Perhaps what is between us"—his hand traced an invisible path from his heart to hers—"simply wasn't meant to be."

Tears sprang to her eyes and with them the vision of Iva Mae Waxler clinging to James's arm. She thought she understood then. Perhaps she had misunderstood James's intentions all along. Maybe she had read something into his kindness, into his warm smile that wasn't really there. At least not the way she'd imagined.

Feeling like a fool, she struggled to her feet and ran through the snow. She didn't stop running until she reached the sanctuary of the library. She hurried through the stacks until she found a quiet corner at the back of the massive room. There she silently wept until there were no more tears.

Chapter 6

James Collingwood stood in front of Andrews Hall and watched Stella run away from him. He knew by the slump of her shoulders as she fled that she was crying. Twice she nearly tripped as her skirt became heavy with accumulated snow. Everything in him wanted to go after her, take her in his arms, and comfort her. But what good would that have done either of them? It would only make the inevitable more difficult.

Dr. Whitestone had called him into his office that morning to inform him of Marcus Bradford's request for a new tutor for his daughter. Bradford wanted James Collingwood to have nothing to do with Stella.

"I don't understand," James had told his mentor. "Have I done something wrong?"

Dr. Whitestone hung his head. "James, I'm afraid I'm unwittingly to blame for this."

James looked at him, confusion in his eyes.

"Marcus asked me about you and I—I foolishly took it upon myself to tell the man your story. I had no right, James. I'm sorry. The man is a good friend of mine and an honorable gentleman. I promise you, I told him your story because I believe it to be one of the finest testimonies to the power of God to redeem a man that I've ever heard. But I didn't take into account that Marcus was asking after you because of his daughter's. . . um, shall we say. . .interest in you. He reacted in a way I never expected. "

James was stunned by Dr. Whitestone's revelation. On more than one occasion, Stella had warned him that her father was overly protective. That was one of the reasons he'd been reluctant to tell her his story. But he'd never expected repercussions of this magnitude.

Apparently Marcus Bradford had also requested that James not be allowed to substitute in any class Stella attended. Arthur Whitestone had drawn the line there.

"I informed Marcus that I would not allow his mollycoddling of his daughter to interfere with the way we conduct the department," the professor told James. "Having no daughters myself, I can't say that I understand the man's obsession. I'm sorry, James, but I did promise him that I would assign Stella a new tutor. I apologize. What he's requested is not fair, but I know you'll understand that I need to accommodate the man as much as I possibly can. He's not only my friend and the father of a student of St. Bartholomew's, but he's a generous benefactor of the academy, as well."

James nodded and dared to ask his superior if he thought Marcus Bradford would ever change his mind.

"Well, I wouldn't hold my breath, Son." Arthur Whitestone sighed. "I'll be glad to put in a good word for you. Not that it will do any good. I already sang your praises when Marcus approached me, and you can see where it got me."

James had declined the offer. If he couldn't win Stella's

father over himself, there was no use sending someone else to do it.

Now with the damage done, James sighed, brushed the snow from his pant legs, and retrieved his valise from the bottom step. He had papers to mark and a lesson to prepare for tomorrow. He'd always known that his youthful transgressions might catch up with him. No sense in being surprised and hurt over it now.

But his heart was heavy as he trudged to Voorhaven Hall. He gathered his belongings from the office and started across town. He would work in his room at home tonight. Maybe he'd talk over his troubles with Sylvia. His sister always had a sympathetic ear and a wise word for him.

The following Monday, Stella walked into Dr. Whitestone's class to find James Collingwood substituting in the professor's stead.

He nodded a barely perceptible greeting as she entered the room. She took her seat and began copying the sentences from the board with trembling fingers. For the rest of the hour, she felt his eyes upon her. Looking at him made her ache with longing. Her emotions were so muddled that she feared she would burst into tears at any moment. When the class period ended, Stella stayed in her seat, meaning to linger until the room cleared and she could talk to James alone. But several students went forward with questions, and when fifteen minutes had passed and one young man still stood in line waiting to speak with the instructor, she began to feel awkward. She knew James was aware of her presence in the back of the room, for he glanced her way every few minutes. But she could not read in his expression whether he wished her to remain or was imploring her to leave.

Finally, she slipped out of the room, feeling lower in spirit than she could ever remember.

For the rest of the week, Stella merely went through the motions of living. She rode with her father each day to the academy, she attended classes, she even worked with the new tutor Dr. Whitestone had assigned. The young graduate student was a perfectly pleasant—and quite handsome—fifth-year student. But for Stella, the lessons had become drudgery.

She did not see James again that week. She was ever watchful, hoping to catch a glimpse of his broad-shouldered form striding across the campus grounds or huddled in a study carrel in the library. But it was as though he were purposely avoiding the places where he knew she might be.

She tried to put the vision of James and Iva Mae Waxler head-to-head in the study room at Robinson Library out of her mind, but the image refused to leave. When Iva Mae approached Stella after their English grammar class on Friday morning, asking if Stella knew what had happened to Mr. Collingwood, Stella became alarmed. "What do you mean?" she asked.

"I just wondered if you knew where he's been. You seem to have the inside track where Mr. Collingwood is concerned," she drawled.

"But. . .isn't he tutoring you, Iva Mae?" she asked the girl, ignoring the sarcastic dig.

Iva Mae shook her head sadly. "Some other gent showed up, and he's the one been coming ever since. You don't suppose Mr. Collingwood's left St. Bart's, do you?"

Stella didn't know, and she began to worry that something was wrong. If Iva Mae hadn't seen James, then that quashed Stella's fears that James's interests had turned to the Southern belle. But what had happened to him? Her thoughts churning, she extricated herself from Iva Mae's diatribe about the English department and hurried toward Dr. Whitestone's office.

A new girl sat behind the desk in the anteroom, and Stella took advantage of the fact. "I'm here to see Dr. Whitestone," she said, trying to make it sound as though she had an appointment.

The girl glanced at the ledger on the desk. "Why, I don't believe he's expecting anyone this afternoon. What did you say your name was?"

"I'm Stella Bradford. Please tell Dr. Whitestone I'm here."

Looking again at the schedule, then shaking her head in bewilderment, the girl went back to the office suite and knocked on Dr. Whitestone's door before opening it a crack. "Sir? There's a Stella Bradford to see you."

Stella could not make out the professor's reply, but the girl motioned for Stella. She slipped into the office, a sheepish smile on her face. "I'm sorry, Dr. Whitestone, but I had to talk to you. I'm worried about James. . .Mr. Collingwood. No one has seen him all week and—"

Arthur Whitestone interrupted her with a raised hand, then gestured toward the leather-seated chair in front of his desk. "Please, Miss Bradford. Have a seat." He gave her a smile that she knew was meant to reassure.

She sat down and waited while Dr. Whitestone seemed to scrutinize her face.

Finally, he told her. "You were inquiring about Mr. Collingwood's absence?"

She nodded anxiously.

"James's sister was taken ill on Monday. He requested the rest of the week off to care for her."

Stella knew that her relief must have been written on her face. "Is Sylvia—is his sister seriously ill?"

"I believe she suffers chronic health problems. But James stopped by the office here midweek to pick up some papers to mark, and at that time he thought she seemed to be improving. I don't believe it's anything for you to worry about."

Dr. Whitestone had a strange look on his face, and for a moment Stella was afraid he was going to reprimand her for barging into his office to inquire after things that were none of her business. Instead, he cleared his throat and leaned forward over the desk. "Miss Bradford," he said haltingly, "I feel I owe you an explanation."

Stella's puzzlement must have been apparent because he held up a hand and promptly continued.

"I don't know what your father—or James, for that matter—has said to you regarding my part in. . .well, in your father's decision to have Mr. Collingwood replaced as your tutor. I suspect one of them has told you that I had something to do with all that."

He paused, and Stella could sense that he was hoping she would tell him precisely what she did know. She was grateful for his honesty and quickly reassured him. "I know you meant no harm, Dr. Whitestone. It's just that Papa is—"

The professor saved her from having to finish the sentence. "Your father is a good man, Stella. And I trust you know that I had no idea my telling him about James would have the effect it did. As I'm sure you know, he loves you dearly and would not see you hurt for the world. On the other hand, I happen to believe that there is a young man who loves you equally dearly, though in quite a different way."

Stella's heart began to pound. Had Dr. Whitestone just said what she thought he'd said? "I–I don't understand. . ."

The professor thought for a moment. "If you truly don't understand, then it's not my place to say more, Miss Bradford. Let me only say that I believe your father will come to his senses. I'm praying that he will. For James's sake."

As Dr. Whitestone rose and came from behind his desk, he muttered, "If I have to see that lovesick young pup moping around here much longer. . ."

"What did you say?" Stella asked. But she had heard the man's words perfectly well. And they set her heart soaring.

"Nothing, nothing," he replied. "I'm glad you stopped by, Stella. I'll give James your greetings."

"Y–yes," she stuttered. "Please do."

She practically ran from the building. Dr. Whitestone, James's confidant, had called him—what was it?—a lovesick pup. That had to be a good sign.

Chapter 7

As she guided the horses down the land, Stella waved good-bye to Mama. Helen snuggled close beside her in the sleigh, and the horses trotted onto the country road. It would only take a few minutes to get into town. At her feet, wrapped in newspaper and a heavy quilt, was the basket of fried chicken and brown Betty she and Mama had fixed for James and Sylvia. Mama had even added some of her home-canned peaches.

Papa hadn't been crazy about the idea, but Mama had worked her wiles with him. Mama didn't very often argue against Papa, but when she did, he usually listened. He had finally agreed that Helen would accompany Stella. They could hitch the team on the street in front of James's boardinghouse and deliver their offerings. "But you come directly home after that, you understand?" he'd warned. Stella didn't care. At least she would get to see James, if only for a minute.

The horses picked up their pace on the open road, and Stella reveled in the feel of the wind in her face. She had forgotten how free she felt riding in the sleigh. Though she was always a little nervous to have the team under her control, it was exhilarating to glide so smoothly along the road. So different from riding in the wagon, which seemed to emphasize every little bump and rut. Since the storm, sleds and sleighs that had traveled over the road had forged a fine path, and the sleigh and team seemed to obey the slightest sway of the reins. Stella began to relax and loosened her grip on the reins a bit. She didn't even mind the cold.

She glanced over at Helen. Her sister's face reflected her elation, her cheeks rosy from the icy bite in the air, her lips parted in a wide smile.

"It's fun, isn't it?" Stella shouted over the jangle of the harnesses and the clatter of the horses' hooves on the hard-packed snow.

"Can I drive, Stella?" Helen shot back.

Stella shook her head vigorously. "Papa would have my head! Besides, I was almost seventeen before Papa let me take the team out on my own. You'll have to be patient and wait until you grow up a little."

Helen pouted for a moment, but it wasn't long before the smile was back on her face and she was reveling in the ride again.

When the silhouette of Clairemore appeared ahead, Stella slowed the team. As they came into town, she saw that the snow had been shoveled into tall heaps along the street corners. After standing through two bitterly cold nights, the piles of snow had turned into veritable icebergs. They made it more difficult to maneuver the sleigh, and Stella's muscles tensed as she watched the street in front of her carefully.

Fortunately, she didn't need to change direction until she reached James's house. They glided smoothly through town on

Main Street, past the mill, until the older neighborhood where Sylvia's boardinghouse stood came into view. The street narrowed, and an avenue of icicle-draped trees formed a canopy over the brick pavement. The sun had begun to thaw the ice that encased each branch, and the air was filled with an odd popping sound as branches broke loose from their frosty cocoons, followed by the sound of shattering glass as icicles hit the brick. Occasionally, a spray of freezing water and ice shards would land on the blanket that covered their laps, and Helen would let out a little squeal of delight.

Carefully steering the team, Stella called a low "Whoa" and brought the horses to a halt along the curb. She jumped down from the sleigh and reached over the side to retrieve the wrapped basket of food.

"You wait right here, Helen," she told her sister. "I'll only be a minute."

"Why can't I go with you?"

"Because," she said evasively. "Now sit still. Don't scare the horses."

With her heart racing, Stella walked up to the front entrance and rapped the brass knocker against the oaken door. Within a few minutes, she heard footsteps. Her heart pounded in her ears.

The door opened slowly. She faced James. "Stella? Hello. What. . .what brings you here?"

She held out the basket. "I heard Sylvia was ill. We wanted to bring you some chicken and some other things—to help out a bit. I hope Sylvia is feeling better."

"She's improving, I think. Slowly." He took the basket from her hands, but his eyes never left her face. "Thank you,

Stella. This is very kind of you."

"Well, I didn't make it by myself. Mama fried the chicken. I—I helped make the brown Betty. And there are peaches from Mama's orchard. She canned them this summer. We thought you might enjoy them. They're really quite good. Oh. . .and Mama would like to have the jar back." She was babbling like a flustered old woman, but she couldn't seem to stop herself.

"Thank you, Stella. It. . .it's so good to see you." She suspected that the expression in his eyes was much like what he must be seeing in her own. In that moment, all her doubts about James—his past, his character, even his relationship with Iva Mae Waxler—vanished. She knew that the man who stood in front of her, this man who had taken time away from a job he loved to care for his ailing sister, was as kind and generous and honorable as she'd always thought him to be.

"Oh, James, I've missed you so."

"I've missed you, too, Stella," he said softly. "You said your mother helped with the food. Does. . .does that mean your father knows you're here?" He looked to the street beyond her as though he half-expected to see Marcus Bradford waiting for her.

She inclined her head toward the sleigh. "Yes, Papa knows. He sent Helen with me—to chaperone, I think—and he gave strict instructions that I'm not to stay for any length of time."

His shoulders slumped. "So he hasn't changed his mind about us seeing one another?"

She shook her head sadly. "I don't think so, James." She stamped her foot on the porch. "Oh, I hate this!" she cried out in frustration. "I hate it that Papa has practically exiled me. I hate it that we—"

Her words were lost in a deafening *boom*. A few yards in front of the sleigh, a heavy branch had fallen under the weight of ice and snow, crashing to the ground and spraying ice and water in every direction.

Startled, the horses bolted, but the fallen branch was directly in their path. One steed veered to avoid the obstacle, but the other reared up on its hind legs, causing the sleigh to tip precariously.

Helen's screams pierced the air, and even from the porch, Stella could see that her sister's face was a mask of terror as the team dragged the sleigh over the curb and onto a sloping lawn. Narrowly missing the broad trunk of the sturdy oak from which the branch had fallen, one runner under the sleigh slid up over a rock-hard drift of compacted snow.

Stella stood paralyzed as the sled toppled over onto its side. Helen was thrown from the seat like a rag doll. The child flew through the air and landed in a heap on the snow with a sickening thud. Stella watched in horror as the overturned sleigh skidded across the lawn, shuddered, and came to rest on the very spot where Helen's crumpled form had landed. The dead silence that filled the air in the aftermath of the calamity caused Stella's heart to cease beating.

Chapter 8

Before Stella could cry out his name, James flew off the porch and raced to the neighboring yard where the overturned sleigh rested. He bent to peer under the body of the sleigh, then quickly placed his hands beneath it. Straining under its weight, he lifted the carriage a few inches off the ground.

"Stella!" he shouted. "I need your help! She's trapped underneath."

The urgency in his voice brought her to her senses, and as the meaning of his words registered, Stella ran to his side, her breath coming in short, painful gasps. Together, they lifted the sleigh, and when they got it a few feet off the ground, James wedged one shoulder underneath its frame to hold it steady.

One horse was down, forelegs flailing in an effort to stand. The other pawed at the ground, trying to free itself from the dead weight of the sled, which tethered it to the spot. James spoke low, soothing syllables meant to calm the beasts.

"Oh, please, God. Please don't let her be dead," Stella prayed through sobs.

"Crawl under there and see if you can drag her out," James ordered, breathless from bearing the heavy weight on his back. "Check for broken bones first."

Stella knelt in the snow and scrambled under the sleigh. Helen was lying prone on the ground, her red coat a startling stain on the pristine snow. Her form was as still as a hitching post on a windless day, and Stella feared the worst. She bent and put her head beside her sister's face. Helen's breathing was shallow and uneven, but Stella silently thanked God that the girl was breathing at all.

The canopy made by the sleigh blocked out what was left of the waning sunlight, but Stella did her best to feel Helen's limbs through the girl's heavy coat and boots. Gently, she rolled her sister's slight form over, and throwing off her gloves, she worked the large buttons on Helen's coat. The little girl gave a low moan.

"Helen! Helen? Can you hear me? Say something, Helen," she pleaded.

James's voice came from above her, muffled and tight with fear and exertion. "Do you think you can drag her out into the open, Stella?"

"I'll try," she panted.

Stella pulled the red coat snug around the little girl and fastened the topmost button. Then moving to huddle near Helen's head, she rose to her knees and grabbed onto the collar of the coat. She backed out, inch by painful inch, dragging Helen from beneath the precariously balanced sleigh.

All the while, his back to them, James held the thing steady, anchoring it upon one strong shoulder as he continued to speak softly to the frantic horses.

When Stella was sure she and Helen were clear of the sleigh, she shouted, "We're out, James. You can let go now."

"You're sure?"

"Yes, we're clear."

He lowered his shoulder and staggered back. The carriage dropped with a resounding *bang*. Stella saw him rub his shoulder and wince, but he turned and hurried over to where she was working over her sister.

"Is she breathing?" he asked, reaching up to lift each pale little eyelid.

"Yes, but just barely."

The commotion had brought a parade of neighbors from surrounding homes. Stella heard someone shout that they'd go for the doctor. A group of young men worked together to right the sleigh and get the downed horse on its feet.

James had taken off his vest and folded it into a pillow to place under Helen's neck. Together, he and Stella inspected the girl for blood and bruises, finding only the latter. Several times Helen's eyelids fluttered, but each time she gave a breathy sigh and drifted from consciousness again.

Stella suddenly realized that Dr. Pulliam and Papa were standing beside her. With deep relief, she left Helen's side to make room for the doctor. Even as Dr. Pulliam quickly examined Helen for broken bones and internal injuries, the little girl started to come around.

Stella ran into Papa's arms and he held her close.

"What happened?" he whispered, his gaze trained on Helen's piteous form.

"Helen was waiting in the sleigh while I delivered the food to. . .to Mr. Collingwood and his sister."

She looked around for James and spotted him helping with the horses.

"That branch fell and spooked the team," she continued, pointing to where the limb had landed. "The horses bolted and overturned the sleigh. Oh, Papa, it was awful! Helen was trapped underneath."

"Underneath?" her father gasped. "However did she get out?"

"James held the sleigh up so I could drag her out from under. I thought she was dead, Papa!"

"He held it up by himself?"

"Yes, Papa. And it took me a long while to get her out."

She told her father the whole story then, but before she could finish, Papa put his hands on her shoulders and looked her in the eye. "Wait right here," he said.

He spoke briefly with the doctor, then strode to where James was working to untangle a badly twisted harness. Stella watched with wide eyes as Papa shook James Collingwood's hand and spoke quietly to him. She couldn't hear all their words, but she knew by Papa's demeanor and the timbre of his voice that he was expressing his deep gratitude to James.

As he started to step away, Stella heard her father tell him, "I'd like you to stop by our house tomorrow evening if you could, Mr. Collingwood. I know my wife will want to offer you a proper thank-you."

Though Stella had been waiting on pins and needles for James's knock, when it finally came, she began to tremble inside. "He's here!"

Helen giggled and ran to admit their caller. Stella was right behind her.

Helen opened the door. James stood on the porch, looking handsome as ever.

"Hello, Stella," he said, tipping his hat.

"Hello, James." They stood staring at one another, and Stella felt unexpectedly shy.

She felt a tug on her skirt. "Aren't you going to ask him in?" Helen's silvery voice cut through the fog in her brain.

"Oh, my," she breathed. "Of course. What am I thinking? Please, James. Come in."

She opened the door wider, and he ducked under the lintel, removing his hat as he stepped inside.

Papa and Mama came into the hallway and stood, waiting to be introduced.

James nodded in their direction, and Stella finally came to her senses. "Papa, you remember Mr. Collingwood?"

"Pleased to see you again, Sir," James said, extending his hand. The two men shook hands, then James turned toward Mama. "And you must be Stella's mother. I can certainly see the resemblance."

Mama blushed at what was obviously meant to be a compliment. As she took James's hand, her gratitude poured out, mingled with tears. "Oh, Mr. Collingwood, how can we ever thank you?"

"No need, Ma'am. I didn't do more than any other man would have done under the circumstances. Stella is the one who should get the credit." He gave her a smile that turned her knees to jelly.

"You were both very brave," Mama told him. "Stella couldn't have gotten to Helen if it hadn't been for you. We are mighty grateful, Son, mighty grateful."

James knelt beside Helen, who stood in the hall staring up at him with a gaze of absolute adoration. "And how is Miss Helen feeling this evening? Have you recovered from your little adventure?"

She gave him her sweetest smile. "Yes, Sir. I'm feeling fine." She bowed her head shyly. "Thank you for. . .for saving me."

"You are very welcome, Helen," James said, putting a gentle hand to her cheek. "I couldn't have done it without your sister's help."

Helen nodded solemnly.

"Please, come into the parlor," Mama urged. "I have cocoa on the stove, and Stella made a cake."

Stella and her mother served refreshments in the parlor. Papa and James seemed to have found several common interests, and the women could scarcely get a word in edgewise. Stella couldn't have been more delighted.

Later, as James got ready to leave, Mama surprised Stella by issuing an impromptu invitation. "James, we're having dinner at the hotel Saturday night. Why don't you come along and be our guest?"

"Well, Ma'am. Thank you, but that's not necessary. That cake and cocoa were plenty of thanks—"

Papa jumped in. "Please, James. We insist. We'd be honored to have you."

Stella could scarcely believe her ears.

James looked at her, then back at her father. "Well, thank you, Sir." He looked to Mama and nodded his thanks. "Ma'am, I appreciate the invitation. I'd be honored."

Mama beamed, and Stella knew that James had succeeded in charming his way into each of their hearts.

Chapter 9

The dining room was crowded, and the tinkle of silverware and crystal and happy voices made pleasant music to accompany the Bradford party as they dined. But Stella Bradford's thoughts were focused in one direction only. James Collingwood sat across from her at the table, and by the way his eyes had held her gaze throughout the evening, she knew that his thoughts were directed toward her as well.

She could hardly believe that Papa had not only *allowed* James to be here with them but had extended the invitation himself. Helen sat at a place of honor at one end of the table, and she giggled every time James looked her way. He was Helen's hero, but more importantly, James had become Papa's hero.

Mama turned to James. "I hope your sister is feeling better, James. Sylvia, isn't it? I'm sorry she could not be with us tonight."

"Yes, Ma'am. Sylvia is much better, thank you. She asked me to give her regrets. She would have joined us, but there was a special gentleman coming to call this evening."

Stella turned to James with a cry of delight. "Is it John Matthews?"

He nodded, a smile of satisfaction on his face. John worked for Papa at the mill, but he and Sylvia had met when James hired him to do some carpentry work on the boardinghouse.

"Oh, James. I'm so happy for her."

The young girl who was waiting on their table came with the coffeepot, and they fell silent. The girl refilled Mama's cup and began clearing empty dishes from the table.

"Thank you, Miss," Papa said politely as she took away his dinner plate. "Might I ask your name?"

The lass gave him a shy smile. "It's Mariette, Sir."

"A very pretty name," Papa said. "Thank you for serving us tonight. You did a fine job."

Stella could tell the young woman wasn't accustomed to having gratitude shown in such a genuine manner.

"You are most welcome, Sir. It was my pleasure," she said, bobbing her head in a tacit curtsy.

Stella smiled as she thought of the surprise that awaited the girl a few minutes from now.

As though he'd read Stella's mind, Papa reached into his breast pocket and slipped out a small envelope, along with his fountain pen. Before they had left for the hotel, Stella and Helen had watched Papa tuck a five-dollar bank note inside the envelope. Helen had been more fascinated with the intricate depictions of Christopher Columbus on the paper bill than she had been with the idea of what it could buy.

As was their tradition, the Bradfords had prayed at home for the then-unknown person who would serve them their meal. Having observed the girl during the evening, Stella knew that this gift would make a significant difference in the life of young Mariette. She was proud of Papa's generosity and elated—as she

had been every Christmas for as long as she could remember—
to be taking part in this family tradition.

Papa wrote something on the ivory parchment, then closed
the flap and laid the envelope on the table, tucking one corner
beneath the porcelain saucer that held his empty cup.

Stella watched from the corner of her eye. Sure enough,
Mariette's name was spelled out across the front of the envelope in Papa's loopy scrawl.

Stella knew that Papa was trying to be unobtrusive for
James's sake. He had always said that it canceled the deed to
blow your trumpet about it. But Helen was watching, too, and
her eyes lit up. "Can we stay and watch her open it, Papa?"

"Hush," Mama chided, shaking her head.

Papa smiled at his youngest daughter. "You know the rule,
Shortcake."

Helen pouted, and James turned to Stella, his knit brows
indicating puzzlement.

"It's one of our holiday traditions," she whispered.

"I don't understand."

Leaning toward him and lowering her voice, she explained,
"There is a five-dollar note inside the envelope. Every year before Christmas, we choose a night to eat dinner at the hotel. It
gives Mama a break from cooking during the busy holiday season, but the real reason we do it is to bless someone who might
not be as fortunate as we are. We always pray before we come
that God will send the person to wait on us who most needs
an extra Christmas blessing. But the rule is that we can't stay
to watch them open the envelope. We want it to be a good deed
done in secret." Listening to herself, she realized that she sounded
like Mama explaining the special tradition to Helen.

James had a strange expression on his face.

Stella put a hand to her mouth. "Oh, and now I've ruined the secret part by telling you about it, haven't I? I'm sorry, James. I don't mean to crow. But it seemed rude not to explain it to you."

He put up a hand and shook his head. "No, it's not that," he said.

Concern filled Stella's heart. His complexion was pale, and he looked as though he might be sick.

"James? What's wrong?"

Without saying a word, James Collingwood pushed his chair back from the table and hurried from the dining room.

Chapter 10

Papa and Mama exchanged worried glances and turned to Stella for an explanation, but she couldn't begin to offer a motive for James's strange behavior. She shrugged and excused herself from the table.

Weaving her way through the other diners, she went to the lobby. The expansive room was empty, save for an elderly couple waiting at the front desk.

Hurrying through the front doors, Stella stepped into the cold night. Wisps of snow blew across the boardwalk, and she shivered involuntarily. Looking both ways down the darkened street, she spotted a lone figure at the north end of the building.

It was James. He stood, leaning against the brick facade, his head bent against the bitter wind. Though the frigid air bit painfully through her light wool dress, she went to him.

"James? Is everything all right?" *What a silly question.* One glance at his face told her that something was terribly wrong. "James, what is it? What's wrong?"

Without looking at her, his voice a monotone, he asked one question. "Stella, how long has this tradition been going on in your family?"

"The tip, you mean? The five-dollar note?"

He nodded.

"Why, as long as I can remember, I guess. What on earth does that have to do with anything, James? What is going on here? Why——"

"Did your family ever eat at the hotel in Barton's Grove? At Christmastime?" he interrupted.

She wrinkled her brow and tipped her head to one side. "I'm sure we did. We lived there for several years while Papa ran the mill. But I was little. I—I don't remember for certain. Why?"

James stood straighter, and for the first time, he seemed to notice that she had come out into the bitter winter night without her coat. He quickly removed his jacket and wrapped it around her. Keeping his right arm around her shoulders, he gently turned her toward the hotel. "Let's go inside," he said. "I. . .there's something I want to tell you."

They went back inside, and James led her to a narrow settee in a quiet corner of the lobby. Her mind was reeling, unable to imagine what had precipitated James's strange conduct.

He took her hand and looked into her eyes, confusion and awe oddly mingled in his expression. "Do you remember when I told you about that Christmas when I was working at the hotel in Barton's Grove? How I prayed that God would make it possible for me to enroll in the academy?"

"Yes. It was when your boss gave you the envelope—the money, right?" A hint of a memory began to niggle at her consciousness. There was some connection here that she couldn't quite fit together. "That was at Barton's Grove?"

James nodded. "But the money wasn't from Mr. Browne, Stella. It was a tip, a gratuity left on the table in an envelope with my name on it—by a family who had dined there that evening." His words gathered steam as they spilled out.

Stella gasped, and a broad smile spread across James's face.

"Oh, James, are you thinking what I'm thinking? Do you really think it could have been us—our family—that you waited on that night?"

A faraway look came to his eyes. "You know, Stella," he said, "for the longest time I wanted so badly to know who my benefactors were. I couldn't imagine why anyone would show such generosity to a stranger. For a time, I suspected that Mr. Browne just made up that story because he knew I wouldn't accept the money as charity from him. But he always insisted that he knew nothing about it. Finally I just quit asking and accepted the money for what it was—a gift from a God who loved me more than I could imagine."

"James," she breathed. "This means that you and I met each other before—before I ran into you on campus."

"You know," he laughed, "the night I got that envelope, I was so bowled over by God's answer to my prayer that I could scarcely think straight. I wracked my brain to remember something—anything—about the people I waited on that night. But the only thing I ever recalled was this family—a family with a baby and a pretty little towheaded daughter who chattered like a magpie through the entire meal."

Stella didn't know if James was teasing or not. Neither did she care, but she gave his arm a playful punch for good measure. She was still trying to wrap her finite mind around the amazing possibility they'd just stumbled upon. "Oh, James, can we tell Papa? Can we tell the others the story?"

He thought for a moment. "I think it's only right that they

find out—after all these years—just how much your little tradition blessed a certain young man."

He took her hand in his, and a little shiver of joy ran its fingers down her spine.

"Yes, Stella, I'll tell your father what he could not possibly have known on that long-ago winter night." A twinkle came to his eyes as he continued. "That the anonymous boy he prayed to bless with that envelope would someday come to him asking to become a part of his family."

It took a moment for his words to register, and even then, she wasn't sure she had heard him correctly. "I don't. . .what are you. . . ?" she stuttered.

He slid from the settee and knelt before her, gazing into her face. "Stella, I know we haven't known each other very long, and right now all I have to offer you are two feet to walk beside you and these hands to hold you." He held his hands palms up before her, as though they held all the promise of his offering. "But I have come to love you with all of my being, and if you will still have me when the day comes that I can provide you with everything you deserve, I intend to request your father's permission to ask you to be my wife."

At that moment, Stella knew in the deepest part of her soul that this was the man God had made for her. The knowledge filled her with joy. "Oh, James," she breathed. "Yes! A thousand times, yes!"

She bent to receive the tender kiss he offered as a promise of his love—a token of the thousands upon thousands of kisses they would share in the hopeful ribbon of years that spooled out before them.

Epilogue

Dakota Territory, 1876

That was a fine, fine dinner, my darling," James said, wiping his hands on the white linen napkin, then rubbing his midsection contentedly.

Stella laughed, looking around the elegant dining room of the Clairemore Hotel, where they sat at a small corner table. "Well, I certainly can't take any praise for the meal. But you are right. That new chef the hotel hired is marvelous." She patted her husband's hand. "Thank you, Dearest, for the break. It was nice not to have to cook tonight."

"Thank your father," he told her with a wry smile. "This little tradition was his idea."

"I will do that—when I see him at Christmas dinner next week." She intertwined her fingers with his across the table. "I think I might even have the house plans ready to show Papa by then."

"I certainly hope so." That familiar, endearing glint she knew so well came to James's eyes. "As much as I do love her," he continued, "I am growing a little impatient with my architect. I am very anxious to begin filling up all those carefully drafted bed-rooms with children."

She smiled and squeezed his hand. "I'm nearly finished with the plans. Truly. But before I turn my drawings over to the builder, I want them to be perfect."

"Well, I couldn't say about the *design* of our house. . . ." He rubbed a warm thumb across the back of her hand, then brought it to his lips and kissed each fingertip. "But as long as you are living within its walls, it will be perfect as far as I'm concerned."

Their waitress came just then with a pitcher of water in one hand and a fresh pot of coffee in the other. They waited in silence while she served them.

The dining room was crowded, and the girl seemed harried and tense. Stella watched their waitress surreptitiously as she replenished their water glasses. The young girl's shoes were scuffed and worn, and her uniform was a size too small. Her hands were red and chapped as though perhaps she spent the hours after the restaurant closed scrubbing pots and saucepans in the kitchen.

James leaned away from the table so the lass could reach his coffee cup more easily. "Thank you, Miss," he said, then cleared his throat. "I'm sorry—what did you say your name was?"

"I didn't say, Sir. But it's Annie."

"Well, Annie, we thank you for your service this evening."

"Quite welcome, Sir," she replied. "You folks have a merry Christmas now."

"And you," James and Stella said in concert.

Annie gave a half-curtsy and, with a weary sigh, moved on to the next table to pour coffee.

Smiling at his wife, James reached into his breast pocket and withdrew a small ivory envelope. Stella watched as he lifted the flap and inspected the contents. Apparently satisfied, he sealed the envelope and placed it on the table in front of him. Withdrawing a fountain pen from his pocket, he wrote Annie's name across the face of the envelope in his fine, precise script. He put away the pen, but his hand returned and lingered for a moment over the name he'd penned, as though he were asking a blessing upon it.

Then he pushed his chair back from the table, rose, and held out a hand to his wife. "Come, my love. Let's go home, shall we?"

DEBORAH RANEY

Deborah began writing in 1994 and is the author of five novels, including *After the Rains, Beneath a Southern Sky,* and *A Vow to Cherish,* which inspired World Wide Pictures award-winning film of the same title. She has also published many short stories, magazine articles, and works of nonfiction. Deborah and her husband, illustrator/author Ken Raney, are the parents of four children and make their home in Kansas. Visit Deb's Web site at www.deborahraney.com.

A Letter to Our Readers

Dear Readers:

In order that we might better contribute to your reading enjoyment, we would appreciate you taking a few minutes to respond to the following questions. When completed, please return to the following: Fiction Editor, Barbour Publishing, Inc., P.O. Box 719, Uhrichsville, OH 44683.

1. Did you enjoy reading *A Currier & Ives Christmas?*
   ❑ Very much—I would like to see more books like this.
   ❑ Moderately—I would have enjoyed it more if _____
   _____
   _____

2. What influenced your decision to purchase this book?
   (Check those that apply.)
   ❑ Cover   ❑ Back cover copy   ❑ Title   ❑ Price
   ❑ Friends   ❑ Publicity   ❑ Other

3. Which story was your favorite?
   ❑ *The Snow Storm*   ❑ *Dreams and Secrets*
   ❑ *Image of Love*   ❑ *Circle of Blessings*

4. Please check your age range:
   ❑ Under 18   ❑ 18–24   ❑ 25–34
   ❑ 35–45   ❑ 46–55   ❑ Over 55

5. How many hours per week do you read? _____

Name _____

Occupation _____

Address _____

City _____ State _____ Zip _____